The Diversity of Modern Capit[...]

The Diversity of Modern Capitalism

BRUNO AMABLE

OXFORD
UNIVERSITY PRESS

OXFORD
UNIVERSITY PRESS

Great Clarendon Street, Oxford OX2 6DP

Oxford University Press is a department of the University of Oxford.
It furthers the University's objective of excellence in research, scholarship,
and education by publishing worldwide in

Oxford New York

Auckland Cape Town Dar es Salaam Hong Kong Karachi
Kuala Lumpur Madrid Melbourne Mexico City Nairobi
New Delhi Shanghai Taipei Toronto

With offices in

Argentina Austria Brazil Chile Czech Republic France Greece
Guatemala Hungary Italy Japan South Korea Poland Portugal
Singapore Switzerland Thailand Turkey Ukraine Vietnam

Oxford is a registered trade mark of Oxford University Press
in the UK and in certain other countries

Published in the United States
by Oxford University Press Inc., New York

British Library Cataloguing in Publication Data

Data available

Library of Congress Cataloging in Publication Data

Data available

ISBN 0–19–926113–X (hbk)
0–19–926114–8 (pbk)

3 5 7 9 10 8 6 4 2

Typeset by Newgen Imaging Systems (P) Ltd., Chennai, India
Printed in Great Britain
on acid-free paper by
Biddles Ltd., King's Lynn, Norfolk

051399

ACKNOWLEDGEMENTS

The origin of this book goes back to a research project on the comparative dynamics of innovation systems undertaken with Pascal Petit, Yann Cadiou, Sandrine Paillard, and Saad Salman at CEPREMAP and funded by the European Community under the Targeted Socio-economic Research Programme. Although stressing the importance of innovation and technology, the project was in fact a comparative analysis of modern capitalist economies. The theoretical and empirical work performed in the course of this project led to examinations of the coherence of the various systems and the complementarity relationships between the various institutional forms characteristic of these systems. Discussions with David Soskice, Bob Hancké, and Donatella Gatti at the WZB were very helpful for the advancement of my research. But I am most indebted to my CEPREMAP colleagues Ekkehard Ernst and Stefano Palombarini, with whom I undertook a research project on institutional complementarity funded by the French Ministry of Education and Research. The many discussions we had during this research project were a great stimulus for writing this book. My research has benefited from the comments of Masahiko Aoki, Peter Hall, Bruce Kogut, David Marsden, and Wolfgang Streeck during the seminars on institutional complementarity held at CEPREMAP in November 1999 and April 2002 and the conference on 'The Sources of Innovation' organized in Paris by the Centre Saint-Gobain pour la Recherche en Economie in June 2001. I would like to thank Helen Callaghan for reading the final draft of the book, Sonja Wiemann for her patience and support, and David Musson for his encouragement.

CONTENTS

LIST OF FIGURES

LIST OF TABLES

LIST OF ABBREVIATIONS

CEPR	Center for Economic Policy Research
CEPREMAP	Centre d'Etudes Prospectives et d'Economie Mathematique Appliquées a la Planification
CNRS	Centre National de la Recherche Scientifique
EC	European Commission
ECB	European Central Bank
EMU	European Monetary Unification
EP	European Parliament
ETUC	European Trade Union Confederation
ETUI	European Trade Union Institute
EU	European Union
FDI	Foreign Direct Investment
FGLS	Feasible Generalized Least Squares
ICT	Information and Communication Technologies
ISCED	International Standard Classification of Education
MPIfG	Max Planck Institut für Gesellschaftsforschung
NBER	National Bureau of Economic Research
NHS	National Health Service
NYSE	New York Stock Exchange
PISA	Programme for International Student Assessment
SASE	Society for the Advancement of Socio-economics
SPD	Sozialistische Partei Deutschland
WZB	Wissenschafts Zentrum Berlin

1

Introduction

1.1 The Institutional Diversity of Capitalism

At the start of the twenty-first century the role of institutions and the conditions for institutional change are at the core of the economic debate in Europe. The debate has its roots in a comparison of economic performance within the triad of Europe, Japan, and the USA in a context of globalization and the emergence of a new growth trajectory associated with what is commonly dubbed the 'knowledge-based economy' (OECD 2000). At the end of the 1980s the discussion about the relative merits of different models of capitalism seemed to be very clear. The context was that of the long-term economic success of Europe and Japan, as opposed to what was perceived as a long-term decline in the USA. Comparative analysis showed that Europe and Japan had all but caught up with the USA in terms of GDP per capita, not simply by adopting the US methods of work organization, but by developing specific modes of organization that proved to be superior to their American counterparts. As a result, the USA was losing ground in terms of industrial competitiveness, as witnessed by the growing trade deficits and the loss of market shares in manufacturing. The feeling in the USA was that something drastic needed to be done in order to 'regain the productive edge' (Dertouzos et al. 1989). Deficiencies in the US model were observed in a number of areas, the most prominent being the financing relationship and the pattern of corporate governance, as well as the employment relationship. The financing pattern reflects the pressure that firms' owners exert on firms' strategies. A major deficiency in the American model was held to be its focus on short-term profits, which are necessary to please shareholders and financial markets. On the other hand, the long-term relationships established between banks and firms in Europe and Japan allowed for the implementation of more long-term strategies financed by 'patient' capital. This explained why the manufacturing sector was in much better shape in Germany or Japan than in the USA. Also, differences in the degree of centralization of wage bargaining, employment protection, and more generally the labour-market institutions encouraged different attitudes with respect to cooperation in the employment relationship. The short-term nature of employers' and employees' involvement in the USA was often held to be detrimental to the accumulation of skills and competence necessary for manufacturing competitiveness.

The terms of the debate have changed drastically since the late 1980s. The comparative economic performance of Japan, Europe, and the USA has led to a reappraisal of the respective qualities of the institutions supporting the different models. The Japanese economy experienced a decade of near-zero growth, while the USA enjoyed the longest ascending phase in the American business cycle since the end of the Second World War: a high average growth rate, low unemployment, a rebound in productivity growth, and low inflation, as well as the rise of privately funded R & D expenditure, a wide diffusion of computers and the Internet, and a high rate of creation of new-technology-intensive firms. By contrast, Europe did rather poorly on average, particularly as regards unemployment, even if some small economies fared better than the large ones. As a result, talk of the American decline and the pitfalls of the American model was forgotten. Far from being the example of industrial decline and economic stagnation, the USA was regarded at the end of the 1990s and the beginning of the new millennium as the epitome of modernism, economic dynamism, innovation, and adaptability to the new socio-technological context. Technology played an important role in the reaffirmation of its supremacy. The USA seemed to be at the vanguard of the 'new economy'; i.e. a new long-term growth trajectory based on a few 'generic' technologies— mainly information and communication technologies (ICT) but also biotechnologies. More generally, the new 'knowledge-based' economy— meaning, generally, that knowledge creation and diffusion play a more important role in competitiveness and growth than they did before— seemed to blossom in market-friendly societies and wane in over-regulated environments. The new competitive conditions were such that innovation was crucial for the survival of firms that had to compete on a permanent basis. The ability to innovate depended on the adaptability of the workforce and its capacity to acquire the necessary skills. Intensification of competition and frequent modifications of production methods called for constant skill-upgrading and high mobility in the workforce. The stable pattern of employment characteristic of Europe and Japan, i.e. job security and seniority wages, could no longer be guaranteed. On the other hand, the flexible labour markets and the strong incentive mechanisms of the USA seemed perfect for gearing the economy towards the new trajectory. A well-functioning price mechanism oriented agents towards the acquisition of the skills most in demand, which allowed them to find employment and enabled firms to use these skills to keep the competitive edge. Well-developed financial markets made low-cost financing of firms easier, and structural change was facilitated by market-based corporate governance and the ability to hire and fire cheaply. No wonder then that the US and Anglo-Saxon economies in general enjoyed superior economic performance whilst other models stalled. The institutions of Europe and Japan may once have been perfectly appropriate for catching up with the USA in the post-war 'golden age', but they had become inadequate in a period of new growth where innovation and adaptability were crucial.

One might pause for a moment and wonder whether all this makes as much sense as it seems to. As Richard Freeman recalls (Freeman 2000), the advent of a new ideal economic model is proclaimed about once a decade: central planning of the New Deal in the Great Depression years, French-style indicative planning in the 1960s, German-style co-determination in the 1970s, the Japanese model of kanban during the 1980s—and finally the American-style New Economy in the 1990s. Should we take this seriously? Are institutional factors so strong that they can explain the differences in macroeconomic performance? Taking a long-term view, capitalist economies have developed with a fair amount of diversity among themselves, which should have resulted in dramatic differences in levels of development. The fact that these differences are for the most part not noticeable might be an indication that capitalism is based on such robust mechanisms that it accommodates varied institutional environments. In other words, institutional differences would be akin to national folklore, with few if any consequences for economic dynamics. Under these conditions, could the good macroeconomic performance of the USA simply reflect a more sensible macroeconomic policy mix than that of Europe? The relatively weak macroeconomic performance of the EU in the 1990s would be largely the result of fiscal retrenchment and the restrictive monetary policies implemented in the context of European Monetary Unification and the launching of the single European currency, the euro. Besides, the USA and Europe could be regarded as not that different after all. Of course, there might have been in the 1960s and the 1970s a Rhine model and a dirigiste model within Europe, but these specificities have disappeared over time. First, as a result of the process of economic integration, which has made economic legislation more homogeneous within Europe, particularly with respect to competition and the intervention of the State in the economy. Privatizations and the completion of the single market have standardized firms' competitive environment within the EU. Second—as an outcome of worldwide institutional convergence—the pressure of globalization and worldwide liberalization, particularly of financial services, has evened out differences between the EU and the rest of the world. Therefore, the institutional differences that are left across countries simply reveal differences in societal preferences, with very little effect on macroeconomic performance differentials. If institutional specificities did have an effect, competition among nations would sooner or later lead to the adoption of international 'best practices'.

This book challenges these views on several counts. There are some elements of truth in the statement that differences in macroeconomic policy mix could explain in part the differences in economic performance, for instance growth and employment, between the USA and Europe. But this does not amount to saying that institutional specificities do not matter in explaining important differences in the basic economic mechanisms of the different countries. There is a considerable amount of theoretical and historical work that insists on the central role of institutions in economic dynamics.[1] Institutions define incentives and constraints that will lead agents to invest in certain assets, acquire certain skills, cooperate, or be opportunistic. These individual decisions will affect macroeconomic growth performance. However, it is in general difficult unambiguously to relate one particular institutional form to 'superior' economic performance when it comes to empirical testing. One reason could be that institutions do not affect economic decisions independently of each other. Interrelations between institutions are likely to lead to a complex of influences that is hard to analyse and whose empirical effects are difficult to unravel. Economic models are characterized precisely not by one but by many institutional forms that exert their effects in interaction. This implies going beyond a step-by-step comparison of the USA and Europe with respect to labour-market institutions, financial sectors, etc. These comparisons are useful and reveal the extent of the diversity among developed economies. The labour market may be more or less regulated, wage bargaining more or less centralized, and the financial systems more or less reliant upon banks or financial markets. The most natural way to perform a comparative institutional analysis would probably be to consider that, for instance, the specificities of labour-market institutions are likely to have an effect on the performance of the labour market, measured by variables such as participation rates or the rate of unemployment. Indeed, many economic theories predict such a link (Layard, Nickell, and Jackman

---

[1] See North (1990) for an overview.

1991). The institutions of the financial intermediation sector are likely to exert an influence on the performance of that sector, measured by the volume of investment, the cost of capital, etc. (Allen and Gale 2000). Making a 'sectoral' comparison across nations would then produce conclusions regarding which set of institutional forms leads to low unemployment, high investment, high skills—and ultimately a high rate of growth. This analysis would then enable the USA to escape the comparison of countries understood as a comparison of models to follow. The efficient economic model would not necessarily be Japan or the USA, but could mix the financial-sector institutions of the UK with the social-protection system of Denmark and the US education system.

1.2 Institutional Complementarity

There are however several difficulties related to such an approach of comparative institutional analysis. First, there might not be one but several institutional forms associated with 'good' performance. A well-known example is given in Calmfors and Driffill (1988), who proposed to take into account a non-monotonic, hump-shaped relationship between centralization of wage bargaining and wage levels or unemployment. The basic idea is that organized labour may be harmful to employment when it is powerful enough to impose a certain wage level on firms but not sufficiently encompassing to take into account the possibly detrimental effects of high wages on the employment level. Therefore, wage moderation can be achieved either through decentralization of wage bargaining or through all-encompassing trade unions. In the former case, bargaining units would be too small to have significant price- or wage-setting power; in the latter case, unions would recognize the possible adverse effects of wage increases on inflation and employment. The intermediate case would correspond to unions strong enough to exert wage pressure but neglecting the macroeconomic consequences on inflation and unemployment. There are thus clearly two ways of achieving superior economic performance, and institutional benchmarking may thus deliver ambiguous conclusions regarding what 'model' to follow. But, more importantly, interaction between institutions may be such that it is necessary to consider them jointly in order to understand their effects on the economic decisions of agents and hence on economic performance. Following Aoki (1994), one can consider the complementarities between institutions. The standard economic notion of complementarity applies to goods entering a utility function, or inputs in a production function. Roughly speaking, two goods are complementary when increasing the amount of one good raises the marginal contribution of the other to the relevant function. In the field of institutions, two institutions can be said to be complementary when the presence of one increases the efficiency of the other. If institutional complementarity prevails institutional benchmarking becomes more complex, since it is not possible to consider the effect of one institutional form independently of the other institutions in the economy. Flexible labour markets may be more efficient when financial markets allow for a rapid mobilization of resources and creation of new businesses that in return sustain labour demand. Conversely, a more stable employment relationship may be more efficient when a specific pattern of monitoring is implemented in the context of a close relationship between a firm and a bank. Institutional complementarity thus has consequences for the comparative analysis of capitalism. Economic 'models' should not be considered just as a collection of more or less random institutional forms, but also as a set of complementarity relations between these institutions, which form the basis of the coherence between the specific institutional forms of each model. Complementarities should not be construed as similarities, as if, for instance, one could refer to a unique 'principle' that applied to all institutional forms whatever the area concerned. Institutional complementarity is different from structural isomorphism. The latter would suppose that a basic similarity in mechanisms could be found in the influence of different institutions present in various areas, such as financial and education systems, labour and product markets, etc. A complementary explanation to the structural-isomorphism approach is often that agents adopt a common way of doing things in diverse settings in conformity with social norms or cultural dispositions, because institutions are 'socially embedded'. If, for instance, State intervention characterizes most or all institutional domains, one may sensibly talk about structural isomorphism and give a simple name to the economic model; i.e. 'Statist' or dirigiste. But it would be too restrictive to suppose that this is a general pattern. Complementary institutions can exist that each appeal to very different 'principles', so that their combination cannot be reduced to a unique dimension. In fact, structural isomorphism and institutional complementarity are most probably independent. Conformity to a single 'logic' does not a priori guarantee the complementarity of institutions, which may itself exist without structural isomorphism.

Institutional complementarity also makes the question of the hypothetical optimal institutional structure more difficult to answer. The efficiency of institutions in a specific domain cannot be appreciated independently of the effects that they have in other domains. This also means that institutional change may not necessarily stay 'localized'. Changing one institutional form in a specific area may have effects that will not remain confined within the limits of this area but extend to the whole institutional structure through complementarity effects. Changing, for instance, labour-market regulation may destabilize financial-sector institutions by indirectly altering their efficiency, which may in turn affect the social-protection system and so on. If this is the case, piecemeal institutional change may sometimes gradually turn into major institutional change and a transition between economic models. This could also explain why institutional change is difficult; i.e. why there is always some degree of institutional inertia present in most societies, and why one sometimes witnesses periods of substantial transformation affecting several institutional forms at the same time. Institutional inertia is sometimes interpreted in terms of 'path dependency'. In the context of technological choice, Arthur (1994) analyses path dependency as the consequence of increasing returns to adoption and network effects. Prior adoption of a given technology makes current adoption more attractive. There is thus a sunk-cost aspect in diffusion that 'locks' the technological trajectory in a certain direction. This explains why it is difficult to change course once a given path has been followed for a certain amount of time. The mechanisms involved in institutional complementarity are slightly different from this type of path dependency. In the presence of institutional complementarity some institutions are more efficient because of their interaction with other institutions. Changing them may only make sense when complementary institutions are also changed. This might in a way be compared to a network effect in so far as the 'diffusion' of one institution in a given area depends on the 'diffusion' of other institutions in different areas. One would then have periods of relative institutional inertia followed by periods of relatively important institutional change affecting several areas of the economy.

The current period is indeed commonly considered to be one in which all-out transformation is necessary. An often-told story is the following: Some important structural transformations of the world economy have deeply altered the mechanisms linking growth, institutions, and economic policy. The pre-globalization period was characterized by a relative insulation of national economies from the international environment. Firms' strategies were developed nationally or internationally rather than on a world basis, because of the various obstacles to factor mobility, either legal or technological. A set of international institutions actually contributed to the definition of a strongly national or regional character to the growth trajectories: fixed exchange rates until the 1970s, legal obstacles to capital mobility, tariff and non-tariff barriers to international trade, etc. Within such a context, a Keynesian-style macroeconomic policy aiming at regulating the level of aggregate demand could be implemented, making use of budgetary instruments and even monetary policy after the demise of the fixed exchange-rate system. But this whole architecture reached its limits during the 1970s and 1980s. A lax use of monetary policies led to inflation pressures, and budgetary policy lost its effectiveness in a context of more open economies. Hence the growing difficulties demand-management policies have faced in the attempt to cure high and rising unemployment, particularly in Europe. A context of increasing internationalization, and even globalization, by which is meant that firms' strategies are devised at the world level and nation-states lose most of their influence on the economy, demands that economic institutions be based on totally different philosophies. Keynesian demand-management policies must be replaced by new classical-economics-inspired measures based on monetary-policy rules rather than discretion, in order to bring about monetary stability, non-activist sustainability-oriented fiscal policies, no intervention of the State in industrial strategies, and in general more autonomy for market forces. This is indeed consistent with the new economic-policy environment of the EU, with an independent central bank for the whole Euro-zone having replaced more or less government-influenced national central banks, and explicit legal restrictions to budget deficits preventing the implementation of discretionary fiscal policies. The 'new times' are also held to be characterized by more uncertainty, increased competition between territories, and a greater independence of economic agents from government decisions. At the same time, the macroeconomic performance of nations is more dependent on agents' decisions regarding human-capital acquisition or innovation, which gives individuals more responsibility, autonomy, and possibilities for self-accomplishment.

If this story is true, the 'new times' are likely to be less kind towards certain economic systems than towards others. Particularly under pressure are the institutions of European countries, which offer a generous Welfare State and a degree of employment stability. The financing of social protection implies a rate of taxation that is bound to become unsustainable in a globalized world, where corporations can shift their production activities to the locations that offer the most advantageous conditions. Besides, rigid labour markets and high employment protection deter job creation and increase unemployment, which amplifies the social-protection burden. One could also add the disincentive effects that high tax rates and solidaristic incomes policies are supposed to exert on the most skilled agents; i.e. precisely those that have become prominent in the definition of a competitive growth trajectory. All this explains why European countries have experienced such inferior performance since the 1990s. The story applied to the Japanese case would consider the negative effects of a sclerotic financial system on the innovation capacity of a country.

The above-told story may be simple, but is not necessarily accurate. By supposing that the 'golden age' was always and everywhere based on a mixture of Keynesian macroeconomics and social-democratic institutions, it neglects the diversity that one could observe at that time among the OECD. Some countries, such as the USA or Japan, never had social-democratic Welfare States, while others, such as the Scandinavian countries, could hardly be described as the closed economies upon which traditional Keynesian policies could be based. In fact, the corporatist arrangements present in some European countries prevented the inflationary tensions that are commonly associated with Keynesian demand management. In other words, the story neglects the diversity of capitalism that existed during the 'golden age'. Could it be that it also neglects the possible diversity in the 'new times'? Why would the 'one-size-fits-all' story be more relevant now than it was then? The usual answer would be that globalization now imposes homogenization, whereas national specificities were much better protected by the institutions inherited from Bretton Woods (1944). But the simple evolutionary argument upon which the globalization story rests supposes that efficiency is associated with one institutional architecture only. Could efficiency take several forms? A positive answer to that question is at the core of the theory of institutional complementarities.

1.3 Institutions and Politics

The notion of the efficiency of institutions has not been questioned so far, but it may be time to leave aside the simple functionalist argument according to which institutions are designed and adopted for efficiency reasons. This position raises two questions. First, what are the mechanisms that ensure that institutions emerge as efficient? Second, how do we define efficiency, or, for whom are institutions supposed to be efficient? An external analyst such as an economist can devise a measure of 'efficiency' of economic systems, for instance the level of GDP per capita or an indicator of development, and check whether some institutional forms are more systematically associated with high measures of the performance indicator than others. But external analysts do not devise national institutions, however strong their desire to do so may be. This book takes the position that institutions are the expression of a political compromise. The design of optimal institutions would be facilitated if agents had a common objective, i.e. if they all agreed on what performance indicator should be taken into account to measure the efficiency of institutions; they might then agree on an efficient institutional design, conditional on their rationality. However, agents usually disagree on what this indicator could be because they often have different and even conflicting interests. Institutions are likely to affect the interest structure and hence the preference that agents may express towards a certain pattern of institutional change. Rather than optimal solutions to a given problem, institutions represent a compromise resulting from the social conflict originating in the heterogeneity of interests among agents. What we consider to be different economic 'models' are therefore based on specific social compromises over institutions. The question of institutional change is basically a question of political economy.

One may easily accept that formal institutions such as laws are the result of a political compromise but be more sceptical regarding non-formal institutions. Going one step further and defining institutions as an equilibrium strategy in a social game, institutions would emerge out of individual interaction and their formalization would only appear as *ex post* ratification of individual practices. This vision of institutions as emerging spontaneously and unintentionally out of individual interaction is widespread in economics (Hayek 1967). This is sometimes interpreted as a guarantee that institutional design is free from conflict motives. Following Knight (1992), I argue that institutional design reflects conflict over distributional issues and that even individual interaction leads to institutional equilibriums reflecting power asymmetries and conflicts of interest. This means that institutions are not primarily designed to solve coordination problems between equal agents with similar interests, but to solve conflict among unequal actors with divergent interests. Institutions will emerge as a consequence of agents' strategic behaviour in a context of power asymmetries. Some agents will decide on a given strategy not because they are perfectly satisfied with it, but because it represents the best solution given the circumstances. Institutions are endogenously determined rules of the game. Once the rules have been agreed upon, they are taken as part of the environment by agents who devise their strategies within the constraints defined by these rules. For instance, labour laws will define the constraints within which social partners engage in wage bargaining. Thus, institutions as endogenously determined rules of the game circumscribe the social conflict within a given area. When social conflict cannot be solved within the existing rules of the game, the possibility of a change of rules is open. This change may take several forms, from rule-circumventing strategies to open political bargaining about the desired institutional structure. As a political-economy equilibrium, institutions need to be supported by a socio-political bloc reflecting common interests and agreement over a political strategy. The formation of this coalition itself depends on the existing institutional structure. The perception of agents' own interests depends on the establishment of a common representation of the world which is itself an institution. The political expression of interest groups depends on the political system; i.e. on the political institutions. Some systems allow for a specific representation of interest groups while others are majoritarian systems. These differences will have consequences for the formation of a socio-political bloc and institutional change.

Another important notion is that of hierarchy of institutions. A first definition of hierarchy would place at the top those rules that define how other rules can be determined. For instance, constitutions would be at the top of the hierarchy, followed by laws, regulations, by-laws, etc. Following from this, institutions at the top of the hierarchy should be those that change least often. A related idea is that the hierarchy of institutions is determined by the pecking order of sunk costs related to each institution. Once again, institutions at the top change less often and other institutions must adapt to them. The notion of hierarchy proposed in this book is based on the definition of institutions as political-economy equilibriums. Institutions are the expression of a compromise and both influence and result from the formation of a stable socio-political bloc. A political coalition will seek to stay in power by finding support with the dominant social bloc; to that effect, it will seek to implement institutional changes that favour the socio-political bloc and try to prevent change that is detrimental to the bloc. The areas where institutional change will be implemented more easily are those where the dominant bloc has little interest. On the other hand, change will be implemented more cautiously in domains where the most powerful socio-political groups have vested interests. Therefore, hierarchically superior institutions are not necessarily those that change the least, since the most powerful socio-political groups might be willing to implement a change that favours them. Institutional hierarchy is also determined by the political system and the representation of interests leading to the establishment of a dominant socio-political bloc. Institutional change may take several forms. Agents may change their strategies under the influence of some exogenous change, change may stem from unintended consequences of actors' decisions, or it may result from conscious strategies aiming at institutional change. This change may stay 'localized', i.e. confined within a certain area, or spread to other areas through complementarity effects. It may give rise to political demands from agents concerned about the consequences of the change. For instance, workers disadvantaged by a new type of organization of production may call for a change in labour regulations that prohibits or limits the modifications implemented by the management. They may try to bargain with the firms' management or call in a 'third party', the State, and directly express a political demand. Whether this demand will be satisfied depends on the balance of power between different socio-political groups. If the political weight of the agents concerned is negligible, no consequences will follow and the outcome of the initial institutional change will be limited to some distributional consequences. If on the other hand they have a degree of political weight, several options are open. The government, seeking political support, may try to implement a specific policy change, or instigate further institutional change. This process may extend beyond the initial area through institutional complementarity. One may, then, devise a typology of institutional change, from local modifications to a crisis of the economic system. When agents fail to find agreement about new 'rules of the game', they may be led to envisage more wide-ranging institutional transformations, which may disturb the dominant socio-political bloc and lead to its reorganization, which may in turn set off further institutional change. The process may end up with a very different set of institutional forms and a very different dominant socio-political bloc.

Such a theory of institutions demands that agents be rational enough to act strategically. They need not be perfectly rational, i.e. have a perfect grasp of all the interdependencies between institutions and a full understanding of all the consequences of their actions, but they need to have enough rationality to be able to decide what constitutes a desirable course of action in a strategic context. But there is no 'social engineer' in charge of the efficiency of institutional design, and there is no pre-established fit of institutions either. Economic 'models', i.e. specific sets of institutional forms and the associated complementarities, are not designed from scratch with all the different pieces intended to nicely complement each other. The coherence of a model is usually defined *ex post* and the complementarities may sometimes come as a surprise even to the agents most closely concerned. An example is given in Streeck (2002). An important element of the German model can be said to be its specific banking sector, whose complementarity with other German institutional forms such as co-determination, i.e. a representation of unions at the monitoring board of large firms, and coordinated wage bargaining has often been put forward to explain the stability of the model. To simplify drastically, close relationships between banks and firms allow the latter to design long-term strategies compatible with skill acquisition, job security, and high wages. One might, then, expect worker representatives to have been highly supportive of such an institutional arrangement. Yet, social actors may initially be totally unaware of the benefits brought to them by key institutions; the German unions and social democrats, for instance, have for decades denounced the 'power of the banks'.

1.4 Five Different Models of Capitalism

Complementarity and hierarchy of institutions explain the possible diversity of models of capitalism. But what are the types of capitalism that we should expect to find? A 'spontaneous' approach would concentrate on the diversity of national arrangements and consider that each country represents a specific type of capitalism. International comparisons have indeed emphasized the differences between national institutions, and we speak casually of 'Modell Deutschland' or 'le modèle français'. But this focus on nations as specific models may run into two different types of problem. First, homogeneity within nations may be questioned. One may object that business practices, patterns of firms' organization, and even sometimes the regulatory environment differ between the regions of a given country. It is sometimes said that there is not one Italian model but three, so that the sub-national level may be more relevant for comparative analysis. The trouble with this approach is that it has virtually no limits. Even within regions, one could probably differentiate according to the sector and actually even consider that the firm is the proper unit of analysis, thereby losing the plot. Second, the consideration of national case studies does not usually define a common framework for analysis. Focusing on national cases leads to the adoption of a nation-specific set of explanations and theories which makes international comparisons difficult and generalizations nearly impossible. An alternative is to define a common theoretical framework for comparative analysis and apply it to the study of modern economies. This approach is exemplified by the classifications of capitalism found, for instance, in Albert (1991) and Hall and Soskice (2001). The former approach is more inductive than the latter, generalizing from the case studies of Germany and the USA, but it in fact leads to the theoretically founded approach of Hall and Soskice (2001). They identify two types of capitalist economy, the liberal market economies (LMEs) and the coordinated market economies (CMEs). The difference between the two is based on one fundamental dimension: coordination. In an LME coordination is based on market mechanisms, favouring investment in transferable assets. In a CME it is mainly achieved through non-market means—the so-called strategic coordination—favouring investment in specific assets. In Hall and Soskice's classification system there are thus basically two types of capitalism. Such a dichotomous approach has both pros and cons. While it simplifies empirical analysis, it is nevertheless fundamentally a one-dimensional analysis. The dimension is the extent of market coordination; it reflects the implicit hierarchy of institutions adopted by the theoretical analysis underlying the typology of economies: Hall and Soskice's approach is centred on the firm. Placing other institutions in the fore-ground could lead to the consideration of more diversity than a dichotom-ous opposition between two types of capitalism. In Amable et al. (1997) four types of 'social systems of innovation and production' were distin-guished: a market-based model, akin to the LME of Hall and Soskice, a 'mesocorporatist' model, representing Japan, a social-democratic model, representing the Scandinavian economies, and a European-integration model. These models were characterized by differences in institutional forms in areas such as the financial sector, the employment relationship, and the education sector, and the consequences of these differences on scientific, technological, and industrial specialization. Other typologies could be found in the literature (Jackson 2002) which are broadly consist-ent with the four types in Amable et al. (1997). They usually concentrate on one specific institution, for instance the Welfare State or the pattern of State intervention, and establish ideal types of capitalism.

The method used in this book is different from the usual ideal-typical method. I start from the consideration of five fundamental institutional areas: product-market competition; the wage–labour nexus and labour-market institutions; the financial intermediation sector and corporate gov-ernance; social protection and the Welfare State; and the education sector. Different complementarities between institutions are envisaged, based on the theoretical work on this topic accomplished over the last few years. Then, on the basis of both the theoretical results and the previous charac-terizations of capitalism found in the literature, I posit the existence of five types of capitalism, each characterized by specific institutional forms and particular institutional complementarities: the market-based model; the social-democratic model; the Continental European model; the Mediterranean model; and the Asian model. Except for the market-based model, which is akin to the LME of Hall and Soskice (2001), all other types of capitalism have a geography-based denomination. This is for the sake of simplicity and should not be taken too literally. It does not mean that geo-graphical or 'cultural' factors are the most important common factors or explain the coherence of the different types of capitalism. Since they are not in general reducible to a single 'logic' that would pervade all institutions, there is no simple denomination that could adequately reflect the institutional complementarities at the origin of the models.

Product-market competition is an important element of the market-based model. It makes firms more sensitive to adverse shocks which cannot be fully absorbed by price adjustments. Quantity adjustments will matter, which implies that competitiveness is based on labour-market flexibility. This allows firms to react quickly to changing market conditions. Financial markets are also instrumental in this capacity of firms to adapt to new competitive environments. They also supply individuals with a large range of risk-diversification instruments which are particularly welcome in the absence of a well-developed Welfare State. The social-democratic model is organized according to very different complementarities. A strong external competitive pressure requires some flexibility in the labour force. But flexibility is not simply achieved through lay-offs and market-based adjustments. Protection of specific investments of employees is realized through a mixture of moderate employment protection, a high level of social protection, and easy access to retraining thanks to active labour-market policies. A coordinated wage-bargaining system allows a solidaristic wage-setting which favours innovation and productivity. The Continental European model possesses some common features with the social-democratic model. It is based on a higher degree of employment protection and a less developed Welfare State. A centralized financial system facilitates long-term corporate strategies. Wage bargaining is coordinated and a solidaristic wage policy is developed, but not as much as in the social-democratic model. Workforce retraining is not as easy as in the social-democratic model, which limits the possibilities for an 'offensive' flexibility in the labour market. The Mediterranean model of capitalism is based on more employment protection and less social protection than the Continental European model. Employment protection is made possible by a relatively low level of product-market competition and the absence of short-term profit constraints as a result of the centralization of the financial system. However, a workforce with a limited skills and education level does not allow for the implementation of a high wages and high skills industrial strategy. The Asian model of capitalism is highly dependent on the business strategies of the large corporations in collaboration with the State and a centralized financial system, which allows the development of long-term strategies. Workers' specific investments are protected by a de facto protection of employment and possibilities of retraining and career-making within the corporation. Lack of social protection and sophisticated financial markets make risk diversification difficult and render the stability provided by the large corporation crucial to the existence of the model.

1.5 An Empirical Investigation of the Diversity of Capitalism

The five-type partition of capitalism can thus be justified on theoretical grounds, but can it be supported by empirical work? If the distinction between these varieties of capitalism makes sense, one should be able to find systematic similarities between countries when analysing indicators reflecting institutional characteristics. However, since institutional complementarity differs from structural isomorphism, one should not expect always to find the same countries close to one another whatever the institutional area under consideration. There are many international comparisons concerning the five institutional areas mentioned above. In fact, some of the typologies of capitalism are usually derived from applied work in one or several of these areas. There are nevertheless very few systematic attempts at making a comparative analysis of a large number of countries focusing on institutions. Most studies either consider a large sample of countries and a limited number of indicators concerning mostly one institutional area, or concentrate on an encompassing institutional comparison between a limited number of countries. This book proposes an empirical analysis of twenty-one OECD countries based on a series of indicators concerning the five institutional areas considered in the theoretical analysis of the types of capitalism. The method used will be cluster analysis based on principal-components analysis. The aim is to identify clusters of countries with common characteristics as well as obtaining a representation of the main dimensions that contribute to differentiating countries within a given institutional area. The indicators taken into account concern the 1990s— either averages over the decade or data applying to the late 1990s.

The empirical analysis on product-market competition uses indicators related to competition regulation devised by the OECD. Although product-market liberalization was set in motion in most OECD countries during the 1990s, there is still substantial variation among them with respect to competition. Initial expectation in this respect would be that countries usually classified as LMEs would be clearly distinguished from other countries, particularly those which represent the traditional CMEs. This is to some extent true. Countries such as the UK and the USA are characterized by a very low level of product-market regulation, but the other countries are not simply distinguished from this cluster on a one-dimensional basis. This is a pattern, indeed, that will be found in other institutional areas. Along a dimension reflecting the intensity of product-market regulation, countries such as Greece, Italy, Korea, and Spain are the most different from the USA or the UK. Traditional CMEs such as Germany occupy a central position. In addition, a specific dimension representing regulation of foreign trade emerges which distinguishes countries such as Norway and Canada from Belgium and Germany. This dimension does not reflect the usual distinction between CMEs and LMEs so much. The cluster analysis itself groups Anglo-Saxon countries together, with the exception of Canada. The other countries are distributed in two or five different clusters, depending on the chosen degree of disaggregation. These countries exhibit on average more product-market regulation. The analysis of labour-market regulation delivers a similar conclusion. Some countries are characterized by a low level of labour-market regulation and are clearly distinguished from several other groups of countries which exhibit differentiated patterns of regulation. Once again, Anglo-Saxon countries are characterized by low levels of regulation, and are neatly separated from Greece, Spain, and France, which possess more regulated labour-markets. Nevertheless, Europe as a continent is not homogeneous. Some countries that would be readily classified as CMEs exhibit in fact a non-negligible degree of labour-market deregulation: Denmark, Switzerland, and even Belgium. Mediterranean countries appear to possess more regulated labour markets than other European economies. Analyses of industrial relations and wage bargaining present a different picture. Market-based economies are not the only ones where wage bargaining is decentralized or uncoordinated. The clustering pattern is broadly consistent with the classification of Crouch (1993), who distinguishes three modes of interest intermediation: contestation, pluralist bargaining, and neo-corporatism. The latter can be organized as 'extensive neo-corporatism', which presupposes strong and centralized unions, and 'simple corporatism', where unions are relatively weak but endowed with a strategic capacity. Australia, Canada, the USA, the UK, the Netherlands, and Switzerland represent pluralism; France, Belgium, Spain, and Italy exemplify the contestation model; Germany, Austria, and Ireland are near a model of simple neo-corporatism; Finland, Sweden, and Denmark represent extensive neo-corporatism. A cluster composed of Norway and Japan appears as unique, but closer to extensive corporatism than to other country groupings. The analysis of employment policies delivers straightforward conclusions. The USA, Norway, Greece, Switzerland, the UK, Canada, Australia, Korea, Austria, and Spain are countries where employment policies are limited in every dimension. The other countries are distributed in three clusters differing with respect to

the favoured dimensions of active employment policies: youth programmes for Italy, Portugal, and France, hiring policies for Germany, Finland, Ireland, Belgium, and Denmark, and handicapped persons programmes for Sweden and the Netherlands.

The analysis of financial systems takes into account variables in the financing structure of non-financial firms, the type of control and corporate governance, and the structure of financial intermediaries. The most common typologies of financial systems distinguish between a bank-based and a financial-markets-based system. This distinction applies not so much to differences in the source of funds of non-financial firms as to the type of relationship between the firm and its financiers: close in the case of banking intermediaries, arm's-length with financial markets. In addition, two types of corporate control are differentiated. In 'outsider' systems there is a potential agency problem between managers and a widely dispersed ownership of the firm. In 'insider' systems the potential conflict is between controlling shareholders, or 'blockholders', and weak minority shareholders. Using a large number of indicators, our analysis shows that if on average accurate, this dichotomy could be refined. Four clusters of countries emerge out of the data analysis. There is a distinct group of countries that epitomize the decentralized financial system. The USA, Canada, the Netherlands, the UK, and Australia have financial systems where institutional investors and particularly pension funds are prominent; stock markets and venture-capital markets are active and well-developed. There is high mergers-and-acquisitions activity, and firms' ownership is dispersed. However, the other countries are not grouped together in a homogeneous ideal bank-based system. Three groups can be distinguished. The financial systems of Belgium, Denmark, and Sweden are certainly bank-based, but the banks have a somewhat 'passive' role: bonds and securities represent a large part of the banks' assets and the debt:GDP ratio is significantly lower than in other countries; control of firms is concentrated, with families playing an important role. In small countries such as Finland, Norway, and Ireland foreign banks are particularly important. A cluster grouping Germany and Japan, but also Austria, France, Italy, Portugal, and Spain, is more representative of the ideal bank-based, insider system: a less developed market for corporate control, a weak development of accounting standards, and a lagging venture-capital sector. Ownership is concentrated and the State plays a relatively important role in the control of some large corporations.

There are also many typologies of social-protection systems. The most widely used is probably that of Esping-Andersen (1990), which distinguishes three basic types of Welfare State. The liberal model is characterized by low and means-tested assistance, flat-rate benefits providing incentives to seek income from work, as well as the predominance of limited social-insurance plans. In the social-democratic model, the social-protection system is universal, based on citizenship, promotes social equality, and implies decommodification and detachment from family; i.e. individuals can achieve a reasonably high standard of living without market participation and independently of family support. Finally, the conservative-corporatist model is committed to preserving status and providing solidarity within rather than between social groups and therefore does not redistribute as much as the social-democratic model. Welfare benefits are linked to activity and employment. The regime favours moderate decommodification and familiarization. Our empirical analysis based on the structure of social expenditure leads us to distinguish three or six groups of countries, which are broadly compatible with the typology of Esping-Andersen. Sweden, Denmark, Norway, and Finland represent the typical social-democratic welfare approach. Japan, Canada, and the USA exemplify a private social-protection system. For once, the UK is not in the same group as the USA, breaking with the usual market-based clustering of countries. A distinct Continental European public system of social protection emerges, in France, Germany, Austria, and Belgium. Finally, an analysis of education systems is made, using data on the structure of educational expenditure as well as indicators of schooling and students' specializations and achievements. Education is an area where international comparisons are rarely conducted within a systematic methodology. The 'varieties of capitalism' approach of Hall and Soskice (2001) centres on vocational training and the relations between the firm and training systems. Other approaches concentrate on the patterns of differentiation and standardization of education. There is therefore no widely agreed-upon typology of countries in this area, as opposed, for instance, to the typologies of the financial sector or social-protection systems. The results of our analyses give a clustering pattern which partly overlaps with some other attempts at establishing a common basis for international comparisons of education systems (Hannan et al. 1996). Germany, France, the Netherlands, and Ireland may be characterized by a high degree of homogeneity in primary and secondary curricula and certification procedures. A cluster gathering Italy, Spain, Portugal, and Greece involves limited initiative from either employer or employee in continuing training. This is also the group of countries where the employer's role is weak in continuing training and weak to moderate in vocational training. The USA, Canada, Japan, and the UK could be interpreted as a group where differentiation of individual paths is moderate or low, as opposed, for instance, to Germany. Scandinavian countries are not all gathered in a homogeneous group, but they nevertheless exhibit some common features, such as a relatively high level of public spending and a high average quality of primary and secondary education.

The conclusions that one could draw from all these analyses are that the usual typologies of capitalism are far from evident whatever the institutional area. This could be interpreted as a rejection of 'naive' structural isomorphism, which would predict that the same clustering pattern should be found in each domain. This also explains why one usually finds different classifications of countries in the literature. Usually, one specific institutional area (labour market, Welfare State, etc.) is privileged even when others are taken into account, and the typologies derived are necessarily partial. This is why it is necessary to take into account all the possible complementarities between the five institutional areas in order to come to an empirical classification of capitalism. The different varieties of capitalism are defined as specific architectures of complementary institutions, and the complete picture can only be grasped by putting all the pieces together. Indeed, a cluster analysis performed on all the active variables of the preceding analyses can be interpreted in terms of the different varieties of capitalism. The final analysis gives five or six clusters of countries, which can be linked to the five different models of capitalism presented above. The difference in the alternative groupings concerns Switzerland and the Netherlands, which may constitute a separate group in the six-cluster typology or join France, Germany, Austria, Belgium, Ireland, and Norway in the Continental European grouping. The market-based economies, the USA, UK, Canada, and Australia, constitute a highly homogeneous cluster, which is opposed to the Mediterranean cluster (Italy, Spain, Portugal, and Greece) on an axis separating 'flexible' markets (financial and labour markets) from 'rigid' markets. A second dimension may be taken into account, which basically expresses the extent of social protection. The social-democratic model (Sweden, Finland, and Denmark) is located at one end of this axis, and the Asian model (Japan and Korea) at the other. In a two-dimensional plane, the 'restricted' Continental European model, i.e. without the Netherlands and Switzerland, appears as intermediate between the social-democratic and the Mediterranean models, whereas the sub-group formed with the two excluded countries appears as intermediate between the market-based and the social-democratic models. Ireland and Norway appear also as slightly separate cases within the 'Continental' model. Thus, the analysis broadly confirms the relevance of the typology of five types of capitalism.

Since institutional design both reflects and influences the structure of interests for individual and collective agents, one may expect to find some correlations between the institutional structures of countries and their political choices, as well as the structure of their political systems. Political choices expressed in terms of partisan politics reflect both the structure of political supply in terms of parties and platforms, but also the constitution of political demand and how this demand is integrated into party politics in order to be implemented by a coalition in power. Expectations regarding the relation between partisan politics and varieties of capitalism are that a larger representation of centre-right parties should be more favourable to the establishment of the institutions characteristic of market-based capitalism whereas the social-democratic model should be associated with a greater importance of left-wing parties. One also usually expects market-based economies to be associated with the Westminster type of government, which concentrates power in the political executive, while varieties of capitalism where non-market coordination plays a crucial role should rely on more consensual or corporatist regimes (Hall and Soskice 2001). These types of capitalism base their competitiveness on a certain degree of stability and guarantees that specific investments will be protected. Political regimes characterized by coalition governments, multiple-veto players, and proportional representation are more likely to supply the type of assurance that incentivizes investment in specific assets. Using various databases of political variables with indicators of electoral results as well as characteristics of government systems, one can check for the robustness of these predictions. A larger share of votes for parties on the left is indeed associated with countries distant from the market-based model, and votes for left and left-libertarian parties are positively correlated with proximity to the social-democratic model. The relationships between variables characterizing the system of government and the type of capitalism are less straightforward. As expected, a large number of veto players seems incompatible with similarity with the market-based model. Some indicators of the consensus-based system of government (Lijphart 1999) seem to be systematically associated with proximity to the social-democratic model, but a robust association between the characteristics of the Westminster system and similarity to the market-based system cannot easily be found.

One of the most distinctive predictions of the 'varieties of capitalism' approach is that there should be a strong link between a country's institutional structure and the type of economic activities it specializes in. This was already hypothesized and checked in Amable et al. (1997). The different 'social systems of innovation and production' were characterized by specific patterns of scientific, technological, and industrial specialization. A summary of the argument underlying the correlation is that competitiveness in specific activities entails investment in particular assets. These invest-ments may be facilitated or hindered by institutional arrangements, so that a specific institutional structure will contribute to the emergence of comparative advantage in the activities dependent on the factors whose accumulation is made easier by the national institutions. In return, agents' situations will depend crucially on the competitiveness of these activities; they are thus bound to express political demands supporting the stability of the relevant institutions. For instance, agents specializing in high-risk activities are bound to favour institutions which allow for easy risk diversification; a specialization in industries whose competitiveness is a function of highly specific assets will be expected to be correlated with the presence of institutions that favour the protection of these assets; agents with vested interests in the survival of complex State-coordinated indus-tries will be more willing to bring political support to strategies based on State intervention. One would then expect the different models of capital-ism to exhibit marked differences with respect to their pattern of special-ization. Institutional differences in product-market competition, labour-market flexibility, or social protection will define specific incen-tives that influence competitive advantage. A comparative analysis of country specialization in scientific publications, patents, and international trade at a disaggregated level of 20–30 activities broadly confirms these expectations. Market-based economies specialize in activities where fast adaptation and good industry–university links matter: biotechnologies, computer science, and electronics. Social-democratic countries have a comparative advantage in health-related activities as well as industries linked to their natural resources (paper and printing). Countries on the Mediterranean model specialize in light industries and low-tech activi-ties. Asian-capitalism countries have a comparative advantage in com-puters, electronics, and machines. The only model which does not seem to exhibit a strong pattern of specialization is the Continental European model. Three types of capitalism also show strong correlations with vari-ous aspects of the 'new economy'. One would expect the market-based model to be particularly favourable to the emergence of new technologies such as ICT and start-up firms exploiting the new opportunities supplied by the technological paradigm. On the other hand, the Mediterranean model of capitalism, characterized by a low technology intensity and heavy product-market regulation, should be particularly unfriendly to entrepreneurship and new technologies. Indeed, these expectations are confirmed. Market-based economies are characterized by a higher production and diffusion of ICT. By contrast, Mediterranean economies suffer from a significant lag in the diffusion of ICT. But social-democratic economies are in fact also very specific in their pattern of diffusion of these technologies: in the education sector, for health-related matters, and in communication between the population and local administrations; i.e. a pattern broadly consistent with the major features of the social-democratic model and its focus on education, the Welfare State, and democracy.

1.6 Institutional Change and Political Strategies in Europe

The debate on the possible convergence between economic systems of the late 1990s has focused on the issue of economic performance. A simple evolutionary argument would predict the elimination of institutional forms that lead to inferior macroeconomic performance and the adoption of those institutions that prove to be efficient; dissatisfied agents would press for institutional change and adoption of the best-practice institutions. As we have seen, this functionalist argument neglects the political conditions necessary for institutional change. An important aspect is precisely the political strategies implemented in order to bring about a change of economic models. It remains true that prolonged differences in macroeconomic performance may certainly initiate a political process leading to substantial institutional change. One of the conclusions of the institutional-complementarities approaches is that there is no such thing as a 'one best way' for achieving superior economic performance. Different combinations of institutional forms may in the end produce similar macroeconomic performance. Some tests of this hypothesis are proposed; their results indicate that there may be several combinations of complementary institutions conducive to high growth, low unemployment, and a high rate of innovation. Yet, the Continental European model is at the centre of criticisms against its alleged inability to reform itself, its inferior economic performance, particularly with respect to unemployment, and its lack of sustainability in a context of globalization intensifying the competition between systems. The most often mentioned deficiencies of the Continental European model are the following. Labour-market rigidity would prevent labour-force adjustments and structural change and would be at the root of mass unemployment. A dwindling employed labour force would endanger social-protection systems which would be unable in themselves to prevent an increase in social exclusion, and would impose levels of taxation detrimental to the competitiveness of European territories. Bank-based financial systems would be too rigid to allow the financing of small, technology-intensive firms upon which the dynamism of the new technological paradigm is based. Two institutional areas are particularly under scrutiny: the enlarged wage–labour nexus, i.e. labour market and social-protection institutions, and the financial system. These two domains have experienced some change during the 1990s in most countries of the Continental European model—more pronounced in the case of the financial system than for the Welfare State. Significant alterations to the institutional forms of these two areas would endanger the institutional complementarities that form the coherence of the model. Attempts at reforming Continental economies towards the adoption of more market-based principles have met with some political opposition. The most important political strategy supporting a transition towards the market-based model has been followed on the left, with the so-called Third Way. Unsurprisingly, the Third Way is a strategy originating from a country belonging to the market-based model. Its economic-policy recommendations are geared towards competition, labour deregulation, financial liberalization, and a reform of the Welfare State emphasizing inclusion in the labour market rather than benefits. This strategy was followed with political success in the UK, and its main proponent, Prime Minister Tony Blair, was very active in its promotion on the Continent. European social-democratic parties were all the more willing to adopt the stance of the 'new left' because they believed it would bring them the same electoral success that 'New Labour' enjoyed. In fact, the attempts at implementing the Third Way in Europe were very modest, basically because it amounts to grafting market-based institutional forms and policies onto a model organized according to very different complementarities. This is bound to be inefficient and raise some serious political concern. Indeed, far from being the key to success, the Third Way proved the best way to electoral defeat for social-democratic parties in Europe. Only parties that differentiated themselves from the 'new left' and reaffirmed their will to defend Continental European or social-democratic institutions such as the Welfare State could escape electoral losses.

This leaves the Continental European model without a supporting political strategy either on the left or on the right. A new socio-political bloc supporting the transformation and renewal of the Continental model might be found in a compromise between large manufacturing employers willing to resist all-out financial liberalization and the resulting shareholder pressure, and unions who would like to maintain a high level of social protection; i.e. basically an alliance between stakeholders. Unions or worker representatives could trade some employment protection and accept some flexibility in exchange for more responsibility in the firm's management. At the EU level this strategy represents one of the variants of the project of 'regulated capitalism'; i.e. an attempt at setting up a social market economy beyond the confines of the nation-state. This project would require a non-negligible degree of bargaining coordination at the EU level, which was lacking at the start of the twenty-first century; this coordination would also allow wage moderation and be compatible with the anti-inflation policy of the ECB. Whether the project of 'regulated capitalism' will succeed in renovating the Continental model of capitalism depends on the strategic capacities of the actors involved.

Chapter 2 provides the theoretical background for the book. It proposes a theory of institutions as political equilibriums and presents the concepts of institutional complementarity and hierarchy. A comparative analysis of capitalism based on these notions is found in the following chapter. Going further than a dichotomy between LMEs and CMEs like that proposed in Hall and Soskice (2001), the chapter presents five possible models of capitalism and the set of institutional complementarities between five institutional forms that these models are based on. The following two chapters test the relevance of this theoretical typology. Chapter 4 presents results from cluster analyses of five institutional areas: product-market competition, the labour market, the financial sector, social protection, and the education system. It is shown that the clusterings of countries are not necessarily identical to the theoretical typology of capitalism presented in the previous chapter. Chapter 5 gathers the results of the analyses of Chapter 4 and proposes a cluster analysis of types of capitalism. Empirical clustering patterns are discovered that are interpretable in terms of the typology of Chapter 3. Specific characteristics concerning political systems, specialization in scientific, technological, and industrial activity, as well as macroeconomic performance are shown to be associated with particular types of capitalism. The last chapter focuses on one particular type of capitalism. It reviews the main transformations that have taken place in the Continental European model of capitalism in connection with the opposition between the main ideological and political currents. It analyses the opposition between a project of regulated capitalism, which corresponds to a renewal of the Continental model, and a neo-liberal project, which aims at transforming the EU countries into market-based economies. It is argued that the Third Way was one political strategy compatible with the neo-liberal project, and that its relative failure can be explained with the help of our theory of the diversity of capitalism.

2

Institutions, Complementarity, and Hierarchy

2.1 Institutions and Economics

2.1.1 Why Institutions Matter

A simple look at the evolution of the literature since the late 1960s leads to the conclusion that the study of institutions is once again a dominant preoccupation in economics. By contrast with the pre-war period, when economic sociology in France[1] and institutional economics in the USA[2] took a prominent position, modern (i.e. post-war) economics that developed during the 'golden age' of capitalism around a rigorous exposé of Walras's 'general equilibrium' has for a long time limited its analysis of institutions to markets. Roughly speaking, other institutions were mostly regarded as hindrances that stood in the way of a proper price mechanism through which a socially optimal equilibrium could be reached without centralized planning. As a consequence, the appropriate institutions that a modern economy needed were those that allowed for a functioning of real existing markets as close as possible to that featured in general-equilibrium theory—at least when no external effects were involved—i.e. basically institutions that guaranteed stable property rights[3] and the enforcement of private contracts. The presence of externalities altered this position somewhat. In their presence it was up to the State, assuming the role of a benevolent planner, to provide the necessary corrections, by means of preferably non-distortive taxation, for instance, in order to preserve as much as possible the free functioning of markets and enjoy the allocative benefits related to market mechanisms. The State's mission was also to care for the supply of goods that the market was ill suited to provide, i.e. pure public goods. This conception of institutions and public intervention corresponded to the prominence of the Keynesian practice of economic policy-making during the golden age. Short-run disequilibrium was corrected by means of active demand-management macroeconomic policy,

---

[1] In particular the works of François Simiand and Maurice Halbwacs, inspired by Durkheim (see Steiner (2001)).

[2] The works of Veblen, Commons, Mitchell, etc. (see Rutherford (1994)).

[3] The rights of an agent to use valuable assets, in Alchian's definition (Eggertson (1990)).

granting that the economy would return to a neoclassical equilibrium in the long run.

In the 1960s and 1970s monetarist and new classical economists initiated a critique of the Keynesian pattern of State intervention and demand-management policy and advocated a free functioning of market mechanisms. The pillars of new classical economics were the various propositions associated with the broad thesis of the inefficiency of macroeconomic policy (Sargent and Wallace 1975) on the one hand, and the prominent role given to microeconomic, supply-side policies on the other. The latter are oriented toward giving proper market (price) signals to firms and individuals in order to increase production, reduce unemployment, and augment welfare. In the context of the post-war developed economies, questioning the efficiency of Keynesian demand management and promoting the implementation of supply-side policies is a call for significant institutional change: the former led, for instance, to a move toward the independence of central banks in Europe and other developed countries and more generally significant restrictions on the 'discretion' with which governments can implement economic policy, from monetary interventions to budget-deficit and public-debt management. This general trend initiated a move towards the diffusion of market-signals-based policies: competition policy for product markets, financial liberalization, and deregulation of labour markets. Such an institutional transformation corresponded also to political changes: the conservative counter-revolution of the 1980s most significantly heralded by the Reagan administration and the governments of Margaret Thatcher, but also the progressive move of left-of-centre European parties away from social democracy towards Third-Way-type politics in the 1990s.[4] The basic idea behind all these changes is that the institutional framework matters a great deal for sound economic performance, and that a move towards greater importance for market mechanisms is desirable.

The resurgence of institutional preoccupations can also be linked to two lines of academic research: one is comparative economics from a long-term perspective and the other is linked to the theory of the firm or the organization. The latter takes a micro/organizational perspective. This research programme, whose origins can be found in Coase (1937), proposed a theory of the firm based on transaction costs, defined as agents' opportunity costs of establishing and maintaining internal control of resources.[5] Firms exist because some transactions must be made outside the market-price

---

[4] See Ch. 6 for a more thorough discussion of this matter.

[5] Eggertsson (1996). External control of resources depends on the system of property rights, the institutional environment of agents; internal control is established by the agents themselves through various decisions: monitoring, fencing, etc.

system because there are costs related to using the price mechanism: discovering the relevant prices and establishing contracts for each necessary transaction. Later developments[6] also considered costs related to opportunistic or morally hazardous behaviour of agents. Other costs are incurred, related to contract enforcement and possible sanctions. The existence of transaction costs explains the existence of the firm, which provides an answer to the make-or-buy decision. There can be different 'governance structures' for solving the problems associated with the existence of transaction costs, which will define the range of activities that will either be internalized or externalized. For Williamson (1985), the frequency of transactions, the specificity of a supplier's investment, and the uncertainty of the transactions are factors which have an effect on the internalization decision. More generally, several branches of economic theory have investigated the functioning of organizations (Milgrom and Roberts 1992; Hart 1995) and the way activities could be coordinated by price and non-price mechanisms: hierarchies, contracts, and incentive schemes are devices that purport to overcome problems related to information exchange, opportunistic behaviour, lack of cooperation, insufficient coordination, shirking, or any type of moral-hazard or adverse-selection problem.

But firms or organizations cannot be considered in isolation. They compete under the influence of 'macrolevel' institutions, and these institutions influence the growth paths of nations. Comparing long-run growth performance of nations is not limited to a growth-accounting exercise, however sophisticated that might be. It means above all performing a comparative institutional analysis.[7] More precisely, the only way to make sense of macroeconomic-growth accounting would be to interpret its findings in the light of a comparative analysis of institutions. Such preoccupations were present in the work of Abramovitz (1986), who, following Okawa and Rosovsky (1973), made use of the notion of social capability to account for the fact that less developed countries possessed no necessary advantage in backwardness independent of the presence of certain institutional features liable to boost technology, skills, and knowledge acquisition, leading to an improvement in productivity and fast growth. Thus, contrary to the conclusions of the standard neoclassical growth model,[8] one should not necessarily expect poor countries to grow faster than rich countries and catch up with them in terms of development level. Going one step further, economic historians such as Douglas North explicitly

---

[6] Williamson, Alchian, Demsetz, etc. (see Eggertsson (1990) or Rutherford (1994)).
[7] See Aoki (1995, 2001).
[8] See Barro and Sala-i-Martin (1995) for a discussion of the convergence problem.

linked growth performance to the institutional structure of the economy, explaining how institutions shaped the growth trajectory of nations through their influence on the behaviour of agents (North 1990). Institutions define incentives and constraints that will lead agents to invest in certain assets, acquire certain skills, cooperate, or be opportunistic. These individual decisions will affect the macroeconomic growth perform-ance. Therefore, the micro/organizational and macro levels are linked. Macrolevel institutions will partly determine the level of transaction costs, and thus the structure of organizations that agents will be led to adopt at the microeconomic level. This institutional architecture will have conse-quences for the economic development of nations. In such a perspective, institutions 'matter' because they—partly and imperfectly—solve problems of coordination among agents: they help promote cooperation and over-come opportunistic behaviour; they make agents internalize externalities, either intertemporal or interpersonal; and they reduce uncertainty. Institutions 'matter' because some institutional arrangements may be more or less effective than others in performing these tasks. Therefore, economic outcomes are likely to depend on institutional configurations; and the characteristics of national institutions, along with more strictly technological characteristics, will determine, for instance, the accumula-tion of physical capital, the investment in R & D, the type of education of the labour force, etc.—and hence the growth path.

If one takes the example of the various growth factors considered by the theory of endogenous growth, one may identify institutions likely to affect the growth and development paths of countries (Romer 1993; Amable et al. 1997; Boyer and Didier 1998). In many endogenous growth theories the growth-inducing actions of some agents have positive effects on the actions of others. Neglect of these positive external effects is detrimental to one's own investment in the growth-inducing factors. Social institutions may help to develop positive interactions. To foster such positive effects, institutions can operate at various levels and use a variety of means, facilitating human-capital investment or physical-capital infrastructures, for instance. One can first take the simplest form of endogenous growth with externalities, i.e. that with capital accumulation and positive externalities (Romer 1986). In this category of models, positive externalities are linked to capital (or knowledge) accumulation through learning by doing or because new knowledge is embodied in new equipment; because of the public-good aspect of knowledge, an individual firm's investment bene-fits all firms. One can identify several institutional features likely to influ-ence the growth path in such a framework: the financial system, which conditions the efficiency of the channelling of saving resources towards investment and ultimately the volume of investment and the rate of growth; the internal organization of the firm (Gatti 1999), which will influence the investment decision in several ways; and any public intervention which affects the cost of capital, such as tax policy, for instance. Institutions are also important in human-capital-based models of endogenous growth. Positive externalities are related to human-capital accumulation, through the presence of interpersonal effects (having educated people around makes one more productive, because of informal information exchange or other channels of transmission) or intertemporal effects (learning now makes further learning easier). The features of the general education and training systems, either public or private, as well as firms' internal training systems or more generally any institutions that affect education and training decisions of individuals, will matter for growth. In empirical work such effects are usually accounted for by the inclusion of one or more schooling variables in growth regressions.[9]

The financial sector has an effect on the efficiency of investment (Levine 1997). Banks not only passively channel saving resources to investment needs, they screen entrepreneurs and sometimes monitor the firm's management either directly or indirectly. Financial intermediaries process information, helping individual savers to find profitable investment opportunities. Regulation of entry into the financial-intermediation sector will determine the structure of competition among banks, hence their levels of profit, and their financial fragility. Financial intermediaries subject to stricter competition have smaller interest-rate margins; this lowers the cost of capital and fosters investment, but banks cannot use their small profits to cushion large adverse macroeconomic shocks, and incur a greater risk of bankruptcy. This increased uncertainty may deter savers and lead to a drop in investment and slower growth (Amable, Chatelain, and De Bandt 2002). Concerning other sources of endogenous growth, the accumulation of knowledge, new ideas, and the innovation process are also subject to various positive externalities. Many institutions or organizations will affect the efficiency of the growth-generating processes: the scientific system, the higher-education system, the pattern of organization of R & D inside the firm, and so on. Therefore, when taking a comprehensive view of the growth-generating factors, many and various mechanisms are likely to be shaped by institutional features.

Finally, without trying to be exhaustive, one could also mention the influence of institutional features on other traditional measures of macroeconomic performance, such as inflation and employment. A wide

---

[9] See Barro and Sala-i-Martin (1995), for instance.

literature has assessed the links between the independence of the central bank and the rate and variance of inflation (Cukierman and Lippi 1999; Gatti and van Wijnbergen 2001). Independence is defined as the degree of autonomy of the central bank from the political authority in monetary policy-making. Governments are supposed to be more responsive than dedicated authorities such as central banks to pressures favouring inflation. Only a very conservative government could be as inflation-averse as a central banker. Therefore, delegation of authority to an independent central bank reduces inflation. The argument is generally exposed with reference to the time-inconsistency problem (Kydland and Prescott 1977); policies once announced induce private-sector strategies which in turn alter the policy-makers' strategies. Applied to monetary policy by Barro and Gordon (1983), the time-inconsistency problem would be such that governments would announce low monetary growth, private agents would set prices according to it, and policy-makers would try to stimulate the economy by cheating on the agents' expectations. Aware of this, private agents would modify their pricing strategies, leading to a higher level of inflation. A way to avoid this suboptimal outcome is to delegate monetary policy to a conservative and sufficiently autonomous central bank, which can credibly announce and provide lower inflation without real economic costs.

The links between wage-setting institutions and employment performance have been a major topic of research since the 1980s at least. The traditional view is that real wage levels will be higher the further wage-setting institutions are from perfect competition, i.e. the more centralized wage-setting is. This institutional arrangement would lead to less than full employment, and presumably high inflation. The literature on corporatism opposed this view and argued that centralization of wage bargaining would be a guarantee that wage setters would take into account broader interests. It would also favour the emergence of a consensus among social partners, which would be beneficial to the employment level and would facilitate work reorganization. Thus, the more centralized wage bargaining is, the higher employment and the lower inflation should be. Calmfors and Driffill (1988) proposed to take into account a non-monotonic, hump-shaped relationship between centralization of wage bargaining and wage levels. The basic idea can also be found in Olson (1982): organized interests are harmful when they are powerful enough to cause major disruptions but not sufficiently encompassing to internalize the costs of their actions. In this perspective, wage moderation can be achieved either through decentralization of wage bargaining or through all-encompassing trade unions. In the former case, bargaining units would be too small to have significant price- or wage-setting power; in the latter case, unions would recognize the possible adverse effects of wage increases on inflation and employment. In the intermediate case, unions would be strong enough to exert wage pressure but would neglect the macroeconomic consequences on inflation and unemployment.

Therefore, there is a large consensus in the economics literature on the importance of institutions. However, this does not mean that there is a unified economic theory of institutions. The following subsection will attempt to present some elements that could help to set up such a theory.

2.1.2 Elements of a Theory of Institutions

The starting point of an economic theory of institutions is certainly that agents' economic decisions are not simply determined by a set of intertemporal prices, as in general equilibrium, but also by 'non-price' factors such as institutions. Institutions impact on economic behaviour not only because they have a bearing on the determination of prices on existing markets, but also because they influence decision-taking when there are missing markets. As seen above, a wide economic literature is willing to acknowledge the effects of institutions on the economy. Yet, stressing the importance of 'institutions' does not answer the question of what an institution is from the point of view of economics. There are several definitions in the literature. According to North (1990), institutions are 'humanly devised constraints imposed on human interaction'. With reference to the framework given by game theory, institutions can be defined as the rules of a game where individual agents or organizations such as firms would be the players. Together with technology and preferences, these rules define the constraints imposed on and the possibilities open to each agent. It would be misleading to consider that institutions merely narrow the possibility set of agents; institutions also enable interactions, coordination, cooperation, and information exchanges among agents. They are thus also humanly devised arrangements opening up and monitoring new possibilities. Agents' strategies are devised under the influence of institutions; i.e. formal or informal rules that define the set of choices available to them. The most formal of rules, such as constitutions, laws, or regulations, cannot be changed by an individual player of the game; agents' strategies must be devised taking these rules as given, as shaping the set of possible actions. In North's view, the conception of institutions as rules of the game does not mean that the institutional structure of an economy never changes. Some players can take the role of rule makers. Playing a certain game and obtaining the corresponding pay-offs may generate a latent demand for new rules of the game, i.e. institutional change. Politics will decide whether this latent demand can be formally expressed, and whether and how a new set of rules should be adopted.[10]

However, the institutions-as-rules view raises some further questions. In order to be effective, rules need to be enforced; there must thus exist a set of enforcement mechanisms which are part of the institutional structure of the economy, since not all rules are necessarily self-enforcing. In fact, many rules are not, and they call for specific enforcement devices: courts of justice, penalties, police, army, etc. More generally, in order to be effective, rules need to be acknowledged as binding by agents. As pointed out by Aoki (2001), the enforcement issue brings a new dimension into the analysis of institutions; the supposed existence of enforcing mechanisms raises an infinite-regression problem—namely, that of who enforces the enforcer. One way out of this infinite regression is to consider all institutions, including the enforcer's actions, as an equilibrium strategy in a game-theoretic framework. This means that the behaviour of the enforcer would not be assumed, as if another enforcer conditioned it, but derived as an equilibrium outcome of the game. The enforcer would behave as expected because doing so is the best he can do given the circumstances. In some cases one could dispense with an enforcer altogether, because institutions would become self-enforcing through the strategic interaction of the players of the game (Schotter 1981; Young 1998). Some strategies are thus excluded by the players, not because there is an external mechanism actually preventing them from adopting these strategies, but because adopting them is not an equilibrium of the game. For Aoki (2001), institutions are then defined as 'a self-sustaining system of shared beliefs about a salient way in which the game is repeatedly played'.[11] They may thus also be defined as the rules governing agents' action, but these rules are endogenous. Institutions emerge as a process of formation of agents' strategies according to their subjective perception of other agents' rules of choice for action. Neither perfect rationality nor perfect information is required for such rules to emerge out of agents' interaction. Institutions cannot be ignored by agents as long as other agents interacting with them take them into account when devising their own strategy. In order to qualify as institutions, endogenous rules must then be self-sustaining. For instance, Aoki (2001) considers that a law cannot be a relevant institution

---

[10] For North, the new rules are negotiated in a 'political market'.

[11] Beliefs come into the picture because agents need elements upon which to form their representation of the equilibrium. An institution must be relevant for all agents, providing them with a common understanding of the way the game is played. Beliefs are important for the emergence of a *salient* way of playing the game.

if nobody abides by it, whereas some informal but observed practices are institutions in this sense. The institutions-as-endogenous-equilibrium-strategies view simultaneously allows us to consider the emergence and stability—through self-enforcement—of institutions and proposes a vision of endogenous institutional change. It solves the problem of how the rules of the metagame implicit in the institutions-as-rules view are chosen. However, as pointed out by Aoki (2001), if such an approach allows us to understand the emergence of an institution in one domain,[12] it is nevertheless not conceivable that a model could be obtained which would explain the emergence of all possible institutions in every domain, starting from resource endowments, preferences, and technology alone. In other words, the applied theory of institutions as endogenous rules of the game must find a historically defined starting point in order to be effective.

These two views of institutions,[13] i.e. rules of the game or equilibrium strategies, shed some light on how institutions influence the behaviour of agents and the economic outcomes that derive from it. Each conception has its pros and cons, and a synthesis could be envisaged. When conceived as rules of the game, institutions shape the incentives agents are faced with and determine what their strategies are going to be. This accounts for the fact that agents—individuals or organizations—take institutions as given, do not question them, and develop their strategies accordingly. This also reflects the role of institutions as coordinating and uncertainty-reducing devices. Taking them as given allows agents to implement their best-response strategies.[14] Without such a stabilized environment the game agents would play would be permanently to reinvent society and the economy, with a complete set of constitution, laws, regulations, practices, and conventions. However, the rules of the game do change sometimes, and agents work out new rules, i.e. institutions, which emerge as equilibrium strategies. We may thus define a two-tier or nested game structure for the behaviour of agents.[15] The lower tier defines

---

[12] The domain of a game is the set of agents and the actions open to them.

[13] Aoki (2001) actually considers three views of institutions in a game-theoretic perspective. The missing view sees institutions as players of the game; this means taking the common-sense definition of institutions as a concept of an economic institution. We choose to ignore it here since we will make a distinction between institutions and organizations.

[14] Again, neither perfect rationality nor perfect information need be assumed.

[15] The structure could of course include more than just two levels, but we use this simplification for expository purposes. One could extend the set of nested rules by considering other 'meta' levels.

agents' strategy in a given institutional framework; for instance, a given legal or regulatory environment. Institutions in such a setting are taken as rules of the game. This corresponds to a situation of relative institutional stability, in so far as the rules of the game are not significantly altered by playing the game, i.e. by the individual strategies devised by agents. On the other hand, the upper tier, which is the level of the metagame in the institutions-as-rules view, defines the framework of the lower-tier game. It corresponds to the game analysed by Aoki (2001), where institutions emerge as self-sustaining equilibrium strategies. Such a two-tier view can be further elaborated by explicitly considering the political aspect in the emergence and stability of institutions. We now move towards sketching a theory of the emergence, stability, and dynamics of institutions affecting the economy and polity. Institutions are not only considered as endogenous equilibrium strategies, but more specifically as political-economy equilibriums, i.e. as the outcome of strategic interactions among agents in a specific power structure.

2.1.3 Institutions and Conflict of Interest

Economic theories of institutions sometimes take as a starting point that agents must develop their individual strategies in a context of uncertainty about the future consequences of their decisions, for instance the pay-offs associated with certain investment levels, and above all what other agents' strategies could be. Let us consider, for example, the typewriter game whose pay-off matrix is presented in Fig. 2.1.[16]

Secretaries must decide which type of keyboard they will learn to type on and employers must decide which type of computer to provide them with.[17] The 'institution' resulting from this game is the equilibrium choice of a

		Secretaries	
		Dvorak	Qwerty
Employers	Dvorak	5,5	0,0
	Qwerty	0,0	4,4

FIG. 2.1 Pay-off matrix for the typewriter game

Source: Young (1998).

---

[16] This example is taken from Young (1998).
[17] See David (1985) for an exposition of the economics of Qwerty.

keyboard. Although this represents a simple coordination problem, choice of the optimal keyboard by all concerned is not guaranteed. Two equilibriums are a priori possible: either everybody chooses the Dvorak keyboard—which is represented here as more efficient—or the Qwerty keyboard is chosen. Which equilibrium is chosen depends on the process of choice.[18] If a decentralized procedure prevails, without explicit coordination, it is possible that the less efficient keyboard will be chosen, depending on agents' expectations regarding diffusion.

Why can this technology choice be considered as an institutional choice? In order to answer this question we need to have a definition of what an institution is. There are different definitions in the literature;[19] I propose the following. Institutions will be defined as a set of rules[20] that structure social interactions in particular ways. Knowledge of these rules must be common to all members of the relevant group or society. Institutions are rules that provide information about how agents are expected to act in certain situations, and can be recognized by those who are members of the relevant group as the rules to which others conform in these situations. They structure the strategic choices of agents in such a way as to produce equilibrium outcomes. The fact that they are rules means that not complying with them implies a sanction. Formal rules are openly codified; non-compliance with them is followed by a sanction delivered by a legitimate authority. Legitimacy is relative to the relevant group or community concerned with the rule and defines what agents agree upon. Institutions or actions may thus be legitimate. In the case of a constitution or a law, the legitimate authorities are courts of justice and the State; in the case of the internal rules of an organization, the legitimate authority may be the management. The legitimacy of the relevant authority is backed by a set of formal as well as informal rules. The sanction accompanying non-compliance with the formal rules is itself codified and formal. These sanctions may be fines, sentences, etc. Informal rules are not fully codified and non-compliance does not in general involve a formal sanction delivered by a legitimate authority. Informal rules are conventions or social norms. One may distinguish between the two with reference to individual behaviour. Norms are observed irrespective of others' behaviour, conventions' value depends on the fact that others respect

---

[18] Although the Dvorak equilibrium is risk-dominant (see below for a definition), we still keep the possibility of the adoption of the Qwerty keyboard.

[19] See Crawford and Ostrom (1995).

[20] Several meanings are given to the word 'rule' by Black (1962): a regulation, an instruction, a precept, or a principle. We will consider that rules are shared prescriptions indicating what may, must, or must not be done.

them. Norms are defined with reference to a set of values; conventions are defined with reference to socially accepted behaviour. The two notions are interrelated, and social conventions may be elevated to the status of social norms. No formal sanction is associated with non-compliance with an informal rule, but informal ones prevail. The sanctions (and rewards) related to informal rules are thus diverse: social exclusion and change in social status, self-esteem, or reputation, or a mere utility loss.

Not all rules are institutions. Rules of thumb, for instance, cannot be considered as institutions since they are strictly private and specific to the individual. Habits cannot be considered as institutions either, because they have no social dimension; institutions are socially shared. The case of regularity of behaviour is more complex. Institutions structure social interactions by providing information about one's own and others' behaviour. Plain regularities of behaviour are not institutions because they do not provide enough information on the future course of action of other agents. An institution must be a rule which applies to all the cases that the rule is supposed to govern, guiding the actions of agents and providing them with expectations regarding the future course of actions of other agents with whom they will interact (Knight 1992). The general applicability of rules guides not only agents' future actions but also their expectations about the future actions of others. Regularities only provide information about past actions. Unless there is some unambiguous and socially shared way to connect present and future actions to observed past actions, it is not possible to rely on regularities in the same way as on an institution. Besides, regularity is strictly contextual by necessity, whereas a rule is more general. One may use a famous example given in Kripke (1982) to illustrate this point. How can one be sure that someone is using the addition rule by observing past actions? If someone has always added numbers no greater than 56 in the past, and has obtained as a result numbers which are in accordance with the adding rule, does it mean that he follows this rule? The observed regularity could be the outcome of another rule, called quaddition and symbolized by $\oplus$. The rule of quaddition is that $x \oplus y = x + y$ if $x, y < 57$ or $= 5$ otherwise. The observed regularity in behaviour is consistent with both addition and quaddition, and there is no way of knowing which rule is being applied. Knight (1992) gives the example of an instance of bargaining between a firm and a trade union. In past negotiations over wages the union has always adopted a strict no-strike policy, but this is a mere regularity since no explicit (or implicit) rule prevents the union from going on strike. Should the management always count on the no-strike regularity for all future negotiations? What if new workers' representatives are elected? Should one expect the same behaviour? Will workers go on strike if the negotiation includes topics other than just wages? In each of these cases mere regularities do not provide the same certainty as institutions, and reducing uncertainty about agents with whom one interacts is precisely the point of institutions. Following from the definition of institutions given above, organizations are not institutions but collective agents who may be subject to social constraints. Organizations possess an internal structure which is made of rules that qualify as institutions since they govern the interactions of the members of the organization.

Going back to the typewriter game, a choice of keyboard will be an institution or a convention if it becomes the common choice of all secretaries and all employers, and knowledge of the choice is shared, or common, among all agents.[21] Sanctions related to non-compliance are merely the utility loss given in the pay-off matrix and expressed by the fact that a secretary who has learned to type on the wrong keyboard will not find employment and an employer in a similar situation will not find employees. There is a particular aspect to the typewriter game; it is a mere coordination problem, because there is no fundamental conflict between players on the solution that should be chosen. It is usual to present the emergence of institutions or conventions in a game-theoretic context as the answer to a coordination problem (Schotter 1981; Batifoulier 2001). Yet, not all games, and not all institutions, address coordination problems only. Some games may be of the 'mixed-motive' type; i.e. where both coordination and distribution issues are present. One can take another example from Young (1998)—that of two people approaching a doorway. The question of who shall give way to the other is a coordination problem. This situation is known as the etiquette game. Young (1998) posits two players: 'women' and 'men'. The game possesses two (pure strategy) equilibria,[22] according to which group will systematically give way to the other. In this case, the institution, i.e. the convention that men (women) defer to women (men), is a coordinating device preventing people from bumping into each other.

The etiquette game suggests that institutions are not *just* coordination devices; they also regulate conflicts. There was no conflict present in the typewriter game because the equilibriums did not bring any asymmetry

---

[21] One may also make a distinction between shared and common knowledge. *Sensu stricto*, shared knowledge means that every agent knows the rule. Common knowledge means that not only do agents know the rule, but they also know that other agents know that they know, etc. Because of the social character of institutions, it is common knowledge that matters.

[22] There is also a mixed equilibrium, which is Pareto-dominated by the pure strategy equilibria.

Women

		Not yield	Yield
	Yield	$1, \sqrt{2}$	0,0
Men			
	Not yield	0,0	$\sqrt{2}, 1$

FIG. 2.2 Pay-off matrix for the etiquette game

Source: Young (1998).

in pay-offs. Both types of agents had the same interest in reaching any equilibrium. There is however a potential conflict in the etiquette game. Although both equilibria of the game have the same social value in terms of aggregate welfare,[23] they have very different welfare values for each player. Coming to a solution regarding who must yield is better than coming to no solution, but one player will win more than the other. The presence of distributional issues in economic situations is probably much more frequent than that of 'pure coordination'. The origins of conflict can be said to arise out of agents' heterogeneity. Following Drazen (2000), one may state that heterogeneity is central to much of economics: it stems from gender in the etiquette game, but could arise from tastes, wealth, skills, expectations, etc. Out of heterogeneity come divergences in agents' interests. In many instances, the possible incompatibilities between strategies cannot simply be reduced by coordination. Drazen (2000) distinguishes between *ex ante* and *ex post* heterogeneity. In the example above, *ex ante* heterogeneity would stem from the existence of two separate groups, men and women. *Ex post* heterogeneity, i.e. after institutions have emerged, would add the fact that one group has lost, and must yield to the other, making lower gains. Therefore, institutions do not necessarily erase heterogeneity and causes for conflict. The equilibrium solution of the game, institutions, may thus partly neutralize conflict, in the sense that agents will agree on a solution, but not necessarily suppress the reasons for conflict altogether, since they do not remove heterogeneity.

We can indeed argue that a choice of institutions is directly or indirectly a political choice,[24] or at least reflects the political equilibrium that prevails in the society, i.e. the compromise that has been reached over distributional conflicts. It is very clearly so if we consider institutions such as statutory laws or regulations, or any formal rules, that have to be ratified

---

[23] Assuming that there are as many men as women in the society concerned.

[24] The political nature is defined by a collective as well as a conflicting aspect.

by a political body, which means that they are the explicit result of a collective choice. This collective choice emerges out of a series of compromises between heterogeneous interests. The process of mediation of these interests is most obviously a political process. But it would be too limiting to think that only formal collective choices of institutions are political-economy outcomes. Other institutions, including patterns of organization and conventions, which appear to be the spontaneous result of decentralized individual choice or are simply informal rules, can also be regarded as the outcome of a conflict. Choices seemingly emerging out of individual interaction, i.e. that are not collective choices, can be the expression of a political equilibrium.

As a first approximation, one could argue that the conception of institutions as 'spontaneously' and unintentionally emerging out of agents' interaction is probably the most widespread in economics,[25] in opposition to political science, for instance, where conceiving institutions as the outcome of intentional design is more common, if only because the emphasis is put on formal rather than informal rules.[26] The economic approach to institutions seems at first sight not to allow for the consideration of conflict motives in the emergence of institutions, all the more so that the absence of intentionality indicates that institutional design is free from the influence of particular agents. Indeed, many theories present institutions as Pareto-improving moves (Schotter 1981). The prevailing idea is that the decentralized emergence of institutions shields the process from the control of agents who would want to devise institutional rules according to their own interests alone. Also, arbitrariness plays an important role in the definition of conventions.[27] The seeming arbitrariness of institutional outcomes, as in the etiquette game, appears to hint at the non-importance of power or income-distribution asymmetries in the design of informal rules. Contrary to formal rules, conventions must be self-enforcing, which

[25] For Adam Smith, the market prevents agents from using their bargaining power to produce institutional arrangements that would harm other individuals. It also encourages the efficiency of existing institutions. For Hayek, social institutions are the unintentional outcome of individual action; agents lack the knowledge to design socially optimal institutions, which leaves open the possibility for a wide diversity of institutional forms, social selection ensuring the collectively beneficial nature of the emerging structure (see Knight (1992)).

[26] See Hall and Taylor (1996) for an exposition of the different conceptions of institutions in political science.

[27] For Lewis (1969), a convention is an arbitrary solution to a coordination problem. Favereau (1999) defines the convention as having four attributes: it is arbitrary, it is not associated with juridical sanctions, its origin is unknown, and it is vague. Arbitrariness also plays a role in Hayek's theory of institutions (1967). Since people do not have the knowledge necessary to design institutions, the spontaneous order can take any direction.

can be held to imply that the outcome is universally acceptable, otherwise rational agents would not comply with those rules.

One could go further and extend this result to formal rules as well. A common argument is that formal rules can only represent *ex post* codifications of informal rules; i.e. once codes of behaviour have been established as equilibrium outcomes (Sugden 1986). In this case, formal collective choice merely follows individual equilibrium strategies, so that there is a fundamental 'bottom-up' character in the emergence of institutions. If on the other hand the law codified a practice which was not an equilibrium outcome for individual agents, it would neither be enforced nor complied with, and would therefore not be an equilibrium strategy for agents. In other words, the legislator cannot impose anything on society; on the contrary, society imposes the enactment of laws on the legislator, based on individual strategies. But asymmetries between agents' situations—in terms of endowments, pay-offs, or influences—and the interdependencies between agents' choices and pay-offs must be taken into account. I follow Knight (1992) and adopt here a theory in which agents act strategically in order to influence institutional choice. For Elster (1986), there are three reasons for the existence of strategic interdependencies among agents: (1) the reward of each depends on the rewards of all; (2) the reward of each depends on the choices of all; (3) the choice of each depends on the choices of all. Under these circumstances agents must choose their course of action strategically, i.e. taking into account the consequences of their choice on the actions of others. Social institutions affect the strategic decision-making of agents. Social agents learn the information necessary to formulate expectations about the actions of others, and with these expectations they choose the strategy that they think will maximize their individual benefits. The distributional effects of social institutions are the consequences of individual strategies and thus indirectly of the social expectations produced by institutions. The strategy of agents may be to orient other agents' expectations in a direction that will induce them to take decisions of a certain kind. In other words, an agent may have incentives to make other agents behave in a way that benefits him by influencing their expectations regarding his future course of action, and have them adopt a certain strategy that would be beneficial for him. This strategic pattern of decision-making is not new in economics,[28] but it has a particular meaning with respect to asymmetries of power and institutional design: some agents can affect the alternatives available to others so as to get them to act in a way that they would otherwise not have chosen.

---

[28] Particularly the economics of imperfect competition.

Women

		Not yield	Yield
Men	Yield	$1,1+w$	o_m, o_w
	Not yield	o_m, o_w	$1+m,1$

FIG. 2.3 Modified pay-off matrix for the etiquette game

In order to improve his own situation the strategic agent would want to prevent some agents from playing certain strategies, or even prevent himself from playing a strategy, so as to induce others to play in a certain way or even call in a third party who might have objectives of his own. This last move may be interpreted as the expression of a political demand when the third party is the government. Social institutions are the result of human interactions; their emergence and their design reflect the conflict between agents with opposing interests and their attempts to establish rules that structure economic interactions in a way that benefits them the most. The outcome depends on the relative ability of agents to impose their preferred solutions. Only in particular cases will the institutional architecture be neutral with respect to the structure of interests: when 'pure' coordination is at stake or when distributional asymmetries are evened out.[29] There might be compensation mechanisms whereby agents benefiting the most from a certain institutional change would compensate other agents for possible losses, but this scheme seems to apply to formal rules—and be the result of political bargaining—rather than to the emergence of informal institutions. Unless compensation itself has emerged as an institution it should play no role in the emergence of informal rules.

We may reconsider the etiquette game using a more general pay-off matrix. We consider the possibility of asymmetric pay-offs, not only at the equilibriums, but also when agents fail to come to a solution. o_m and o_w (<1) can be regarded as the 'breakdown value' available to agents when they fail to agree on a rule; m and w (>0) are the distributional advantages accruing to one or the other player.

Men dissatisfied with the rule that they should yield to women have several options. If they could commit themselves to playing the 'not-yield'

---

[29] Sugden (1986) argues against the relevance of distributional issues on the grounds that most social institutions evolving in these types of case are 'cross-cutting'; i.e. that each individual will sometimes find himself on one side of the asymmetry sometimes on the other. One may question the truly cross-cutting character of most institutions. Cross-cutting cases are likely to be exceptions.

strategy, this would force women to adopt a 'yield' strategy as a best reply. Is this commitment a possible course of action? This depends on a series of other institutional arrangements. Any arrangement which eliminates the 'yield' strategy for men will reinforce their position in the etiquette game. If men have sufficient political weight to impose the prohibition of the yield strategy for them, it would be in their best interest to do so. If women are unsure about the strategy that men will follow, they may consider the risks attached to choosing either strategy. Which institutional equilibrium will emerge will depend on the relative pay-offs. The risk factor of the equilibrium not yield/yield for men/women is defined as the smallest probability p such that if men believe women will yield with probability strictly greater than p then 'not yield' is the optimal action for them. The smallest such p satisfies

$$(1 - p) + o_m \cdot p = o_m \cdot (1 - p) + (1 + m) \cdot p$$

for men. Let p_m denote the solution to the above equation. For women, the smallest p satisfies

$$(1 + w) \cdot (1 - p) + o_w \cdot p = o_w \cdot (1 - p) + p.$$

We denote p_w the solution to this equation. The risk factor of the equilibrium where men do not yield and women yield is the smallest value of p_m and p_w, denoted $p_m \wedge p_w$. The risk factor of the equilibrium where men yield and women do not yield is the smallest value of $(1 - p_m)$ and $(1 - p_w)$, i.e. $(1 - p_m) \wedge (1 - p_w)$ (Young 1998). The equilibrium where men do not yield is risk-dominant when

$$p_m \wedge p_w \leqslant (1 - p_m) \wedge (1 - p_w)$$

which is equivalent to

$$w \cdot (1 - o_m) \leqslant m \cdot (1 - o_w).$$

If $w = m$, the asymmetry of power between men and women boils down to an asymmetry between breakdown values. The player that suffers most from the absence of a rule is the one that should yield. If $o_w = o_m$, the player that wins less is the one that should yield.

This asymmetry in breakdown values or in gains at the equilibrium reflects an asymmetry of power. If the etiquette game is taken literally, losses associated with non-coordination mean collision. One may think that men are on average heavier than women, so that a collision between a man and a woman is likely to inflict more damage on the latter than on the former. Less literally, the breakdown values reflect, for instance, the distribution of income in the absence of a rule. The most favoured agent is the one which has the highest breakdown value. The fact that the strategy most likely to be adopted, i.e. the risk-dominant one, gives precedence to the stronger group is a clear indication that the convention embodies asymmetries of power. Less literally, the more resistant group, defined as the group that loses less than the other group should an equilibrium not be reached, or wins more than the other when the equilibrium has been reached, is more likely to impose its preferred outcome. One may also note that the etiquette game is already played in collective rather than individual terms: 'men' and 'women' instead of individual versus individual. This presupposes a certain form of social organization which has split individuals into two social groups. Why this partition has emerged instead of 'tall' versus 'short', 'old' versus 'young', 'blue-eyed' versus 'brown-eyed', or any other divide can probably be linked to the power asymmetries between players. Through interactions with others, agents with similar resources establish a pattern of successful action in a particular type of interaction; as others recognize that they are interacting with one of the agents who possess these resources, they adjust their strategies to achieve their best outcomes given the anticipated commitments of others (Knight 1992). Salience plays an important role in the emergence of conventions for many authors (Schelling 1960; Sugden 1986). What could be more salient than asymmetries in power or wealth? The process of social recognition leads to the institutionalization of the rule. Asymmetries of power characterizing the fundamental fissures in a society form the basis of the recognition.

Let us for a moment suppose that the equilibrium rule is a convention according to which men should go first. Some women may be tempted not to comply with it because they are not satisfied with this institutional equilibrium. Men may tolerate some degree of non-compliance as long as it does not threaten the rule itself. The odd heavy woman taking a chance against the odd skinny man is not a questioning of the rule as a social convention, it is a case of individual misbehaviour. Incidentally, the establishment of a social convention, i.e. the institutionalization of the rule, would imply a modification of the pay-off structure stabilizing the convention itself. Losses associated with non-compliance are not only related to collision, but also to the social penalties that the group or society imposes on deviants. A woman who does not yield to a man will be considered rude, so that the post-institutionalization of the convention should involve a decrease in o_w. The group benefiting from the rule may seek to further stabilize it and formalize the rule. Formalization may diminish the risk of non-compliance, either by making the rule more explicit or by imposing strengthened sanctions for non-compliance.

A formal and explicit enunciation may be chosen because the rule is ambiguous and this increases the risk of involuntary disobedience. Voluntary disobedience may be a problem when the threat associated with informal sanctions is too weak. A classic result is that effective social sanctioning is weak in large communities. In the etiquette game above the social sanction entails being considered rude; this sanction may be effective in small communities where information about who has done what circulates easily, but is more problematic in large societies where relative anonymity lessens social costs associated with non-compliance. Every institution should be resistant to transgression within certain limits. In the case of the etiquette convention, it is resistant as long as deviance does not become the new convention. Changes in the pay-off structure may destabilize the existing institutional equilibrium in such a way that a sufficient number of deviants would tip the equilibrium over. Therefore, in the absence of formal sanctioning, respect for the rule might not be a rational strategy, which could prompt the most favoured group to look for the implementation of formal sanctions.

This formalization of the rule implies first organizing the favoured interest group, which may involve certain costs, and second gaining the support of an external enforcer, in most cases the State. But, as mentioned above, the external enforcer is a third agent in the game, whose interests and strategies must be taken into account. In democratic societies the State is governed by political agents who compete for power. State agents are therefore looking for political support in order to stay in power (Palombarini 1999). Their own interests are also a function of the distributional consequences of the rule itself, so that conflict over economic resources is intertwined with the conflict over political resources. Also, the presence of the State may serve as a focal point for the organization of some interest groups. The State acts as the external source of legitimacy from which interest groups are going to seek institutional support, in return for political support. Once the State as a source of legitimate power is a focal point for the conflict over institutions, it becomes itself a new source of conflict. This latter conflict will be regulated by the rules governing political competition, which are themselves institutions. The formalization of rules, i.e. the process of institutionalization, is thus itself a product of institutions. This has consequences for the institutional equilibrium; the rules that are going to structure political competition will have an influence on the final institutional equilibrium through the distribution of influence of the various interest groups over the process of legal or legitimate decision-making. This means taking seriously the view of institutions as equilibrium strategies, i.e. as endogenous rules of the game. In other words, there may be several institutional equilibriums: one would entail a certain set of social and economic institutions associated with a certain set of rules for political competition and interest representation; another would involve different social and economic institutions coupled with substantially different rules of political representation and decision-making.

With this representation of institutions, institutional change comes from a change in the pay-off distribution or from a change in bargaining power. In the case of informal rules, a change in pay-offs, i.e. the benefits and sanctions associated with adopting one or the other strategy, may trigger a change in equilibrium behaviour leading to a change in conventions. Bargaining-power changes may be represented as a change in breakdown values, which may cause a reversal of strategies for both agents. In the case of formal rules, a change in bargaining power may come from the modified ability of a group to influence the process of decision-taking, or from a decrease in the net benefits of group organization leading to a weakening or the disappearance of a specific interest group. Some strategic agents may actively try to modify the pay-off structure or the relative bargaining powers in order to set off an institutional change that would be beneficial to them. Lack of institutional change, on the other hand, should not be interpreted as necessarily reflecting a state of satisfaction for all concerned. It may simply reflect the failure of some groups to organize and push their interests through the political representation system. The non-contestation of an informal rule is also an expression of a political equilibrium: there exists no coalition strong enough to oppose the rule. The coalitions involved may be informal and the rule could thus be interpreted as a behaviour that everybody expects to be observed, i.e. as a seemingly 'cultural' trait.

2.1.4 Institutions as a Political-Economy Equilibrium

Conflict of interests is necessary for the existence of political constraints, and the effect of politics on economics stems from the mechanisms through which conflicts are resolved. Institutions, by fixing the 'rules of the game', are one way of settling fundamental conflicts of interest between agents. But institutional design emerging out of the upper-tier game does not abolish conflict. For instance, employed workers may be content with a certain wage-bargaining structure which gives market power to trade unions. It may be a guarantee of high real wages or employment stability. The unemployed on the other hand might prefer another wage-bargaining structure, which would be favourable to employment growth, even at the expense of lower wages. Employers might also prefer a more decentralized bargaining structure, which would give them greater bargaining power. If they are unable to change the bargaining rules, they may still express their discontent and try to obtain some compensation. As acknowledged by the Heckscher–Ohlin–Samuelson theory of international trade, free trade is likely to have detrimental consequences on the owners of the 'rare' factors of production. These agents are thus likely to back up a political programme which protects them against foreign competitors.[30] If they do not possess the power significantly to change the rules of free trade, they may still try to obtain some policy measures that would lessen the loss they incur—by means of transfers, for instance. If they are politically too weak, they will obtain nothing and incur a loss. Divergences in economic interests are conveyed in the political sphere, where agents will express a demand for the implementation of a policy that affects the pay-offs to their benefit. There is thus scope for a policy intervention, even within a fixed institutional frame, modifying the pay-offs associated with one or the other strategy. Policy choices are also the equilibrium strategy of a particular agent, the government, seeking political support; implementing a particular policy must thus constitute an equilibrium strategy for the government.

The framework defined so far is represented in Fig. 2.4. Within a given economic structure, characterized for instance by technology and preferences, we consider a heterogeneity of agents' economic interests. It helps to start with exogenous technology, preferences, and interests but this hypothesis can be relaxed, and will be later on. To a relative proximity of interests corresponds a clustering of agents in different social groups: workers, firms' managers, farmers, pensioners, etc. These groups correspond to an expression of individual interests in a collective form. This expression depends on the perception of agents with respect to their own interests, their situation in society, and their relation to other 'similar' agents. This perception is mediated by the system of representations that individuals have, i.e. by ideas and theories about the state of society (Palombarini and Théret 2001). Heterogeneity survives up to this first aggregation of individual economic interests into groups. The diversity of economic interests is expressed in the economic area: wage earners and firms' management bargain over wages and working conditions, lenders and borrowers must agree on the terms of credit contracts, landlords and tenants negotiate over rents, etc. It also finds an expression in the political

---

[30] See Rogowski (1987) for a political-economy analysis of the Heckscher–Ohlin–Samuelson theory of international trade.

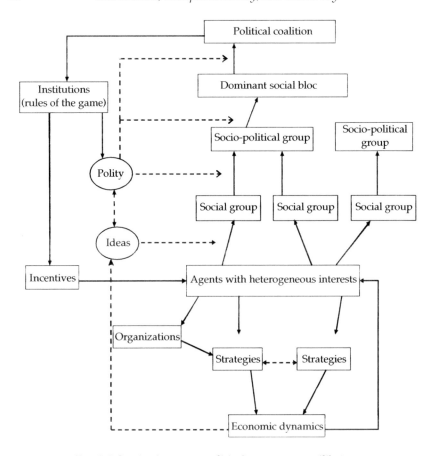

FIG. 2.4 Institutions as a political-economy equilibrium

arena, not only as partisan politics, but as a political demand for protection of specific situations and interests. Social groups, as an expression of a community of economic interests, do not express political demands as such. This is the role played by socio-political groups, which represent a collective action for the expression of a common political goal. Socio-political groups may aggregate several social groups. Their formation is made under the influence of the political process. They are political constructions, and, at this stage, institutional rules governing polity influence the gathering process of agents, their mode of interaction, and the form of their representation. The representation of social and socio-political groups with respect to State decision-making, either policy choices or institutional change, can take several forms: formal negotiation among and formal representation of groups, voting and delegation of power, hierarchical representation, etc. These characteristics have some bearing on the weight that interest groups will have in policy-making or institutional change, and thus on the sensitivity of the institutional structure to the political demand of socio-political agents.

Different types of political system may be envisaged (Lijphart 1999). At one extreme, there is the majoritarian model, where policy choices are made by a unified centre whose power is derived from the delegation to it of a majority of the people, mostly a bare majority and even sometimes a plurality instead of a majority. Once agreement has been reached on the identity of the agent in power, the latter has the ability to take policy decisions and implement institutional change without asking for further agreement. Lacking formal representation, a multiplicity of interest groups will exert pressure on the government in an uncoordinated way. At the other extreme, one may have a consensus-based model, where power is deposited in the hands of a government with broad participation seeking a broad agreement on policies and institutions. A limited number of powerful interest groups are formally represented in the process leading to compromise-based decision-taking. This model makes policy decisions and institutional change conditional on reaching an agreement among the agents representing different socio-political groups. The two models will differ with respect to the number of 'veto points' and the weight of 'veto players' (Tsebelis 1995, 2002; Scharpf 2000). Veto points are any points within the political system where a policy measure, legislation, or any institutional change may be blocked and the status quo preserved; veto players are individual or collective agents who may block such measures. Where a veto may be opposed and who may do it depends on existing political institutions. The consensus-based model is likely to have more veto players than the majoritarian model. As a consequence, the latter system will more easily enable radical institutional change once political change has brought a new government into power. The former system is likely to be much more resistant to radical institutional change and permit a better representation of organized, corporatist interests.

A coalition expressing the common political demand of a group of agents will represent a socio-political bloc, i.e. a de facto alliance of socio-political groups possessing different interests rendered compatible by a compromise over a political strategy. These coalitions should not be considered as pre-existing; they are formed under the influence of political action. Politically organized workers may press for the establishment of labour regulations which favour job protection, managers may want different labour-market regulations, farmers may ask for subsidies, pensioners may seek the preservation of their income against inflation, etc. In the broad economic space, these demands are expressed on a multidimensional basis.

A government strategy is a way to reach an agreement on a series of institutional and policy decisions in this multidimensional space which satisfies the political demands of the dominant socio-political bloc.[31] Similar to the formation of social groups, political demands are not simply a reflection of the 'objective' economic interests of the concerned agents. The expression of a political demand depends on what is perceived as legitimate by the socio-political groups. This perception and the expression of the political demand itself are shaped by the dominant ideas (Hall 1993; Palombarini 1999). Ideas—or ideologies if one refers to an organized body of ideas—provide the frame within which agents' interests can be collectively expressed under the form of political demand. They influence how agents perceive their own interests, shape the formation of social groups, and affect the expression of their demands. Starting from a wide diversity of individual interests expressed in a multidimensional space, ideologies act as focusing devices, narrowing the definition of agents' social identities, making them aware that they belong to the group of workers, or consumers, or entrepreneurs, or whatever, and thus facilitate coalescence into organized bodies. This process is dependent on the structure of institutions in the economy. The existence and expression of the political demands of certain groups is influenced by the representation of interests taken into account in the institutional structure. For instance, the collective expression of workers' interests in the political sphere is likely to be easier in institutional environments where there is a corporatist labour relation, i.e. where workers are already considered as an interest group. This corporatist relation is in turn strengthened by the expression of workers' interests in the political sphere.

As mentioned above, agents devise their individual strategies within a specific institutional frame: once the institutional frame of wage bargaining is established, workers and firms engage in wage bargaining, the outcome depending on their respective bargaining power; lenders and creditors establish financing relationships coherent with the institutional frame for these activities; agents form organizations; etc.[32] Rules defined

---

[31] See Palombarini (2001).

[32] One could argue that our schema reproduces North's distinction between institutions (rules of the game and the enforcement characteristics of these rules) and organizations (groups of individuals bound by a common purpose) and neglects the fact that organizational forms may also define the rules of some games and restrict agents' strategies. As mentioned before, whenever a formal rule of a game is defined we have an institution; in this sense, the rules defined by an organization are institutions. Institutional arrangements can be made at all levels of society. Some arrangements are 'local': the choice of an organizational form, for instance. Others are made at an aggregate level (constitution, laws, etc.) and involve a formal political decision.

at the meta level have a significant influence on the outcome of the game played at the infra level. In the situation described by the typewriter game, what matters most is to know what the process of decision-making for the choice of one or the other keyboard is, considering the fact that this will have a tremendous impact on the final outcome. If the choice is individual and decentralized, i.e. if every individual employer and every individual secretary decides alone, using only 'market' signals to form expectations, both keyboards may a priori be chosen.[33] The economy may thus end up being stuck in a 'low-level' equilibrium (the Qwerty keyboard), depending on initial conditions or early diffusion, for instance (Arthur 1994; David 1985). But this result stems from the particular type of choice modelled in the typewriter game. If on the other hand choice is 'coordinated', i.e. if employers and secretaries exchange information or meet before taking a decision regarding which keyboard they are going to buy or learn to type on, the outcome of this process is that the Dvorak keyboard will be chosen with certainty since it is obviously the most efficient solution for everyone concerned.

The difference between the two procedures is crucial for a comparative institutional analysis, precisely because societies differ in their 'coordination' procedures. The choice of keyboard may be re-expressed as a nested game structure. First, an upper-tier game would define whether secretaries and employers coordinate their decisions or not; this game would set the rules of the lower-tier game. Second, according to the coordination procedure, they would decide which keyboard they should adopt. If coordination prevails, the most efficient technological solution will emerge with certainty, whereas the choice is a priori not determined in the absence of coordination. This is in fact analogous to a decision to internalize or externalize. If, for instance, secretaries' typing apprenticeship is internal to the firm, a large part of the coordination problem disappears. Secretaries would learn to type on the keyboard which the firm that hired them had decided to adopt. From the secretaries' point of view, the problem would be a trade-off between acquiring specific versus general skills; i.e. skills that are only relevant when applied to a specific context, working in a given firm, or skills that could be used in any environment. As we will see later, the issue of specific versus general skills is important when it comes to differentiating types of capitalism. The game above can thus be seen to refer to two different types of 'institution'. The choice over the mode of decision, coordination or no coordination, is clearly of the 'rules-of-the-game' type; the other, the technological choice of a specific

[33] See Arthur (1994) for a modelling of path-dependency.

keyboard, is a rule for behaviour. The outcome of the lower-tier game, the individual strategy, depends on the framework defined by the upper-tier game, where the mode of decision is established.

Strategies elaborated by individual or collective agents may themselves become formal or informal institutions. Patterns of internal organization of firms may become a formal rule applicable to firms; individual strategies may evolve into conventions. Therefore, the scheme of Fig. 2.4 represents also a certain form of institutional dynamics. The question of institutional coherence arises, since agents do not design institutions in a global fashion. It may, for instance, be possible for some formal institutions such as laws to be in contradiction to informal institutions such as conventions. One can envisage a situation in which, for instance, trade unions and the firm's management would agree on a set of internal rules which violate existing labour regulation. If this behaviour stays localized this is a case of deviance which does not question the formal institutions as such. Generalization of this behaviour may nevertheless undermine the institution; if all firms adopt the same pattern and this becomes the conventional mode of business organization, we have reached a different institutional situation. We would have a certain set of institutions which stipulate A, and another set of institutions which stipulate not-A. Which of the two sets defines the rules of the game?

It may be that the law prohibits bribing officials to obtain procurement contracts; yet, it is conventional for firms to bribe them. The law stipulates that cars should stop when the traffic light is red; yet, one may drive past a red light when an injured person on board must be rushed to hospital. The difference between the two situations concerns legitimacy. In the latter case, even a law-abiding citizen would be willing to ignore the traffic light in order to save somebody's life. Why? Because some moral norms (not to mention formal rules) allow him to pass over the prohibition derived from traffic regulation. Institutions with greater legitimacy, under the guise of social norms or moral codes, allow disregard for traffic regulation. In fact, such a possibility is even mentioned in some formal rules; they are to be complied with unless a case of emergency, often not otherwise specified, prevents one from conforming to the rule. Even law enforcers would concur that the car driver is right not to respect the traffic light. The other case of incoherence is different. We have a contradiction between a formal rule, a law which prohibits corruption, and an informal rule, a convention, according to which one must bribe officials in order to do business with the local authority. One could consider that a law which nobody conforms to is not an institution: it does not regulate behaviour the way an institution is supposed to (Aoki 2001). It is not an equilibrium strategy for agents. Therefore, the proper institutional equilibrium would be the conventional equilibrium, where everyone follows the convention of corruption. Firms know that they must bribe officials; officials know that firms willing to obtain a procurement contract must bribe them; firms know that officials know; etc. Corruption is common knowledge. Still, is such an equilibrium the same as one in which 'corruption' is legal? I argue that the two equilibriums are different because of the legitimacy of the practice of corruption, the consequences on economic outcomes, and the stability of the convention and the whole institutional structure. In one case, agents know that their behaviour is not legal and probably not considered legitimate either. This is different from the situation of the injured person in the car, where the driver would consider his disregard of the law legitimate. In the case of the corruption convention, it is always possible for some firm to sue the official that asked for a bribe, and it may be that a judge will sentence him. This case is of course ruled out if no law prevents 'corruption'. French writer Joseph Kessel tells the following anecdote. Walking down the streets of Manhattan in the early 1930s he comes across a man he has known as a US Navy officer in Vladivostok in 1919. The man suggests they celebrate their new encounter and go for a drink. This is however prohibition time and finding a place to drink alcoholic beverages is not so easy. 'No problem', says the American, and goes up to a nearby policeman directing traffic and asks him the whereabouts of the nearest speakeasy. The NYC cop is only too happy to oblige.[34] In this case, one could say that disobedience of the prohibition laws is so much common knowledge in New York that there is no risk attached to asking a policeman how to transgress the law. Is this situation analogous to the non-existence of the prohibition law in New York? The answer is 'no' for several reasons. Had there been no prohibition the former US Navy officer would not have had to take the trouble to ask someone directions to a place to drink; there would have been bars publicly advertising their business. Even a law that nobody complies with can raise transaction costs. The economic equilibrium associated with the no-prohibition convention is substantially different from the absence of legal prohibition, in terms of liquor prices and quality, structure of supply, level of demand, etc. From a comparative-institutional-analysis point of view, the conventional equilibrium has different economic implications. Even if chances are very slim, a policeman might exist who is a 'tea totaller'. Asking this policeman directions to a drinking place would have radically different consequences depending on whether there is absence

---

[34] Joseph Kessel, French radio interview, 1956.

of prohibition law or a no-prohibition enforcement convention. Therefore, even if formal institutions are not complied with on a conventional basis, their superior degree of legitimacy means that they cannot be ignored altogether.

2.2 Institutional Complementarity

Comparative institutional analysis does not, of course, consider institutions in isolation, but taken together and forming an institutional structure. One would expect institutions to be 'coherent' with one another, i.e. that the rules they define should not contradict each other, otherwise they would not constitute an equilibrium. But even this requirement is never fully satisfied, as we just saw. However, interdependencies between institutions are not limited to contradictions or non-contradictions between formal and informal rules. Even if limited rationality prevents a full grasp of the interdependencies between institutions, strategic agents are conscious of *some* interdependencies between strategies applying to different situations, i.e. in the different games they play. This will accordingly influence their decision-taking. Strategic agents may, for instance, accept 'losing' in some games in order to 'win' in others and reach a globally more satisfying position. Going back to the etiquette game, the equilibrium we envisaged, where women yield to men, is not the equilibrium prevailing in most societies. Does that mean that the asymmetry in power is in fact in favour of women or that power plays no role in the conventional equilibrium of the etiquette game? The thesis of neutrality of power asymmetries in the determination of a conventional equilibrium would contradict most studies on informal rules governing gender relations and family organization.[35] In fact, strategic agents may not seek to win in certain games if it threatens the outcome in other, more determinant, games. Therefore, yielding to women when approaching a door may be a rational strategy in spite of a power asymmetry favouring men if this reinforces the domination of men in other areas of social life. Rules of etiquette and politeness soften social exchange but may also be thought of as softening a social domination.[36]

This point hints at the existence of possible complementarities between games, or situations, which will have consequences for the institutional

---

[35] See references in Knight (1992).

[36] 'Above all, beware of teaching the child empty phrases of politeness that only serve as magic words to subdue those around him to his will and to get him what he wants at once . . . It is obvious that "If you please" means "It pleases me," and "I beg" means "I command." What admirable politeness, which only succeeds in changing the meaning of words so that every word is a command!' (J.J. Rousseau, *Emile*, Trans. Grace Roosevelt).

architecture of an economy. A society is not just a collection of institutional forms, but a particular combination of these forms. Institutions' influences on the economy should therefore not be considered independently from one another. Institutions affecting one area of the economy will have consequences beyond that particular area, if only because of general equilibrium effects.

2.2.1 Interaction

Consideration of the link between institutions and economic outcomes is most often limited to one area of the economy at a time. The hypothesis is then that institutional characteristics in the area concerned will have consequences for the type of economic outcome in that area. Labour-market institutions will impact on real wage levels and unemployment; financial systems' characteristics will influence the quality of corporate governance, the cost of capital, or the amount of credit to the economy; features of the education systems will affect the level of education and skills profile of the population; competition regulation will influence competitiveness of industries; etc. In line with this 'local' perspective, the criteria for appreciating the performance resulting from a particular institutional structure are usually area-specific: the level of employment or unemployment for labour-market institutions, the amount of investment for financial systems, price levels for product-market competition, the number of patents or research articles for science and innovation systems, etc. One can then have a multiplicity of performance criteria for the appreciation of the effects of such-and-such an institutional feature on a certain area, according to the area concerned.

The question is then whether one can relate specific institutions to an aggregate measure of performance. In other terms, if we define good macroeconomic performance as a combination of low unemployment, low inflation, high competitiveness, and high innovativeness, is it possible to conclude that it is associated with a combination of institutions that separately produce these performances? One could suppose that an optimal institutional configuration exists in each area of the economy, independently of the institutional configurations that are present in the other areas. One would then be able to define the 'best' institutional context for the labour market, the best configuration for the financial sector, education systems, social protection, etc. The best institutional configuration for an economy—i.e. the one that leads to the best macroeconomic performance in terms of employment, output level, etc.—would therefore be the one that is closest to the sum total of these optimal local configurations. This conception is very probably the driving force behind benchmarking efforts—and the basis of international comparisons such as those that have been carried out by the World Economic Forum (Davos) or by Lehman Brothers (Edwards and Schanz 2001*a,b*). The purpose of such studies is usually to classify countries in terms of their competitiveness. Towards this end, a certain number of categories are defined, and countries are marked for their performance in a given category. An overall mark is then obtained by adding up the scores from each area. The best model is the one that is closest to the profile that has been defined as being the best local configuration. Their findings can be interpreted as follows: the ideal economy of the 1990s should have possessed Denmark's education system, Sweden's technology and employment policy, the competitive environment of Finland's high-tech sector, and the entrepreneurial environment, labour-market regulation, fiscal system, and competitive environment of the USA. It remains to be seen whether this mixture of American and Scandinavian institutions would be viable.

There are several problems related to this and similar approaches. First, it is implicit that only one best institutional configuration exists in each area. For instance, only one type of wage bargaining would guarantee wage restraint and hence high employment levels and low inflation. Like the evidence proposed in Calmfors and Driffill (1988) for the relationship between employment performance and centralization of bargaining, a non-monotonicity in the relationship between a specific institutional characteristic and performance could possibly be found in various institutional areas. For instance, a bank-based system and a financial-markets-based system could both lead to a low cost of capital and a high level of investment, whereas a combination of banks and stock markets could produce poorer results. If generalized to a large number of domains, these results potentially lead to a wide diversity of institutional configurations that would produce sound macroeconomic performance. With n institutional areas, there would not be one best way for the economic institutions of a modern economy, but 2^n. This diversity of possibilities could explain why similar economic performances over the long run have been observed for countries characterized by markedly different institutions. A telling example is that of Switzerland and the USA. According to Maddison's (1995) data, these two countries have followed the same growth path between 1870 and 1990[37] in spite of being characterized by very different institutional features

---

[37] Taking the GDP per capita for these two countries, the difference between the two series is a I(0) process of zero means. This is one of Durlauf's (1996) definitions for absolute convergence in income levels (see Amable and Juillard (1999)).

in terms of labour markets, the structure of the financial system, product-market-competition regulation, etc.[38] In each sphere of the economy these differences should have produced very different results in terms of employment levels or physical and human-capital investment, which should have had consequences for the differentiation of the growth paths of these two countries. The fact that it has not should not be seen as indicating that after all institutions do not matter, but rather the possibility that different combinations of institutions may deliver near-identical economic performance.

This brings us to the second point. Is *any* combination of institutions that proves 'locally' efficient likely to deliver good performance at the macroeconomic level? Would a country adopting the Swiss banking system and the US product-markets regulation fare as well as the USA and Switzerland in terms of economic growth? In other words, is it realistic to consider that there may be as many as 2^n institutional configurations? In order to answer this question it may be useful to consider again the point made by Calmfors and Driffill (1988). They drew attention not only to the importance of wage-bargaining centralization but also to the interaction between wage-bargaining patterns and market competition. The positive effect of either complete centralization or complete decentralization of wage bargaining is reinforced through an interaction with product-markets characteristics. Incentives for unions and firms to exert wage restraint depend on their expectations regarding the responsiveness of competitors' prices to their own. For Calmfors and Driffill, both very competitive and very coordinated structures can induce restraint. With perfect competition in product *and* labour markets, competitors' markets do not respond at all; firms cannot pass wage costs on to consumers. If unions and firms cannot exercise restraint in perfectly competitive markets, they will certainly be driven out of the market. With perfect coordination across the whole economy, all concerns about prices relative to competitors vanish, since all wages rise with one's own. Incentives for restraint stem from national economic-competitiveness constraints. Between the two polar cases, with individual firms having some ability to set their prices, the market power of firm-specific unions is reinforced and they will set higher wages than a centralized union. The interaction of imperfect competition with product and labour markets reinforces the argument for the hump-shaped relationship between centralization and unemployment.

This finding leads to the question of the effects that institutions have on one another. The interaction effects are more precisely analysed in Aoki

---

[38] See Bonoli and Mach (1999) on the Swiss model.

(1994), with the aim of separating an ideal-typical American model from an ideal-typical Japanese model of production. The latter is characterized by team production; i.e. the output of the firm is the result of the efforts of each member of a team and the uncertain environment. The firm relies on outside investors to finance the investments necessary to engage in production. These investors cannot observe the actual output of the firm. Team members must exert a certain effort to produce output, and receive a wage in return. The aim of the firm's management is to promote reciprocal-effort behaviour between workers, but this can only be achieved imperfectly, because monitoring is imperfect. In such a situation it is possible to devise a contingent governance structure where the transfer of decision-making regarding distribution of output residual, i.e. once contractual payments have been made (to outside investors), and the continuation of the team are contingent upon the realization of final output. If output drops below a certain level, an outsider to the team, acting as an *ex post* monitor, becomes the residual claimant and the team is dissolved. This *ex post* monitoring scheme provides incentives for individual workers to make an effort. This is a theoretical representation of the main-bank system that operated in Japan (Aoki and Patrick 1994). The main bank bore the responsibility for the governance of financially distressed firms. If difficulties were temporary the main bank would bail out the firm. If restructuring the firm was impossible, the firm would be liquidated and former employees would find less advantageous opportunities.

The point made by Aoki (1994) is that the particular *ex post* governance mechanism described above is complementary to the organization of production in teams. In other words, the financial system of Japan is an institutional form complementary to the Japanese pattern of work organization. By contrast, the American system associates strong, high-powered financial incentives and the relative absence of teamwork in favour of the individualization of performance and reward. There would in this case be a complementarity between a particular financial system which allows for the provision of high-powered incentives such as profit-related rewards and a work organization which is not based on team production but more focused on individual performance. Complementary relations between financial systems and labour-market institutions have also been modelled by Osano (1997) and Garvey and Swan (1992). In the latter paper the individual worker's performance depends on the 'help' provided by other workers, so that production has the elements of a team organization. A financing relationship based on shareholders does not encourage cooperation among workers, whereas a mixed financing by shares and debt may encourage individual effort and cooperation. In all these cases the presence of one institutional form makes the other institutional form more efficient.

One could envisage a complementarity between other institutional areas. In the case of wage bargaining, for instance, the outcome in terms of wage levels (and employment) depends on both parties' outside options. These outside options are in turn dependent on the institutions affecting areas other than the labour market. The alternative job for a worker may depend on his skill level and hence on the institutions of the education and training system; the alternative option for the firm may depend on its relocation possibilities, i.e. on the regulatory environment or the liquidity of the financial market. Through the effects on each bargaining party's outside options, institutions not directly connected to the labour market will nevertheless have a bearing on the outcome of labour-market bargaining. As shown above, outside options or 'breakdown values' are reflections of asymmetries in power or income, and they determine agents' equilibrium strategies, and therefore institutions. If these outside options or breakdown values are themselves the product of other institutional choices, this means that choice in one area will depend on the presence of institutions in other areas. Strategic agents may then rationally take decisions regarding specific institutional forms bearing in mind the consequences of their strategy choice on other institutions in other areas.

2.2.2 Complementarity

It is therefore necessary to consider the influence of institutions on the whole economy not in isolated ways, i.e. by considering one area of the economy after another, but in terms of the joint influence of institutions. Generally conceived, institutional complementarity stems from the interdependence of institutional influences on agents' decision-making. One could conceive this interdependence in standard terms as a general economic equilibrium. An institution affecting prices on one market will affect prices on all other markets too, by a general-equilibrium effect. This will be the case if institutions produce positive spillovers in different markets and mutually enhance their respective beneficial effect. For instance, institutions that each raise the time horizon of agents or that allow for better protection of specific investments in different markets would be said to be complementary, while those that affect markets in opposite directions—favouring reversible arrangements and liquidity of assets—would not. Therefore, 'local' institutions will not have 'local' effects only but will affect the economic outcome in the whole economy. Each institutional arrangement's existence or functioning within a given area is enhanced by the institutional arrangements that are in effect in other areas. Institutional complementarity is present when the existence or the particular form taken by an institution in one area reinforces the presence, functioning, or efficiency of another institution in another area.

We may illustrate this point with the specific example of the complementarity between financial systems and training systems. One may for the sake of simplicity consider two possible types of institutional form in each area. One financial system is decentralized, in the sense that financial markets play a prominent role; the other is centralized, and banks are the main financial intermediaries. Similarly, there are two possible types of training system. One is of the 'general' type, and employees acquire skills which are not specific to a firm but can be applied everywhere; the other is specialized, in the sense that the emphasis is on firm-specific skills. We further suppose that the two solutions in each area are equally satisfactory in their own area: a low cost of capital can be obtained either with a bank-based or a market-based financial system, for instance. Similarly, the skill level of the labour force is high with either type of training system; only the type of skills differs. The fact that they deliver identical performance in terms of macroeconomic indicators does not mean that the institutions are identical. They may give similar aggregate results through a variety of incentive mechanisms. For instance, financial-markets-based systems favour short-term investment projects over long-term investment.[39] In this situation, two institutional configurations are expected to emerge (Soskice 1999). One will favour the adoption of short-term strategies both in the financial relationship between the firm and financial markets and between the firm and its employees in the employment relationship. Lack of long-term relationships between financiers and entrepreneurs will prevent the establishment of such relations on the employment side. To the emphasis on short-term profits will correspond a non-commitment of the firm towards its employees. As a consequence, workers will be reluctant to invest in firm-specific skills, which may be easily devalued should the employment contract be severed following, for instance, adverse-demand shocks and downward adjustments of the labour force. These are all the more likely to take place in that the management must respect strict short-term-profitability constraints, where temporary losses cannot be accepted against the prospect of longer-term gains. In this setting, facing the prospect of losing their jobs, workers will prefer to invest in general rather than specific skills, augmenting the likelihood of finding well-paid employment in another

---

[39] See Dewatripont and Maskin (1995) for a modelling of this idea.

firm or industry. General skills acquisition augments workers' outside options.

In the opposite case, long-term strategies are favoured and both firms and workers invest in the production relationship, for instance in terms of specific-skill acquisition. This bilateral investment is made possible by the fact that the bank-based financial system supplies 'patient capital', i.e. allows firms' management to devise long-term strategies and social partners to develop long-term arrangements. The result applies also to more general complementarities. If certain conditions are met, negotiations between social partners in a given labour market can create the sort of stable compromises that could help the workforce to receive a high level of training. In addition, physical investment may be facilitated by the existence of close relationships between banks and firms, creating a better information exchange between the two parties. This could reduce the uncertainty perceived by lenders over the prospects of the firm's investments or mitigate the moral-hazard problem by enabling close monitoring. In this scenario the existence of durable relationships, and of proximity between banks and firms, enhances the implementation of long-term investment projects, and this *in return* facilitates the establishment of stable compromises in the labour market. Conversely, a flexible labour market, one that facilitates employee mobility, is seen here as complementing a financial system that facilitates the reversibility of commitments and the liquidation of investments. In both cases the important point is that each institution reinforces the influence of the other. Similar cases could be related to the relationship between financing patterns and the nature of industrial relations. Workers and firms faced with the possibility of adopting cooperative behaviour and sacrificing short-term gains for long-term stability, for instance under the guise of wage restraints which would augment the firm's survival probability, will be discouraged from doing so if an outside short-term constraint exists.

All the cases exposed above exhibit a notion of institutional complementarity which appears to be very similar to the notion of complementarity commonly used in economics. One can try to distinguish several definitions of the notion (Amable, Ernst, and Palombarini 2001). The *differential definition* is derived from the standard meaning of complementarity in economics. The marginal 'efficiency' of a certain institution is positively related to the presence or intensity of another institution in another area. Consider an aggregate 'performance' function $F(.,.)$ and two institutional domains X and Y (labour market and financial system, for instance), respectively associated with specific institutional forms x and y. If x and y are continuous variables, and F is differentiable, the common definition of complementarity in economics is that $\partial^2 F(x,y)/\partial x \partial y \geqslant 0$. For instance, an institutional complementarity between deregulated labour markets and deregulated product markets will mean that less regulation in the labour market increases the marginal gain to deregulation in product markets.

The notion of complementarity is not limited to continuous variables. In fact, comparative institutional analysis is faced with comparing a limited number of institutional configurations instead of a continuum. Let us suppose that we have two possible institutional forms for each area, x_1 and x_2 for x and y_1 and y_2 for y, which may, for instance, represent the degree of wage-bargaining centralization and the importance of banks in the financial system respectively. Let us further suppose for convenience that $x_1 \geqslant x_2$ and $y_1 \geqslant y_2$. Complementarity in this situation is associated with the notion of supermodularity (Topkis 1998). The arguments of the function F are complements and F is supermodular when the following condition holds:

$$F(x_1,y_1) - F(x_2,y_1) \geqslant F(x_1,y_2) - F(x_2,y_2).$$

Increasing wage-bargaining centralization when banks have a large influence over the economy improves performance at least as much as increasing wage-bargaining centralization when banks have a small influence. This introduces another definition of institutional complementarity, related to *comparative performance* (Amable, Ernst, and Palombarini 2002).

With the previous example we can compare four different situations, two of which will be considered as equilibria. The performance matrix in Fig. 2.5 shows that x and y are complementary. Moving from an institutional equilibrium characterized by decentralization and a low influence of banks to an institutional configuration where one institutional form only is modified is costly in terms of performance; the same conclusion applies to the case where the initial situation is wage-bargaining centralization and a high influence of banks. One can check easily that the condition for supermodularity is fulfilled in the example of Fig. 2.5. However, this condition would have been fulfilled too with $F(x_2,y_2) = 0$. In that case, only one institutional configuration would have been worth

Institutions	x_2	x_1
y_2	3	1
y_1	2	3

Fig. 2.5 Performance matrix

	If $y = y_1$				If $y = y_2$	
		Managers				Managers
Strategies		1	2	Strategies	1	2
Workers 1		4, 3	2, 1	Workers 1	1, 1	1, 2
Workers 2		1, 2	1, 1	Workers 2	2, 1	2, 3

FIG. 2.6 Pay-offs for the wage-bargaining game

considering—that with centralization and strong banks—since the situation with decentralization and weak banks would have had a clearly inferior performance and changing one institutional form would have improved the situation.

In order to make a meaningful comparison of institutional configurations it is necessary to have a multiplicity of viable cases. In this case, institutional complementarity would call for a situation where a multiplicity of 'equilibriums' is a priori possible. If we consider that (x_1,y_1) and (x_2,y_2) are the two institutional equilibria, the comparative performance definition of 'strong' institutional complementarity would also demand that:

$$F(x_1,y_1) \geqslant F(x_1,y_2), F(x_1,y_1) \geqslant F(x_2,y_1), F(x_2,y_2) \geqslant F(x_1,y_2), F(x_2,y_2) \geqslant F(x_2,y_1).$$

In this notion of institutional complementarity, the overall performance declines when one changes one institution, leaving the other unchanged.

So far, we have not considered institutional dynamics. We may add a dynamic aspect to the existing definition of institutional complementarity. The *dynamic definition* of institutional complementarity could be that the presence of one institutional form in one area leads to the adoption of an institutional form in another area (Amable, Ernst, and Palombarini 2002). Dynamic considerations beg the question of the factors behind institutional change.

The comparison of institutional configurations has so far been made in terms of global performance of the economy. Complementarity of institutions would be appreciated from a global, outside perspective and not related to choice. However, the theory of institutions presented above defines institutions as resulting from choices. Institutions do not emerge as the result of a welfare-maximizing process. They are the outcomes of a political process. The whole set of institutions is not chosen all at once, by agents possessing a clear view of *all* the interdependencies between institutions concerning *all* areas of the economy. In other words, as we have distinguished between different levels, that of the rules of the game and that of strategies, nobody plays the global 'meta' game. Agents play some games, taking the results of other games as given, if only because of limitations to their rationality, but also because of the various costs associated with institutional change; some rules are de facto exogenous, i.e. not subject to choice. Once again, labour regulations are exogenous for workers and entrepreneurs when they bargain over wages or work organization. If they want to change these rules, this means going through a costly political process of institutional change, which may or may not be undertaken, depending on the relative political influence of interest groups. In the absence of strategic coordination across different domains of games, agents' choices in one domain are parametrically affected by choices made in other domains. Total strategic coordination is not possible if agents do not participate simultaneously in all games. Even if they do, they may perceive the prevailing institutions in other domains as objectified and thus exogenous. The institutions prevailing in other domains constitute the institutional environment. However, there is some strategic coordination, and agents may want to orient the game structure in a direction which is beneficial to them. Whether they can do so depends on their relative power.

Let us suppose two agents are playing two games in an uncoordinated way. The first game concerns the choice of bargaining procedure (x), the second game is the choice of financial systems (y). In each game agents have a binary choice of strategy, 1 or 2.[40] Institution x_1 (x_2) establishes itself if agents choose strategy 1 in the first game; a similar structure applies for the second game. However, the two games are not independent; the pay-off functions in each game depend on the institutional configuration established in the other game. Besides, agents' pay-offs are given in each game as separable functions, i.e. total agents' pay-offs are the sum of the pay-offs they obtain in each game. One could alternatively suppose that the two games are played by different agents, or by the same agents having different social functions. For instance, one may think that the first game is played between workers and managers, and the second between savers and investors. Workers (managers) and savers (investors) may be the same group of agents, but they are for the moment assumed to behave as if they were different agents.

---

[40] We do not consider the possibility of a 'mixed institutional form' which would correspond to a mixed strategy. Most institutions cannot be adequately represented by such a mixed form.

	If $x = x_1$				If $x = x_2$	
	Investors				Investors	
Strategies	1	2		Strategies	1	2
1	1, 1	1, 0		1	0, 0	0, 1
Savers				Savers		
2	0, 1	0, 0		2	1, 0	2, 2

FIG. 2.7 Pay-offs for the financial-systems game

The pay-off matrices for each game are given below. For each game, there are two matrices, according to the prevailing institution in the other game. One can see that if the financial system is bank-based ($y = y_1$) agents choose to adopt a centralized bargaining procedure, whereas they favour wage-bargaining decentralization if the financial system is more financial-markets based ($y = y_2$). There is thus a complementarity between institutions.

Regarding the other game, the outcomes are that agents opt for a bank-based system if there is centralized wage bargaining and a financial markets-based system otherwise. There is a symmetrical complementarity between financial systems and wage-bargaining procedures.

If u_i (v_i) denotes the pay-off functions for agent i in the $x(y)$ game, one can check that these functions are supermodular. If $c_{i,j}$ denotes the choice of agent i for institutional form j in the wage-bargaining game, and $e_{i,j}$ the choice in the financial-intermediary game, the following conditions hold for all i:

$$u_i(c_{i,1}; c_{-i,1}, y_1) - u_i(c_{i,2}; c_{-i,1}, y_1) \geqslant u_i(c_{i,1}; c_{-i,2}, y_2) - u_i(c_{i,2}; c_{-i,2}, y_2),$$
$$v_i(e_{i,1}; e_{-i,1}, x_1) - v_i(e_{i,2}; e_{-i,1}, x_1) \geqslant v_i(e_{i,1}; e_{-i,2}, x_2) - v_i(e_{i,2}; e_{-i,2}, x_2).$$

The game structure exposed above gives two possibilities for the overall institutional arrangements: $\{x_1, y_1\}$ and $\{x_2, y_2\}$; i.e. the combination of a bank-based financial system with centralized wage bargaining and the combination of a financial-markets-based system with decentralized wage bargaining. In the example above, the two institutional equilibria are not Pareto-comparable. The bank–centralization configuration is more favourable to workers whereas the markets–decentralization arrangement favours savers and investors; managers are indifferent between the two equilibria. The total sum of all agents' pay-offs is the same in both equilibria, which could be interpreted as a neutrality of institutional configurations taken as a whole with respect to the aggregate performance of the economy. However, one could have constructed examples where one institutional configuration would have been associated with higher aggregate pay-offs.

The hypothesis put forward so far is that of non-coordination; i.e. agents play games taking the results of other games as given. This is consistent with a multilevel analysis of the emergence of institutions, where some institutions are taken for granted when agents devise their strategies. Again, this reflects the fact that the institutional structure is not plastic; one does not reinvent society as a whole each time a decision is taken. However, the institutional structure is the product of a political equilibrium, itself reflecting the compromise reached between different socio-political groups. The two equilibria above may also be interpreted as different compromises reached between the different groups. It is nevertheless clear that agents have different preferences regarding the type of game they want to play. Let us suppose that we have four different interest groups: worker, savers, investors (i.e. intermediaries between savers and firms), and managers. The $\{x_1, y_1\}$ centralized institutional equilibrium would be supported by workers, possibly allied to managers. The $\{x_2, y_2\}$ decentralized institutional equilibrium would find the support of savers and investors, possibly in coalition with managers. Which of the two coalitions wins politically will determine the institutional structure. In the above setting, managers play a central role because they are indifferent between the two equilibria. On what condition they will side with workers or with savers/investors will have consequences for institutional design. Also, a move from the centralized to the decentralized equilibrium could be prevented if workers have a veto power granted by the political system.

2.3 Institutional Hierarchy

The first section (2.1) argued that the institutional configuration of an economy depends on the formation of a stable dominant social bloc coalescing different socio-political groups prone to support a coalition with a certain political strategy. Implementing this strategy will lead to institutional change in a direction that is beneficial to the dominant social bloc. However, the social bloc itself is a coalition of different and sometimes diverging interests; the institutional structure that will result from the political strategy that it supports will therefore be a compromise, which may be more or less explicit. Because social agents do not generally possess a perfect vision of all interdependencies and complementarities between institutions, the compromise does not apply to all the institutions of an economy, but has to be re-established as changes in the economic environment modify agents' options and strategies. Institutional change takes place continuously, as the result of agents' autonomous action, and may sometimes threaten the interests of some groups within the dominant bloc. Policies will be implemented within the framework given by institutions, as a strategy devised by the government, under the control of the political coalition. These policies will themselves be subject to change, partly in reaction to the demands expressed by the dominant social bloc. Complementarity between institutions makes the implementation of policy, as well as institutional design, more complex. Institutional design in one area depends on the institutions prevailing in other areas. This raises the possibility of considering a hierarchy among institutions. Whereas the notion of complementarity links different institutions and modes of organization in a specific architecture and focuses on interactions between the different elements conditioning the coherence of the whole system, the notion of a hierarchy insists on the relative importance of one or a few institutions for the structure of complementarity and the dynamics of the institutional architecture as such.

Various theories consider that institutions have different levels of manifestation and legitimacy and/or different degrees of permanence. The problem of institutional hierarchy is sometimes pictured as a case of contradicting rules. If rules A and B contradict each other, which one should agents follow? The rule that agents must comply with is the one that is hierarchically superior to the other. Thus, moral norms are supposed to be superior to a large range of institutions, including formal regulations, as in the case of a car driver ignoring a traffic light in order to get to a hospital. But the problem of institutional hierarchy is more general than that. If we return to the example of complementarity presented above, the choice of institutions is dependent on which institutional arrangement prevails in the other area. Therefore, if institutional choice has already been made in the labour-market area, for instance, institutional choice in the financial-intermediation area is a mere consequence of the initial choice of bargaining structure. This brings a first definition of institutional hierarchy, which is that the inner design of one institutional form takes into account the constraints and incentives associated with another. It is thus an extension of the notion of complementarity; one institution somehow imposes the conditions according to which complementary institutions are going to supplement it in a specific institutional structure. In the framework presented above, institutional area X would be hierarchically superior to institutional area Y if the institutional choice in the latter was a consequence of the institutional choice made in the former. In terms of institutional forms, $x_1(x_2)$ would be at the top of the institutional hierarchy and $y_1(y_2)$ would be chosen as a consequence of the previous choice.

But anteriority or 'path-dependency' is not the true source of hierarchy, since institutions can be changed. Agents dissatisfied with the prevailing institutional arrangement in the labour-market area could oppose it and try to alter institutions under the conditions evoked in the previous section. Ostrom (2001) makes a distinction between three types of rule. *Operational rules* affect day-to-day decisions made by participants in any setting. *Collective-choice rules* affect operational activities and results through their effects in determining who is eligible to specify rules to be used in changing operational rules. *Constitutional-choice rules* affect operational activities and their effects in determining who is eligible and the rules to be used in crafting the set of collective-choice rules that in turn affect the set of operational rules. There is thus a clear hierarchy, because upper-level rules determine the design and mode of change of lower-level rules. Institutional hierarchy is thus tightly related to institutional change; the hierarchy is defined according to which set of rules dictate the design and possibilities of evolution of other rules. As a consequence, institutions at the top of the hierarchy are those which should change less often, being the most stable, and simply because change in these rules would generally imply changes in rules at lower hierarchical levels. From an economic point of view, this can be expressed as the fact that higher costs for changing rules are associated with institutions at the top of the hierarchy. The hierarchy of institutions could be interpreted in terms of a pecking order of sunk costs, i.e. the costs that were necessary for establishing those rules. The costs involved here could be seen as political costs or the costs necessary to reach an agreement on the design or change of the rule. Operational rules are relevant for a limited number of agents, and changing them is less costly than changing a collective-choice rule, for which an agreement must be reached across the community concerned.

The institutional hierarchy that I will now consider is related to but distinct from the above notion of institutional hierarchy. Institutions reflect the socio-political equilibrium of a society, and the costs and benefits associated with institutional change affect individuals differently. A political coalition will seek to stay in power by finding support from the dominant social bloc; to that effect, it will seek to implement those institutional changes that favour some or all of the socio-political groups that constitute the dominant bloc and try to prevent change that is detrimental to the bloc, in response to the political demands raised by the different socio-political groups. Therefore, the areas where institutional change will be implemented more easily are those in which the groups of the dominant bloc have little interest. On the other hand, change will be implemented more cautiously in domains where the most powerful socio-political groups have vested interests. If, for instance, the dominant social bloc consists of an alliance between firms' managers and industry workers, change affecting wage and employment bargaining will be of greater interest for the social bloc than change affecting other domains, because the basis on which the different socio-political groups have made an alliance concerns most probably certain features of the employment relation. Therefore, any change affecting this relation is likely to have far-reaching consequences for the stability of the bloc and hence for the solidity of the political coalition. Political agents are bound to tread more cautiously when labour-market and employment issues are concerned. The institutional hierarchy will thus be such that the institutions on top are those that are most crucial for the socio-political groups that constitute the dominant bloc, i.e. those where change is likely to modify substantially the distribution of income for individuals behind the socio-political groups. This is compatible with the notion of costs related to institutional change. Change is less likely to take place with institutions where the related costs are high, as in North (1990), but these costs must be understood as net costs incurred by the dominant social bloc. Since these net costs may actually turn into net benefits in the case of favourable evolution, hierarchy of institutions is not strictly synonymous with immobility or institutional inertia. Hierarchically superior institutions according to our definition are not necessarily those that change the least. A rational political strategy from the point of view of political agents may well be to favour change affecting the most crucial institutions for the dominant bloc as long as these changes are profitable for the bloc and reinforce the political support of the coalition. Therefore, stability of institutions is also a function of the political–representation system, such as the number and weight of veto players. Institutions are less likely to change if they are hierarchically at the top and if changes affect in differentiated ways the different socio-political groups that have some veto power.

The adopted definition of institutional hierarchy is therefore made with reference to a specific socio-political equilibrium and a specific dominant bloc. Changes in the institutional structure of the economy can then be related to political changes and modifications of the dominant bloc. The institutional structure of an economy is always changing under different influences: some 'external' or exogenous forces, for instance. A changing environment can modify agents' strategies. It is commonplace to put technological change at the forefront of exogenous causes of institutional change.[41] Technological

---

[41] We will see in Ch. 6 how technological change is supposed to destabilize the institutional arrangements of European countries in Third Way interpretations of modern capitalism.

evolution may call for certain organizational or institutional change in order to reap the full benefit of the new technological opportunities. Technological changes may also benefit or harm certain social groups, which may then revise their strategies, leading to institutional change. But technology is exogenous only to a certain extent; technological change is in large part the result of deliberate attempts by economic agents to improve the conditions of physical production, to further knowledge acquisition, and to innovate. In such conditions, one might better speak of the institutional consequences of technological change as 'unintended consequences' of deliberate choices. This category is not limited to technology; not all consequences of individual or collective decisions can be taken into account by the relevant agents. Thus, every decision has consequences that have not been foreseen or have been consciously neglected by the strategic agents. These consequences may impact on the institutional structure and provoke institutional change. Last, institutional change may of course result from intentional decisions, as seen in the previous section.

Institutional change may be localized, in the sense that it affects a limited area of the economy. Some firms may, for instance, transform the organization of production or management. This change may have distributional consequences for the agents concerned (workers, managers, capital owners, etc.) and push them to express a specific political demand for another type of institutional change. For instance, workers disadvantaged by a new type of organization of production may call for a change in labour regulations that prohibits or limits the change implemented by the management. They may try to bargain with the firms' management, calling for a modification in the reform plan, or, if necessary, call in a 'third party', the State, and directly express a political demand. Whether this demand will be satisfied depends on the balance of power between different socio-political groups. If the political weight of the agents concerned is negligible, no consequences will follow and the outcome of the initial institutional change will be limited to some distributional consequences. This is likely to be the case if the agents involved are outside the dominant social bloc. If on the other hand they have a degree of political weight, especially if they are within the dominant social bloc and can put forward their demand, several options are open. The government, seeking political support, may try to implement a specific policy change, or instigate further institutional change. Some redistributive measures may be implemented, in an attempt to lessen the effects of the initial institutional change. On a larger scale, negotiation within the dominant social bloc may lead to further institutional change in order to compensate the agents concerned.

Let us take the example of a simple economy, with three institutional areas, A, B, and C. Within each institutional area there may be several different institutional forms, A_i, B_i, C_i (where $i = 1, 2, 3$, etc.). For instance, if domain A concerns the labour market, the different forms could be decentralized or centralized wage bargaining. Let us further suppose the existence of three socio-political groups, G_1, G_2, and G_3, which are themselves aggregations of different social groups. Therefore, these socio-political groups are themselves subject to change according to the modification of political strategies of social groups. The dominant social bloc is a coalition of socio-political groups, supposed to take place between groups G_1 and G_2 at the beginning. The initial institutional configuration is characterized by institutions A_1, B_1, C_1 at the initial period considered, as indicated in Table 2.1. Institution A_1 is supposed to be at the top of the hierarchy for the dominant bloc because the political compromise between G_1 and G_2 crucially depends on the stability of A_1.

An economic system is characterized by a set of complementary institutions. Therefore, change in one institution may have consequences beyond the initial area and affect a whole new range of institutions. As a consequence of change in one domain, agents may be led to alter their

TABLE 2.1 Institutional change and institutional hierarchy

Institutional areas and political support	(1) Initial situation	(2) Local institutional change	(3) Reaction to the initial change	(4) Spread of institutional change through institutional complementarity	(5) Modifications in the dominant social bloc, generalized institutional change	(6) Change of system, generalized institutional change, and break-up of the dominant social bloc
A	A_1	A_1	A_1	A_1	A_2	A_3
B	B_1	B_1	B_1	B_2	B_2	B_2
C	C_1	C_2	C_3	C_3	C_3	C_3
Dominant social bloc	G_1, G_2	G_1, G_2	G_1, G_2	G_1, G_2	G_1', G_2'	G_2', G_3'
Outsiders	G_3	G_3	G_3	G_3	G_3'	G_1'

strategies in a different domain, and this process may lead to institutional change, i.e. change in the formal and informal rules that govern agents' behaviour. Some localized institutional change may thus trigger further changes, so that modification of the institutional structure does not stay localized. The question arises as to whether it is possible to find new institutional forms that would be complementary to each other. The dominant social bloc would be willing to look for institutional change as long as their interests were preserved. It will thus try to back up political strategies that aim at finding policy and institutional solutions compatible with the preservation of the institutions that are at the top of the institutional hierarchy. If this is possible, the economy will undergo a phase of substantial institutional change, which will not be considered to be a change in economic model so long as the institutions at the top of the hierarchy are preserved. A localized institutional change is, for instance, a move from situation (1) to situation (2) in Table 2.1. This change may be the consequence of a deliberate variation in agents' strategies, or the unintended effect of some strategic choice. The economy may stay at situation (2) if a new political-economy equilibrium is reached at this stage, which demands that new institutional complementarities be found. Reaching such an equilibrium may be facilitated by a change in economic policy, for instance. However, the initial change may trigger some political demand for further institutional change in the area concerned, such as a demand for a modification in the level of protection following a variation in competitive practices. If the demand is satisfied, the economy may find itself in a situation such as (3), which may or may not be a political-economy equilibrium. Through the effect of institutional complementarities, the local institutional change may provoke changes in other institutional domains, leading the economy towards a situation such as (4), where substantial institutional change has already taken place in comparison to (1). For instance, deregulated financial markets may put pressure on the arrangements previously made between firms' management and workers regarding employment stability and protection, and modifications in this area could follow. If (4) is not a political-economy equilibrium, more radical institutional change is likely to take place, affecting this time the dominant bloc and the institutions at the core of the socio-political compromise. The change may be more or less incremental, such as in (5), where some modifications of the dominant bloc have taken place, within each socio-political group, accompanied by more or less incremental modification of the dominant institutional form (A_1 becoming A_2). A more radical change is also possible, which can be assimilated to a change in system, as in situation (6), where the former social bloc has broken up and where the hierarchically superior institutions have been substantially modified. Once again, (6) may or may not be a new equilibrium. If it is not, the economic system is in a situation of crisis; if it is, the change of system may be accompanied by a change in institutional hierarchy. The new equilibrium has been reached through a reorganization of socio-political alliances. The new dominant social bloc may have different priorities to those of the previous dominant bloc; i.e. the new compromise reached between the socio-political groups participating in the new dominant bloc can be based on issues other than those that underlay the previous compromise. Therefore, the new institutional hierarchy may place B_2 or C_3 on top.

This formalization of institutional complementarity and hierarchy also provides an answer to the question of 'tight fit' versus 'loose coupling' of institutions in an institutional-complementarity context. The 'tight fit' thesis would argue that any change, however small, in the institutional structure questions the coherence and stability of the whole and sets in motion a process of reorganization and institutional change that will end up with a radical transformation of the model. If 'tight fit' prevails, the only possible institutional change is a move from situation (1) to (6). Interdependence between institutions is so strong that there can be no small modification. At the other extreme, the loose-coupling thesis says that 'anything goes', and is somewhat antithetical to the concept of institutional complementarities. A softer version of the loose-coupling thesis would permit all situations in the Table above and consider them as possible equilibria. In fact, the range of situations exposed in Table 2.1 demonstrates the many possibilities intermediate between the two extremes. Even within a given set of institutional forms and associated complementarities, some alterations are possible which do not question the institutional hierarchy and the stability of the economic 'model'.

We have seen in this chapter how institutions influence the economic equilibrium and how institutions are political-economy choices. An economy is characterized by a set of complementary institutional forms resting on specific political equilibria defining the hierarchy among institutions. We will now turn to the concrete cases of modern economies and assess the complementarities that form the basis of the different economic models.

3

A Comparative Analysis of Capitalism

3.1 Historical and International Differentiation of Capitalism

One can identify two ways in which comparative analyses of capitalism handle the issue of institutional diversity at the international level. A first approach is to consider that there is a stable, theoretically grounded reference for the institutional structure of a market economy, and that international institutional comparison must be made on the basis of that reference. As mentioned in the previous chapter, the standard neoclassical position is to compare any economic system with the Walrasian model of perfect competition. From this point of view, the further an economy's institutions are from those ensuring perfect competition the less efficient this economy should be; economies far from the neoclassical ideal are consequently expected to be lagging behind in terms of growth, welfare, and other performance indicators. As pointed out in Chapter 2, this position is based on strong deductive reasoning, starting from well-established results of economic theory—general equilibrium—and applying these results to concrete cases in the world economy. One can criticize this standard view on the basis that its validity is basically limited to a first-best world; applying all-market recipes in an economy with market incompleteness or other associated 'pathologies' may turn out to be counter-productive (Bohm 1987). Market economies are intrinsically institutional economies.

The standard neoclassical approach is however not the only one to take an implicit or explicit reference against which international comparisons must be made. In the 1960s the observation that France and Germany were in the process of rapidly catching up to the US level of productivity led scholars to look for specific factors that could be at the root of the fast growth that European countries were enjoying, and which contrasted so much with the pre-war situation of the same countries. For Shonfield (1965), France and Germany were not just catching up *in spite* of having very different institutions from the USA but *because* of them. The reasons behind French modernization, for instance, could be found in an increased public intervention in the economy. This intervention could take several forms: State-owned banks or firms, the establishment of a Welfare State, a more or less comprehensive regulation of competition, public investment in research and development, and coordination of private agents through (indicative) planning and information exchange. Compared to the standard neoclassical view, the perspective was thus inverted. Non-market ways of coordinating activity had proved to be superior, not on the ground of their intrinsic quality whatever time and space, but because they corresponded to the dominant trends of contemporary capitalism. Incidentally, this perspective would not so much lead to a diversity of capitalism as to a convergence toward a mixed economy associating market mechanisms and planning.

A consideration of the historicity of the institutions of modern capitalism is also adopted by the French school of *régulation*.[1] Its central problem was to explain the periods of relatively high and stable growth alternating with episodes of slow growth and macroeconomic disequilibria in developed economies, and particularly the crisis of the 1970s which manifested itself under the guise of an association of high unemployment and high inflation—a combination of pathologies a priori ruled out by both the Keynesian and the classical theories—as well as a marked slowdown in productivity gains. In order to explain the crisis of the 1970s it seemed necessary to be able to explain why the post-war 'golden age' of capitalism could have occurred, with its high rates of stable growth. Starting from the case study of the US economy, Aglietta (1979) proposed an analysis of capitalism and its transformations based on the consideration of five 'institutional forms': the wage–labour nexus, the forms of competition, international relations, money, and public authorities. The relations between these five forms characterize the overall mode of *régulation* of an economy. One of the five institutional forms, the wage–labour nexus, had a predominant position in the hierarchy of institutional forms. The story could be broadly summed up as follows. The necessity of a parallel evolution of mass consumption and mass production for the coherence of the Fordist, i.e. post-war, *régulation* put the institutional arrangements of the wage–labour nexus at the centre of the whole institutional architecture. The corresponding capital–labour compromise allowed the implementation of Taylorist methods in the factories in exchange for a certain sharing of the productivity gains obtained thanks to the implementation of these production methods, a certain degree of employment stability, and social protection offered by the Welfare State. This led to a coordinated expansion of supply and demand and moderate competition between national producers, best characterized as oligopolistic behaviour. Inflationary pressures which could—and in the end did—result from this setting were

---

[1] See CEPREMAP-CORDES (1977); Aglietta (1979); Boyer (1986).

alleviated by an accommodating monetary policy in the context of an international regime that permitted discrete currency adjustments. In addition, short-term demand-management policies helped in stabilizing economic dynamics and prevented the occurrence of the type of business fluctuations that characterized pre-Fordist growth.

The idea that there is a 'one best way' for achieving high and stable economic growth is nonetheless quite removed from the preoccupations of the *régulationistes*, if only because their main topic was after all the crisis of the mode of *régulation*. However, because the study of Fordism originated in an analysis of the most advanced economy of the twentieth century, i.e. the United States, the 'vintage *régulation*' approach[2] somehow suggested—rather than expressed—the idea that in order to enjoy the benefits brought by Fordism countries would have to adopt the institutional forms characteristic of that mode of *régulation*, and hence (at least part of) the institutions characteristic of the prominent type of capitalism, the USA. The *régulation* school then developed a study of Fordism applied to other countries, starting with France (CEPREMAP-CORDES 1977). Comparative Studies soon produced the result that there was not one but several forms of Fordism, and that some national forms seemed more apt to dodge the pitfalls of the American brand, as witnessed by the macroeconomic achievements of Germany, France, or Japan in the 1960s, 1970s, or 1980s (Boyer and Mistral 1986). The USA seemed a less than ideal model in that it adopted neo-conservative strategies and 'defensive' flexibility in order to escape the crisis of Fordism; these solutions seemed more akin to the pre-Fordist type of *régulation* than an answer to the problem of finding a successor to Fordist *régulation*. Other countries (the Nordic ones) seemed to turn toward a more 'offensive' flexibility (Boyer 1988), preserving a more cooperative wage–labour nexus and defending the Welfare State; some economies (Japan) were apparently able to implement production methods that could overcome the shortcomings of Taylorist mass production (Boyer and Yamada 2000).

The quest for post-Fordism nevertheless turned out to be deceptive. On the one hand, comparative analysis as well as industry and firm case studies proved that new productive principles were spreading worldwide which were not merely copying the Japanese forms of organization. In a way, a process similar to the diffusion of Fordism seemed to be taking place during the 1980s and 1990s (Boyer and Durand 1998). Just as the post-war years saw national adaptations of the institutional forms of Fordism, the end of the twentieth century could be seen as a process of

---

[2] i.e. the approach of the 1970s inspired by Aglietta (1979).

implementation and hybridization of the Japanese methods of work organization coupled with the specific institutions of the various countries. On the other hand, the Japanese crisis of the 1990s contrasted with the macroeconomic successes of the USA and led some authors to suggest that the future of capitalism was somewhere other than in the Far East (Aglietta 1998). Post-Fordism may lie not so much with Toyota as with Wall Street combined with the Silicon Valley.

The burst of the new economic bubble may have put an end to this last vision among the *régulation* school (Boyer 2002), but the approach itself still contains a tension between two trends: on the one hand, there is a vision of the mode of *régulation* still centred on the US type of capitalism, from the original expression of the theory and Fordism to the 'patrimonial *régulation*' in Aglietta's more recent works. In this perspective, the USA is still the country that defines the future of capitalism. As a consequence, a 'finance-led' or patrimonial type of capitalism is likely to spread all over the world, with its principles of corporate governance as the leading institutional form. On the other hand, some other contributors, such as Boyer, for instance, have been more reluctant to confer on the USA the title of 'home of the future of capitalism'. The study of other countries (France, Japan, etc.), particular industries (cars), and specific time periods (the New Economy decade) has given a more complex picture of the dynamics of capitalism. The conclusion is more along the lines that the USA *should* not be an example to follow and perhaps *could* not play this role anyway.

There is a more or less explicit normative aspect in the works of Boyer ((2001) and (2002), for instance); it is clear that there is a 'good' capitalism (or a 'good' mode of *régulation*) and a 'bad' capitalism. The former is expected to guarantee high and stable growth coupled with low income inequality and high welfare, whereas the latter is more likely to generate sometimes high but volatile growth with an aggravation of income-inequality problems and a low level of social protection. Such a normative idea is also present in a muted form in other authors' works. Generally, the debate is organized around an opposition between the US style of capitalism and an alternative form, which could deliver the same macroeconomic performance but at a lower social cost. The terms of the debate on the comparison between different models of capitalism were very clearly stated in Michel Albert's book, *Capitalisme contre capitalisme* (1991). The main point of the book is to stress the differences between two main types of capitalist economy, the neo-American model and the Rhine model, respectively exemplified by the USA and Germany. The former model is characterized by several features: an emphasis on individual achievement, the importance of short-term financial benefits, and reversibility and flexibility of commitment. The latter rests on long-term commitments, collective achievements, and consensus. An interesting aspect of the book is that although Albert thinks the Rhine model is on many counts 'superior' to the neo-American model, and in any case better suited to European societies, he does not believe that it would win in a free competition among varieties of capitalism, where superior forms of organization would win partisans over by the sheer power of their attractiveness. If the most appealing aspects of the Rhine model are to spread across Europe, it will be through a political process of European integration.

Albert's book does not propose a fully-fledged typology of capitalism as such; countries other than Germany or the USA are either classified under one or the other model or sit uncomfortably between the two, as is the case with France, for instance. The Germany–USA dichotomy has become a classic feature of comparative analysis of capitalism and is analytically presented in the various works of David Soskice and Peter Hall.[3] The starting point of their analyses is the relational firm, defined as an agent seeking to develop dynamic capabilities and the institutional framework within which it operates. They use five spheres in which firms develop relationships to resolve coordination problems central to their core competencies: industrial relations, vocational training and education, corporate governance, interfirm relations, and the coordination problems firms have with their own employees, i.e. 'internal' coordination. They compare two different production regimes, the *liberal market economies* (LMEs) and the *coordinated market economies* (CMEs). This dichotomy is the basis for the consideration of one fundamental dimension separating the different national production systems, namely coordination. In an LME coordination is based on market mechanisms, favouring investment in transferable assets. In a CME it is mainly achieved through non-market means—the so-called strategic coordination—favouring investment in specific assets. LMEs are thus characterized by short-term finance, deregulated labour markets, an emphasis on general education, and strong product-market competition. CMEs are characterized by long-term finance, cooperative industrial relations, high levels of vocational training, weakened product-market competition, and strong information exchanges through more or less formal professional associations favouring the establishment of common industrial standards. The differences extend to the patterns of innovation and technological change as well as industrial specialization, the so-called comparative institutional advantage. LMEs have a comparative advantage in industries where radical

---

[3] The most recent contribution is Hall and Soskice (eds.) (2001).

innovation leads to market-stealing benefits and where competitiveness stems from a fast adaptation to changing market conditions. CMEs have the edge in industries where competitiveness is based on cumulative build-up of knowledge and company-specific skills and where incremental innovation matters.

3.2 Methodological Questions

As with Albert's contribution (1991), Hall and Soskice's binary classification of economies into liberal market economies and coordinated market economies leaves a certain number of national cases occupying ambiguous positions, since they do not clearly rest on market-based coordination principles nor possess strong and organized interest groups upon which non-market coordination could be based. France and Italy are examples of such intermediate countries; for instance, neither country appears in tables 1.1 and 1.2 in Hall and Soskice (2001) (pp. 20, 59), where comparative statistics concerning CMEs and LMEs are presented. When international comparison along the lines of a binary classification is applied to a large sample, countries can either belong to one or the other type, or be classified as 'intermediate cases'. The types considered in dichotomous approaches are usually exemplified by specific countries; the USA is the near-perfect example of an LME and Germany is the corresponding near-perfect CME in Hall and Soskice (2001), for instance. The theoretical construction of the archetypes is generally based on both theory and inference drawn from specific case studies and international comparisons; the theoretical categories always bear the marks of the specific examples upon which they have been constructed. It is always possible to apply the typology to other cases: the UK can also be defined as an LME, Japan as a CME. But some countries cannot be classified so easily, and consequently fall in-between. Not being clearly identified as belonging to any type, these countries are considered somewhat deficient and are expected to have lower macroeconomic performance. As seen in Chapter 2, in many comparative institutional studies the relation between performance and institutional features is U-shaped. In Calmfors and Driffill (1988), countries obtain good employment performance when their wage bargaining institutions are either highly coordinated or totally decentralized. Extending this argument to a more general pattern of coordination versus market-based mechanisms, all intermediate-case countries should have macroeconomic performances located at the bottom of the U shape.

One faces, then, a double problem. Forcing countries into one or the other category runs the risk of ignoring fundamental differences between them, thereby emptying the classification of its meaning. Categories that are too broad tell us very little about what brings countries together in a specific group. On the other hand, having as many types of capitalism as there are countries is to present little more than a series of country-specific case studies, and cannot therefore represent a comparative analysis of capitalism. Building a theory of the *variety* of capitalism on such a basis is probably too easy, since variety is presupposed at the outset. But there is a more fundamental difficulty with the dichotomous approach: by treating a large number of countries as intermediate, 'imperfect' cases one may miss a more complex country grouping than the simple binary taxonomy. The intermediate cases of the dichotomy may belong to other categories that the initial analysis ignores, which suggests that some important aspects of country differentiation are missed by the dichotomous analysis. This raises the question of the bases upon which the diversity of economic systems must be analysed both from a theoretical and an applied point of view. One can indeed argue that binary classifications are always one-dimensional. The dimension opposing two types of capitalism expresses the institutional hierarchy present in the theory concerned. Introducing other possible types is a questioning of the hierarchy expressed in the dichotomy.

We can start from the most fundamental and popular opposition between types of capitalism, i.e. that between a market-based system (i.e. an LME) and a coordination-based model (i.e. a CME). In the former model agents are coordinated through markets and prices; in the latter they are coordinated through non-market means. Such a dichotomous approach has both pros and cons. One advantage is that it provides a clear theoretical basis for an empirical analysis (Hall and Gingerich 2001). On the other hand, it suffers from the defaults associated with a typology of capitalism based on an opposition between two polar extremes. Any such comparison, as noted above, is always bound to be made according to one dimension only, which is an expression of the implicit hierarchy of institutions adopted by the theoretical analysis underlying the typology of economies. The fundamental dimension which splits apart CMEs and LMEs for Hall and Soskice (2001) is the structure of coordination of the firm. It corresponds to a reduction of the complexity inherent in an international, macrolevel, and institutional comparison. The choice of this dimension may reveal two things: (1) the pattern of relations of the firm with its environment is at the top of the hierarchy of institutions in this particular theory of the variety of capitalism; (2) there is a certain embeddedness of institutions, such that the market/non-market-coordination opposition corresponds to a societal logic coming from the whole set of social ties between agents. Therefore, it is pervasive in all institutions and forms of organization, which then justifies the reduction of the analysis to one dimension. The first aspect is undoubtedly present in Hall and Soskice's works, as we saw. Their theory is basically firm-centred.[4] The second aspect is not so clearly present in Hall and Soskice (2001), but more so in works of economic sociology (Streeck 1997*a*; Hollingsworth 2000).

Getting out of a binary classification implies considering other dimensions along which economies are differentiated. Several authors have thus introduced an element deemed crucial for explaining the differentiation pattern of modern capitalism. For instance, Schmidt (2002) identifies not two but three distinct ideal-typical models: market, managed, and State-enhanced capitalism, respectively exemplified by the UK, Germany, and France. One can associate with each type countries other than the three just mentioned: the USA is a clear case of market capitalism, the Netherlands and Sweden belong to the category of managed capitalism, and Italy is another case of State capitalism. The basic advantage of such a threefold classification is that it gives a specific status to a group of countries previously classified as intermediate between CMEs and LMEs, by explaining what ties them together. A consequence is that in finding an identity as well as a 'logic', i.e. a mode of coherence between the specific institutional items in the model, the countries belonging to this model are no longer automatically condemned to inferior macroeconomic performances, as was the case with the U-shaped representation. This classification also provides the supplementary factor of international differentiation. The State is the major agent of differentiation among the types and this explains why one has a distinct third type in addition to the traditional market (LME) and managed (CME) types of capitalism: the liberal State gives a high degree of autonomy to economic agents in market capitalism and acts as an arbiter; the enabling State encourages associational governance and negotiation among private agents in managed capitalism, and acts as a facilitator; the interventionist State directly coordinates and intervenes in private activity in State-enhanced capitalism, and acts as a leader. Other institutional features derive from this characterization: business relations are driven by the market in market capitalism, managed outside the market in managed capitalism, and organized by the State in State-enhanced capitalism. Likewise, the structure of industrial relations is respectively market-reliant, coordinated, or State-controlled in the three different types of capitalism.

---

[4] Ibid. 5: 'By locating the firm at the centre of our analysis...'. For another firm-centred analysis of the diversity of capitalism see Whitley (1999), who proposes an analysis of 'business systems'.

Such an approach questions the hierarchy of institutions underlying the dichotomy between CME and LME in the firm-centred view. In order to see it more clearly, let us suppose that one can analyse the variety of capitalism by considering two institutional areas: interfirm relations and the pattern of State intervention in the economy. Let us further assume that one has identified two different types of interfirm relationship, namely market-driven versus coordinated, and three different patterns of State intervention: arbiter, facilitator, and dirigiste. Deciding whether one adopts a categorization of capitalism based on two or three types amounts to choosing which institutional pattern is most important, that of interfirm relations or of State intervention. If the former applies, the diversity of patterns of public involvement in the economy is only secondary, and any variety in this respect may be neglected in a first outline. Such an option is actually taken in some comparative works. Acknowledging the decline of the role of the State in the economy, the firm-centred view is led to neglect a hypothetical third variety of capitalism, which may have been relevant during the 1960s or 1970s but is no longer so. In this variety, coordination by the State is no longer possible because of the pressures of globalization and Europeanization, which limit the scope for public intervention in the economy. The State is no longer able to supervise coordination in the economy; the economies of the third variety have thus lost a cornerstone of their internal coherence. Their evolution will lead them either towards a CME or an LME pattern, the latter evolution being more likely than the former. If, on the other hand, one believes that State intervention is still relevant and that the pattern of interfirm relations is somehow derived from or influenced by the type of State intervention, then limiting oneself to a dichotomy derived from consideration of the interfirm-relations area means missing a clear understanding of the economic dynamics of the supposedly 'intermediate' cases.

The questioning of the institutional hierarchy present in the dichotomous classification can be seen in the contributions of other authors, who do not consider the pattern of State intervention as that important, but rather insist on the consideration of another area which is held to be essential. Rhodes and van Apeldoorn (1997) have thus identified a third group in addition to the traditional dichotomy: a Latin brand of capitalism, where Spain and Italy would be joined by France. If the countries concerned are more or less those of Schmidt (2002), the reasons for putting them together in a specific category are very different. The supplementary institutional area taken into account for the comparison is here the structure of corporate governance, i.e. the role of banks versus that of stock markets, the type of firms' owners, the structure of management boards, and the role of employees in firms' management. The external environments of firms are also considered: the role of the State, cooperation between social partners, industrial relations, training, labour markets, and innovation systems. Ebbinghaus (1999) bases his typology of capitalism on consideration of the Welfare State, and distinguishes four models within Europe: Nordic, Central European, Southern European, and Anglo-Saxon. The four types of capitalism are each characterized by a specific type of Welfare State, the classification in this area being taken from Esping-Andersen (1990). The Nordic model differs from Germany's Central European model in its universalist Welfare State, which allows for higher labour-force participation. Sweden offers very different types of benefits and criteria for distribution from Germany's conservative Welfare State, where welfare is more closely linked to occupational stratification (Jackson 2002). Labour unions are stronger and play a much more important role in the Nordic, Central, and Southern varieties than in the Anglo-Saxon model.

The idea of an institutional hierarchy is explicit in Boyer's classification (1997) of capitalism into four types according to the distinctive form of the labour market, or more precisely the wage–labour nexus. This hierarchy is totally in line with the *régulationniste* analysis of Fordism. The institutional characteristics defining the four types are entirely derived from the specificities of their labour markets and industrial relations. Market-oriented capitalism exhibits decentralization and external mobility of the labour force; trade unions have a non-important role to play. On the other hand, the corporatist model is characterized by a significant role for trade unions and occupational labour markets. The social-democratic model relies more on a tripartite agreement between labour unions, firms' management, and the government. Unions are strong and play a major role, not only in determining wage levels, but also in the process of defining skills and training. There is a fourth model, the Statist one, where the government plays a central role in the definition of rules affecting economic activity, and most particularly the labour market, and where internal labour markets are dominant. The USA, Canada, and the UK are examples of market-oriented capitalism, Germany and Japan are classified as corporatist countries, Sweden and Austria belong to the social-democratic model, and France and Italy are considered 'Statist' countries.

This brief look at different theories of diversified capitalism suggests that there is a significant overlap in the various classifications. Most authors consider Nordic countries to belong to a specific type of economy where bargaining among social partners plays an important role. Anglo-Saxon countries are often classified in a group where market mechanisms are particularly strong in the coordination of economic activity. There are distinctive elements in the South European countries, with France being sometimes attached to this group. The issue of the distinctiveness of Japan is another problem. For Aoki (2000), Japanese capitalism is a distinct model in itself, whereas the variety-of-capitalism approach would lump this country together with Germany in the CME group. The question of the possible distinctiveness of East Asian capitalist economies may also be raised. Some contributions have not insisted that these countries belong to a separate model, but have rather distributed them within already existing partitions of economies. An identifiable Asian model of capitalism would therefore not exist, because of the significant differences across Far Eastern economies. The importance of large conglomerates in Korea is sometimes opposed to patrimonialism and familial networks in Taiwan (Orru, Biggart, and Hamilton 1997). Three types of capitalism could then be distinguished in Asia: alliance capitalism, which is akin to the CME model in the dichotomous classification; dirigiste capitalism, where the State has a strong role in the economy; and familial capitalism, which relies on small firms and family networks. Japan (and Germany) would belong to the first type, Korea (and France) to the second, and Taiwan (and Italy) to the third.

Other authors are more prone to accept the existence of an Asian model of capitalism, focusing on the existing similarities linking East Asian countries rather than on their differences. One reason for a relative homogeneity within Far Eastern economies is that history links these countries together: Korea operated under Japanese rule for over thirty-five years, for instance. More generally, Japanese dominance led to an integration of these countries into Japanese-led regional economy, functioning along Japanese guidelines (Cumings 1987). Some contributions link the Asian model to 'crony capitalism' and its associated pathologies of corruption, bad loans, financial crises, and bankruptcy (IMF 1998). More optimistic approaches regard the unique attributes of Asian financial systems as instrumental in the fast growth that Japan and the 'tigers' experienced until the 1990s, allowing industry ample supplies of 'patient capital' (Singh 1998). In its 1993 report on development, the World Bank linked the success of the high-performing Asian economies to the ability of the State to overcome coordination failure through its intervention in the economy. More generally, the main features of the Asian model can be said to be the following (ibid.): a close relationship between the government and business—government's interventions are made after consultation with business, and such interventions are carried out through a system of 'administrative guidance' rather than through formal legislation; a specific financial system, with long-term relationships between banks and firms; cooperative relationships between management and labour in the internal pattern of firms' organization in connection with supporting labour-market 'imperfections';[5] a reluctance to consider perfect competition on product markets as more efficient than 'guided competition'; and a strategic pattern of integration within the world economy, leaving finance and science sectors isolated from external competitive pressure.

To sum up, the literature points to the possible existence of several distinct models of capitalism. Besides the opposition between CMEs and LMEs, one can perhaps distinguish between three or four different models within the European Union alone, with in addition a specific model for East Asian countries. Such a diversity was also considered in a comparative analysis of different 'social systems of innovation' presented in the next section.

3.3 Social Systems of Innovation and Production

A theoretical analysis and an exercise in international comparisons in Amable et al. (1997) led to the distinction between several types of 'capitalism', entitled 'social systems of innovation and production' (SSIPs). The theoretical analysis identified why institutions were likely to 'matter' in the differentiation of economies and why this could be expected to have consequences for the scientific, technological, and industrial specialization of countries. A consequence was that different institutional characteristics should be associated with different innovation capabilities and a differentiated pattern of industrial specialization. The theoretical scheme underlying the analysis can be represented pictorially as in Fig. 3.1. The basis of the theoretical scheme is the interaction between the scientific sector, producer of ideas, the technological sector, which turns these ideas into artefacts, and the manufacturing sector, which turns the artefacts into marketable products. Three institutional areas were also of particular importance for the efficiency of the interaction just mentioned: the education and training system, which is responsible for supplying the economy with an adaptable and well-trained workforce, the financial system, which defines an implicit time horizon of innovation and production and plays an important role in selecting and financing investment projects, allowing for a sufficiently high investment rate, and the system of labour relations, which indirectly determines price competitiveness as

---

[5] Allowing for lifetime employment and seniority-based wages, for instance.

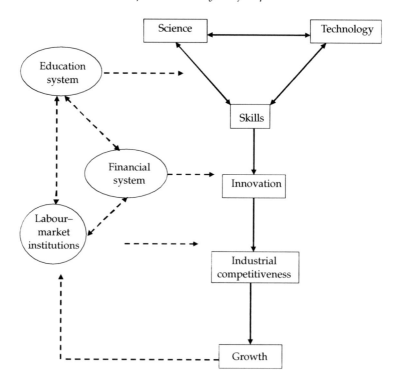

Fɪɢ. 3.1 Social systems of innovation and production

well as some non-price aspects such as the quality of cooperation in production relationships.

The social systems of innovation and production were defined as particular forms and patterns of interaction between six subsystems: science, technology, industry, education and training, labour markets, and finance; each subsystem is characterized by a specific mix of institutions and forms of organizations. The dynamic 'compatibility' of each subsystem with the others defines *ex post* the features of the global SSIPs.

The analysis produced a distinction between four different SSIPs, whose main characteristics are summarized in Table 3.1.

1. *The market-based SSIP*

Principles of competition, between firms and between individuals, are central to this SSIP. Agents are mainly coordinated through market mechanisms, which shape the crucial economic relations upon which the model is based. Therefore, the competitiveness of this model is based on the strength of the incentives given to agents and their ability to respond to them. Individuals invest in education and training expecting high returns from a deregulated labour market which enables a large wage

TABLE 3.1 Four types of social system of innovation and production

SSIPs	Market-based	Mesocorporatist	European-integration/public	Social-democratic
Science	The research system is based on competition between researchers and between research institutions	Academic research is largely disconnected from industry	Public basic research is disconnected from new-product development within firms, but there are large-scale programmes	Social needs are important in the definition of research objectives
Technology	Importance of intellectual property rights protection, patents, and copyrights as incentives towards and protection for innovation	Importance of tacit knowledge and in-house innovation	Importance of public impetus for private research	Gradual evolution towards advanced technologies and new sectors—from natural-resources exploitation to information technology
Competence and skills	Highly segmented labour force; high skills and innovation on one side, low skills and production on the other	Homogenized general education; specific skills developed within the corporation, but labour-market dualism	Internal rather than external mobility of the labour force	Egalitarian ideals in education and wage-setting; limits through public action to the adverse consequences of technical progress
Labour markets	Decentralization of wage bargaining; individualized wage- and labour-market segmentation	Wage compromise within the large corporation but synchronizing of wage rises	Strong institutionalization of employment rules, working hours, and social protection	Centralization of wage bargaining under the external competitiveness constraint

TABLE 3.1 (cont.)

SSIPs	Market-based	Mesocorporatist	European-integration/public	Social-democratic
Competition	Limits to concentration through legal action; constant evolution of oligopolistic competition	Strong competition on internal product markets between large firms	Once moderate competition, because of public intervention or business associations, has intensified within the single market; concentration of capital	Small number of large internationalized firms and networks of small local suppliers
Finance	Market-based finance and sophistication of financial services; financial innovation; strong influence of shareholders	Stable long-term relationships between the main bank and a keiretsu; strong involvement of public authorities (MOF and central bank) in private banking	Importance of banks; relatively low sophistication of financial services	Bank-based financial system; no sophistication of financial services
Products	Important product innovation	Adaptation of products and processes in the catching-up phase; fast product innovation after that	Slow adaptation to market changes	Importance of quality, services, and differentiation
Other characteristics:				
Public Intervention	Fragmented in a series of agencies and monitoring institutions; strong and extensive limits to	Furnishes collective services and acts as a coordinator; small size but significant role	Important public intervention (central State or local authorities): firms' regulation, public	Many forms of public intervention, with financial transfers regulation

	public intervention; political competition		spending, social security, etc.	Largely open economies
	Importance of large public-research programmes (defence, etc.) which supplement private research	No large public programmes of the 'mission' type	Large variability among the different countries concerned	Small countries, strong external constraint
International regime	Adherence to free-trade principles; status and autonomy of nations depends on size (USA vs. UK, etc.)	Economic development conditions all choices in terms of international trade	Regionalism (EU) favoured over multilateralism; political will for European integration conditions economic integration	
Consequences for:				
Innovation	Schumpeterian waves of (radical) innovations; importance of patents and individual rewards to innovation	Ability to imitate, transfer, and transform technology starting with incremental innovation	Both 'mission'-type projects of large size and incremental, quality innovation	Innovation linked to solutions to social or economic problems
Industrial specialization	Sectors linked to 'radical' innovations: information technology, aerospace, pharmaceuticals, finance, etc.	Sectors where coordination is necessary and where competence is localized and cumulative: cars, electronics, robotics	Sectors linked to public infrastructures (France, etc.) and/or where competence rests on a skilled labour force: aerospace, mechanics, cars	Sectors linked to social demand (health, security, environment) or exploiting natural resources
Countries	United States, Great Britain, Australia, and Canada	Japan	France, Germany, Italy, and the Netherlands	Sweden, Finland, Denmark, and Norway

Source: Amable, Barré, and Boyer (1997); Amable (2000).

dispersion according to skills demand. Firms innovate expecting high profits from deregulated product markets enabling an intense competition favouring new entrants. Intellectual property rights are protected through a strict patent system. A financial-markets-based system favours setting up new technological firms, and acts as a discipline device for firms' management through a market for corporate control. Countries close to this model should specialize in activities where knowledge is codified and where drastic innovation matters greatly for competitiveness and service activities.

2. The mesocorporatist SSIP

Labour markets are internalized at the mesolevel, that of large industrial groups, with specific wage-setting practices and a specific type of employment stability for some workers. The financing relationship enables firms to establish long-term strategies. Firms' activities are coordinated within the group, which allows for the implementation of incremental innovations. The education system is oriented towards general skills, specific skills are acquired within the group through internal mobility and on-the-job training. Countries close to this model (in fact, Japan) have an advantage in complex industrial goods requiring a highly skilled workforce and good coordination of activities. It should be weak in activities based on radical and/or science-based innovation.

3. The European-integration/public SSIP

This group of countries is the most unusual compared to other taxonomies found in the literature. The idea was to insist on the fact that public intervention and the process of European unification had brought closer together some countries which were usually very neatly put in different categories. In this model, public institutions play a determining role in the impulse towards and codification and direction of innovation and are at the centre of the processes of economic adjustment. In opposition to the social-democratic configuration, tripartite bargaining is more difficult and a large part of the specialization derives from demand originating in public expenditure: transport and communication infrastructures, health, etc., as well as large public programmes, either civilian or military. Basic research is mainly public, as is the education system, so that the transferability to the private sector of research advances and the closeness of fit between training and the needs of private firms may be a problem. Traditionally, public regulations have a role in the allocation of credit by banks. This bank-based credit system tends to favour large firms over small businesses and new firms. In this model, public authorities are an important agent in the dynamic adjustment between supply and demand in the fields of innovation, production, and credit.

4. *The social-democratic SSIP*

Social partners' interests are well represented by trade unions and professional associations and they are sufficiently powerful to negotiate mutually advantageous compromises. A reactive education and training system gives a well-trained and competitive workforce. The economies close to this type are small open economies which need to adapt to external competitive conditions in order to maintain a high standard of living. A comprehensive Welfare State insures individuals against the risks associated with work reorganization. The economies concerned have a competitive advantage in health and environment-related activities.

The classification into four SSIPs was derived both from theoretical considerations of the differentiation of institutions in the various areas covered and from a systematic empirical analysis identifying clusters of countries among a sample of twelve developed economies. The data for the empirical analysis focused mainly on the end of the 1980s and beginning of the 1990s, a period of intense institutional change and questioning about the stability of differentiated types of capitalism. The question of the evolution of the developed economies and the possible alteration of the SSIPs was then raised, particularly the problem of a supposed convergence towards the market-based system.

New analyses were proposed in Amable, Cadiou, and Petit (2000) and Amable and Petit (2002) which led to a refined typology of SSIPs. In addition, the empirical analysis was extended to 21 countries[6] and data was updated to include the end of the 1990s. This time, six SSIPs were distinguished:

1. A group comprising countries previously associated with the market-based SSIP—the United States, Great Britain, Canada, Australia—now joined by Norway.
2. A group comprising those countries that embody the social-democratic SSIP. The list includes the former countries from this SSIP—Finland, Sweden, Denmark—now minus Norway.
3. The mesocorporatist SSIP, with Korea now joining Japan.
4. The European integration (or public) SSIP, made up of the countries that already belonged to this SSIP—France, Germany, the Netherlands—minus Italy, but now including Belgium and Ireland.

[6] The United States, Japan, the United Kingdom, Canada, Australia, Italy, Spain, Portugal, Greece, France, Belgium, Denmark, Norway, Sweden, Finland, Germany, Austria, Switzerland, the Netherlands, Ireland, and Korea. The empirical data considered related to scientific and technological fields, economic structure, the education system, and the labour market. As such, this is an extended-innovation-system conception.

5. An 'Alpine' variant of the preceding SSIP, consisting of Austria and Switzerland.
6. A 'Mediterranean' variant of the European SSIP, comprising Spain, Italy, Greece, and Portugal.

One can interpret the new findings as a confirmation and a refinement of the previous ones. The broad categories found for economies at the end of the 1980s still existed at the end of the 1990s. This is a weak confirmation of the non-convergence toward the market-based system. Only Norway seems to have made a significant move in that direction. Otherwise, the SSIPs have kept their distinctive features. However, subsystem analysis does not show that the SSIPs have remained unchanged. Quite the contrary, it provides glimpses of a deeper infiltration of certain market-based mechanisms in most economies. This advance of market-based mechanisms is localized in a finite number of subsystems, namely the financial sector and the labour-relations subsystem, and is epitomized by the progressive transformation of the SSIPs rather than by any radical transformation. The European SSIP's heterogeneity, as already stated in Amable, Barré, and Boyer (1997), is noteworthy for its breakdown into three variants. The first is a core group where France and Germany are the pivotal countries. The two other variants differ from the central group in terms of their average income levels, which are higher for the Continental variant and lower for the 'Mediterranean' one. This latter group is also characterized by the economies' lower level of technological intensity. But even this differentiation into three subgroups does not lead to particularly homogeneous groupings in comparison with the other SSIPs.

The results of the analyses of SSIPs are broadly consistent with those of the diversity of capitalism, and complement them in some respects. There are clearly diverse models of capitalism, but there are more than two of them, i.e. it is necessary to go beyond the dichotomy between LME and CME. When making applied analyses, one finds the grouping of countries broadly consistent with other typologies proposed in the literature, although the premises are different, particularly regarding an assumed institutional hierarchy. Nevertheless, the process of classifying countries in different groups in Amable et al. (1997) and (2001) mixed strictly 'institutional' determinants with economic characteristics such as industrial or technological specialization. It was very clear from the beginning that there was a link between the institutional characteristics of economies and their industrial or technological comparative advantage, an idea that is also found in Hall and Soskice (2001).

3.4 Diversity of Capitalism

Comparative analysis of capitalism is based on an identification of a set of key institutional areas, which serves a twin purpose. First, countries exhibit significantly different features in each of these areas; this demonstrates that they are not just slightly different versions of a generic market economy. Second, the interconnection between the different institutional forms outlines the coherence of the different varieties of capitalism. Institutional complementarities define the different models of capitalism; they should therefore be at the roots of the comparison between countries. Five major institutional areas will be found in the comparative analysis performed in the next chapters:

- product-market competition
- the wage–labour nexus and labour-market institutions
- the financial-intermediation sector and corporate governance
- social protection
- the education sector.

We can outline a few elements of institutional differentiation and complementarity upon which the diversity of capitalism is based.

3.4.1 Elements of Differentiation Among Models; Possible Institutional Complementarities

Product markets may differ substantially across countries with respect to intensity of competition. These differences may stem from differences in the average size of firms, or the type of technology used, or more basically from variations in competition regulation (Nicoletti et al. 2000). Competitive pressure impacts on firms' behaviour, as is shown in any economics textbook: the more 'imperfect' competition is, the higher the prices, the lower the quantities and welfare. Therefore, any regulation hindering competition or protecting market positions should have negative consequences for welfare, growth, and employment. Nevertheless, the relation between imperfection of competition and economic performance is not necessarily monotonic if one considers that rents may come as a reward for a specific effort. This is the case with innovation, where protection of invention through patents and the derived monopoly rents act as an incentive to invent and innovate. Many endogenous growth models based on innovation formalize this mechanism (Aghion and Howitt 1998). One would then expect more intense competition in product markets to be detrimental to economic performance. But competitive pressure itself may also act as an incentive to innovate; it may push firms toward seeking competitive advantages in order to escape from this pressure. Incumbents would want to protect their market positions through quality improvements to their products, while new innovative entrants would want to gain new markets through innovation. The overall ambiguous effect of competition on innovation may well result in a hump-shaped relationship between innovation (and growth) and the intensity of competition. At low levels of competition an increase in competitive pressure is likely to augment incentives to innovate; at high levels of product-market competition decrease in rents would discourage firms from innovating. Aghion et al. (2001) find empirical evidence supporting the existence of such a relationship both at the level of firms and across countries.

Differences in labour-market characteristics such as the level of centralization of wage bargaining or the role and relative power of trade unions are likely to have the micro- and macroeconomic effects that have been mentioned in the previous chapter. One may also briefly cite some other effects of labour-market institutions. Centralization of wage bargaining in connection with strong unions will affect not only the level but also the structure of wages. Solidaristic wage-setting is a well-known feature of social-democratic countries such as Sweden (Moene and Wallerstein 1999), but may also be said to characterize Continental European countries. The archetype of a solidaristic wage-setting, the so-called Rehn-Meidner model, is based on the principle of 'equal pay for equal work'; wages should therefore not reflect the specific economic situation of a firm or an industry. High-productivity firms will benefit from this wage-setting mechanism, since it will increase their profit margin, whereas low-productivity firms will suffer from it. This acts as an incentive for firms to innovate and adopt modern technology in order to be able to pay high wages; it reduces the average age of equipment in industry by forcing old plants to shut down, thereby boosting industrial productivity, and favours entry with up-to-date-equipment, since wages are held down at the higher end of the wage scale. However, it also reduces the average lifetime of plants, thereby reducing profits, which may discourage investment. By narrowing the scope for price competition based on low-wage policies, it forces firms to follow a quality-based competition and shun wage-cutting strategies. If high-skilled workers are complementary inputs to modern equipment, this type of wage-setting arrangement calls for a large supply of trained and retrained workers, and hence the implementation of active labour-market policies. Solidaristic wage-setting also entails a redistributive aspect. Real wage increases should be determined relative to the productivity gains of the aggregate economy, not those of specific companies or specific occupations. This will limit wage increases for jobs with higher-than-average productivity growth in favour of those with lower-than-average productivity growth, limiting wage dispersion in the overall economy, i.e. across skill levels.

Solidaristic wage-setting is based on a certain degree of centralization of wage-setting, offsetting the wage-differentiating tendencies of decentralized bargaining. This is linked to the existence of collective-bargaining institutions which allow a coordination of wage-setting across firms, industries, and regions. Cross-industry national wage bargaining was a characteristic feature of Sweden and Denmark until the 1980s and it still exists in Finland and Norway. However, national-level *centralization* of wage bargaining is not indispensable for achieving national-level *coordination*. Even in countries where industry-level bargaining predominates, some institutional devices may coordinate wage-setting, such as wage-policy recommendations made by national unions or employers' associations, or the role of wage setter assumed by a prominent sector in which unions would push for wage increases in line with the productivity gains of the economy as a whole. IG Metall has traditionally played such a role in Germany (Schulten 2001). The government may also play a role in coordination, as in France, through the reference point that minimum wage increases represent.

A certain degree of employment protection is also a characteristic of European countries, as opposed to the United States. A first effect is that employment protection, hiring and firing rules, unemployment benefits, or any arrangements affecting labour-market 'flexibility' may affect workers' and firms' attitude toward risk. By making lay-offs more expensive, employment protection may hinder labour-market adjustments and structural change in favour of new industries (Saint-Paul 2001). Employment protection is also likely to have interaction effects with educational and training regimes, which will influence the availability and quality of the skilled workforce. One must distinguish between specific and general training. In the latter, workers acquire skills that can be applied in different industries or positions in the economy. On the other hand, specific training improves the skills necessary for a specific occupation, firm, or industry. Training may thus be position-specific, industry-specific, or firm-specific. General training not only improves the worker's productivity within the firm, but also his job opportunities with other firms. For Becker (1962), in the case of perfect competition on the labour market, a trained worker would obtain a wage reflecting his marginal productivity whatever the firm he decides to work in. Therefore, the firm that trains the worker would bear the costs of training without deriving any benefits from it, which is an incentive not to provide any general training. On the other hand, workers who invest in firm-specific or industry-specific skills would want either credible commitments for long-term employment with the firm or within the industry, or alternatively some external insurance such as is provided by a welfare system, because technical change or an adverse economic environment may render these investments worthless. General assets are less vulnerable to technological change or the business cycle. In the absence of explicit protection of specific assets, a rational strategy is to invest in redeployable skills in order to improve one's opportunities on the labour market. On the other hand, there may be specific institutional devices such as social protection implemented to insure individuals against economic risks such as unemployment and the associated income loss. Therefore, both market-competition characteristics and Welfare State arrangements are likely to interact with both firms' and workers' educational and training investments. Countries differ with respect to institutional characteristics in this area. American workers receive premium market wages for their skills when there is high demand for them but have no statutory employment protection; they have for this reason few incentives to invest too much in specific skills. Japanese workers are, or were, willing to invest in firm-specific skills because they trust(ed) to lifetime employment in the corporation. German skilled workers are compensated during unemployment by the Welfare State. As analysed by Iversen and Soskice (2001), investment in specific assets strengthens support for the implementation of policies and institutions that protect these investments. In return, protection of specific assets acts as an *ex ante* incentive for investing in such assets. In some countries a well-developed training system improves the average skills level of the workforce and evens out the distribution of skills, thereby reducing earning inequality. Since agents want a welfare system that protects this specific investment in skills acquisition, countries with a high level of training of the workforce will have both a low level of income inequality and a high level of social spending. Agents will also want a stable protection system, i.e. one not subject to threats of being dismantled following a change in the political situation. As seen in the previous chapter, political systems with an entrenched representation of interest groups and a high number of veto players will be more likely to provide guarantees of institutional stability. Therefore, political systems with corporatist interest intermediation, i.e. consensus-based systems, will be more favourable to a high degree of social protection and a high level of investment in specific skills.

Employment protection and coordinated industrial relations drive firms towards internal training and labour reallocations. The institutional framework acts as an incentive for the firm to undertake workforce training, because labour turnover is low and finding a trained labour force outside is more costly. The incentives for a firm to provide non-firm-specific training are mixed; although it improves the productivity of the worker, it also improves his relative labour-market value. If the worker leaves the firm, part of the firm's training costs will have been spent for the benefit of other firms. A cooperative solution could be reached if all firms could coordinate their training investments and eliminate incentives to free-ride on other firms' efforts. Mandatory training might help solve this type of problem. In the absence of such mechanisms, training incentives depend on the degree of competitiveness of the labour market. Stevens (1996) shows how non-competitive labour markets orient incentives towards investing in specific skills whereas competitive labour markets are associated with investment in general skills; to intermediate levels of labour-market competitiveness corresponds investment in neither completely specific nor completely general, but 'transferable', skills. Amable and Ernst (2002) show how investment in specific assets may decline with labour-market liquidity. A tighter labour market improves a worker's chances of finding an alternative job in the event of job destruction. Better outside job prospects are an incentive not to invest too much in the existing production relationship.

One can, then, envisage several configurations: non-competitive labour markets and investment in specific skills; competitive labour markets and investment in general skills. As mentioned before, coordinated or solidaristic industrial relations constrain wage levels at the upper end of the earnings scale and allow firms to appropriate the difference between the marginal productivity of skilled workers and the wage. This is an incentive for firms to upgrade the skills level of their workforce (Acemoglu and Pischke 1998, 1999*a,b*). On the other hand, low employment protection and uncoordinated industrial relations increase wage dispersion and skill premiums, diminishing the rent from training that the firm can appropriate. This discourages firms from sponsoring training. Certification of skills makes them more easily transferable across firms or industries and should therefore act as a disincentive for firms. However, if certification improves the effort put into training by the worker, it may be in the firm's interest to invest in certified-skills acquisition (Acemoglu and Pischke 2000).

Social-protection and industrial-relations systems are also linked through several channels. The level of welfare entitlements determines the level of social earnings as well as non-labour costs. The more or less generous character of unemployment benefits partly defines the outside options of workers, and impacts on the outcome of wage bargaining. The Welfare State and the structure of benefits also influence labour-shedding strategies of firms in cases of structural change, making labour-force adjustments more or less easy. The management of the Welfare State also strengthens the loyalty of employees to organizations—unions or their firm—according to the type of system, whether self-administered or company-based.

The functioning of the labour market may also depend on the specific features of product markets. An increase in product-market competition is often held to be beneficial for the efficiency of the labour market. A higher degree of competition in product markets drives rents derived from market power away. This mechanically diminishes the scope for rent-seeking behaviour: rents available for unions to capture through collective bargaining are reduced, potentially leading to a decline in union power or more decentralized wage bargaining. Therefore, workers no longer obtain wage premiums, allowing the firm to move down on its labour-demand curve, fostering employment. An increase in product-market competition also augments output and shifts the labour-demand curve out, bringing about an increase in firms' labour demand for any given wage level. The positive effect derives from the modification of firms' pricing behaviour when competition becomes stronger. The rationale is straightforward: stronger competition reduces market power for each firm, this lowers the price mark-up that firms are able to enforce and increases employment at any given level of real wages. This is unambiguously positive for the level of employment if the wage-setting process does not lead to a wage increase that abolishes the employment gains. Product-market deregulation also lowers entry costs, augmenting competitive pressure on incumbents, and favouring entrepreneurship, which is beneficial to employment creation (Nickel 1999).

In addition, an increase in product-market competition is likely to lead to a modification in the ability of firms to offer stable employment. Firms enjoying market power may benefit from more stability than firms subject to more intense competitive pressure. Firms with high profit margins are less fragile and less exposed to adverse demand shocks. As a consequence, the labour force may also benefit from this situation in terms of job stability. An increase in product-market competition may make firms more sensitive to adverse demand or supply shocks and will render employment levels more sensitive to these shocks. Ideally, price adjustments could substitute for quantity adjustments, but there may be important causes of price rigidities even in very competitive product markets. Therefore, for a given size of adverse shock, a rise in product-market competition will boost the rate of lay-offs, augmenting job insecurity (Amable and Gatti 2002*a*,*b*). This may have adverse consequences on the level of effort or on the size of specific investment that workers will be willing to make. If there is a trade-off between employment stability and wage levels, through an efficiency-wage mechanism, for instance, increased job insecurity will augment the efficiency wage and labour turnover across firms and industries. Whether one obtains positive or negative employment effects depends on the average size of shocks. Employment-protection measures such as firing costs or specific legislation may mitigate the negative effects of increased product-market competition on employment.

Unions may also play a role in job security when firms cannot guarantee stable employment by an enforceable contract. Unions' activity may augment dismissal compensation and substitute for high wages, fostering workers' effort and firms' productivity. The union would then act as a commitment device for job security, increasing the *ex ante* profit of the firm while lowering its *ex post* controllability of the employment level (Eguchi 2000). Unions and corporatist arrangements as commitment devices are also analysed by Teulings and Hartog (1998); they play a crucial role in the distribution of surplus created by specific investments. An employment contract specified *ex ante* has the advantage of removing the necessity to renegotiate it *ex post*. *Ex post* renegotiation, as in the case of spot markets, would undermine *ex ante* incentives for investment. Corporatist institutions enable the firm to make a stronger commitment.

Managing risk and protecting assets is one of the most important tasks of financial systems. Financial systems may and actually do have very different characteristics across countries (Allen and Gale 2000). The most basic distinction is between systems based on arm's-length finance, i.e. financial markets, and systems based on financial intermediaries—banks—which may have more or less long-term relationships with firms. Long-term relationships may be instrumental in promoting cooperative behaviour between the firm and its financiers and discourage morally hazardous behaviour. Close relationships between banks and firms may help to solve information-related problems, such as with the Japanese main-bank system or the German *Hausbank*. By contrast, financial markets are better at imposing a 'hard budget constraint' on firms and maintaining a commitment to refuse further funding to firms in case of default (Dewatripont and Maskin 1995). This may act as an *ex ante* incentive for the firm and prevent managers from investing in too risky projects; this bias may however not be socially optimal if it puts too high a 'short-termist' pressure on firms. Financial systems also share risks, and the most common view is probably that financial markets do a better job than banks in this respect, because they favour liquidity and reversibility of commitments for savers. However, Allen and Gale (2000) point out that financial markets also create risks through changes in assets' value. Furthermore, some risks cannot be diversified at a given point in time, but can be averaged out over time so that their impact on intertemporal welfare is reduced. Allen and Gale (2000) show that bank-based and financial-markets-based systems have very different abilities at intertemporal risk-smoothing. The former are much better so long as they are not under competitive pressure from the latter. Intertemporal risk-smoothing is much better provided by long-lived institutions accumulating reserves over time. But these intermediaries are fragile, because individuals are likely to choose markets in good times, when the accumulation of reserves may not benefit them. Financial markets are on the other hand better at insuring against cross-sectional risks. Financial systems and social-security systems are two ways through which individuals are insured against risks. Countries differ with respect to the relative importance of private versus public social insurance or private versus public pensions. In some countries the amount of public insurance is rather small, leaving a large role to private schemes. Institutional investors such as pension funds are therefore major agents on financial markets and contribute to their growth. International differences also exist in the regulation of the insurance industry. In the UK the insurance industry is lightly regulated in comparison to Germany. Insurance companies also tend to invest more directly in financial markets and equity than on the Continent.

Countries also differ with respect to the nature of their corporate governance: whether managers have a strong incentive to act in the shareholders' interest (fiduciary duty); the channels through which shareholders monitor and influence managers; the type of election for the board of directors (whether it is one share one vote or not); the number of external directors; etc. The market for corporate control, as a means of disciplining management and replacing it if the firm does not pursue a policy in the shareholders' interest, is more or less active country by country. It may operate through various means, such as friendly mergers or hostile takeovers. The latter are more or less facilitated by the existing legal framework, which may authorize the implementation of various measures by the management in order to resist the takeover. Cross-shareholding, for instance, makes the success of a takeover much more uncertain. Roe (1993) showed how the US model of corporate governance emerged from a specific legal and law-making tradition prone to limiting the activities of banks under populist pressures, privileging managerial over workers' rights, and taxing the dividends obtained from cross-holding of shares. This does not mean that US corporations are necessarily easy prey in takeover attempts. There are other ways to resist takeovers, such as minority-shareholders' protection and explicit anti-takeover rules. In most American states corporate law allows the board of directors to fight off hostile takeovers. This is what Mayer (2001) calls a 'market-control bias', in opposition to a 'private-control bias' stemming from weak minority protection and leverage-control devices, such as in Germany: dual-class shares, pyramids,[7] and non-voting shares allow dominant investors to retain control as outside ownership comes in. The legal framework in the USA also privileges competition over coordination by specifying tight constraints on collaborative arrangements between firms in the same industry. In Germany and Japan on the other hand different banking, labour, and competition regulations support models of corporate governance that facilitate regular interactions between owners and managers and extensive collaborative ties between financial institutions and firms or between firms themselves (Roe 2001). Therefore, the principles of corporate governance are different on each side of the Atlantic and rest on different political-economy equilibria (Roe 2000). In the USA, agency costs relative to the separation between management and ownership (Berle and Means 1932) are controlled by specific institutions and organizations: independent and active boards, incentive compensation of managers, an active market for corporate control, securities-markets signalling from financial analysts, competitive capital and product markets, etc. On the other hand, in most European countries more rigid labour markets make it more difficult to lay off workers, diminishing incentives for mergers and takeovers, boards are less active and effective, and so on.

La Porta et al. (1997, 1998, 2000a,b) have stressed the importance of legal determinants in the structure of financial systems and their differences across countries. Legal systems differ with respect to the extent of protection given to shareholders and creditors. This will have an impact on firms' financing, ownership structure, and governance. They make a distinction between countries where common law predominates (the UK and the USA, for instance) and countries where civil law prevails (France, Germany, and Scandinavian countries). Civil-law systems give weaker

---

[7] Pyramids are structures in which a holding company controlled by an entrepreneur issues shares in a subsidiary that it itself controls.

legal rights than common-law systems, where shareholders' and creditors' rights are stronger. However, the quality of enforcement of legal rules is highest in Scandinavian and German civil-law systems. An important point is that substitutes for legal protection have been developed in systems where there is more risk of appropriation by managers. There, investors require powerful mechanisms for exercising control through holding large ownership stakes in companies and exerting voting power that is disproportionate to the amount invested in firms. Concentrated ownership is a means of preventing the abuse of minority shareholders' rights when legal protection is weak, and acts as a monitoring device. Blockholders and private owners have the means and motivation to monitor managers; dispersed shareholders in a 'Berle and Means' corporation have not. There is a free-rider problem associated with dispersed ownership. No single shareholder has an incentive to incur costs for actively monitoring the firm. On the other hand, shareholders with a significant wealth commitment have such an incentive, so that the firm's value may increase with the concentration of ownership. Banks may play such a role, but there is a specific risk attached to this configuration. Acquiring information about the firm, banks may use it to extract rents. For Hellwig (1998) there is also a risk of collusion between banks and management, at the expense of outside owners. Blockholding may persist on the Continent because managerial agency costs are potentially higher there and stockholders have no other alternatives for monitoring managers. In countries where investors' rights are well protected, firms' ownership tends to be widely held, whereas the reverse is true when investors' protection is low: shareholders control large blocks of shares, or companies are controlled by a single family or the State. On the other hand, a high level of creditors' and shareholders' rights favours the development of capital markets, which in turn fosters the dissemination of ownership. In addition, firms in common-law countries pay more dividends than firms in civil-law countries.

3.4.2 Five Types of Capitalism

The mechanisms exposed above suggest that a variety of institutional complementarities is possible, generating a diversity of models of capitalism. Based on previous results on the diversity of SSIPs, and other contributions to the literature surveyed in this chapter, the existence of five different models of capitalism can be proposed:

- the market-based economies (aka liberal market economies or the Anglo-Saxon model)
- social-democratic economies

- Asian capitalism
- Continental European capitalism
- South European capitalism.

The characteristics of the different models in each institutional area are presented in Table 3.2. The pattern of interaction between institutional forms determines the set of institutional complementarities at the origin of each model. Based on the theoretical considerations outlined above, Table 3.3 presents the main institutional complementarities that characterize each model of capitalism.

The qualifications 'market-based' or 'Continental European', for example, cannot express the whole set of complementarities that characterizes the different models, and are chosen for the sake of simplicity. Since the various models are not in general reducible to a single 'logic' that would be pervasive in all institutions, there is no simple denomination that could adequately reflect the coherence and complexity of the types of capitalism. Therefore, adopting a geography-based denomination for a type of capitalism does not indicate the prominence of geographical influences in the founding of the model.

Product-market competition is an important element of the market-based model. Intense product-market competition makes firms more sensitive to adverse demand or supply shocks. When price adjustments cannot fully absorb shocks, quantity adjustments matter, particularly concerning the labour force. Therefore, product-market competition leads to de facto flexibility of employment. Competitive market pressure demands that firms react quickly to changing market conditions and modify their business strategies. This is made possible by quickly reacting financial markets, which favour a fast restructuring, itself facilitated by flexible labour markets. This economic model favours fast adjustment and structural change and therefore entails a high degree of risk for specific investments. Risk-diversification for financial investments is guaranteed by sophisticated financial markets, but specific investments are particularly at risk in this model, since social protection is underdeveloped. Therefore, there is little incentive to invest in specific skills, since these skills would not be protected either by the Welfare State or by job security and a rapid structural change would devalue them. Competition extends to the education system. A non-homogenized secondary-education system makes competition among universities for attracting the best students and among students for entering the best universities more crucial.

The social-democratic model is organized according to very different complementarities. Strong external competitive pressure requires some

TABLE 3.2 Five ideal types of capitalism

Institutional area	Market-based economies	Social-democratic economies	Asian capitalism	Continental European capitalism	South European capitalism
Product-market competition	High importance of price competition, non-involvement of the State in product markets, coordination through market (price) signals, openness to foreign competition and investment	High importance of quality competition, high involvement of the State in product markets, high degree of 'coordination' through channels other than market signals, openness to foreign competition and investment	Importance of both price and quality competition, high involvement of the State, high degree of non-price 'coordination', high protection against foreign firms and investment, importance of large corporations	Moderate importance of price competition, relatively high importance of quality competition, involvement of public authorities, relatively high non-price 'coordination', low protection against foreign firms and investment	Price- rather than quality-based competition, involvement of the State, little 'non-price' coordination, moderate protection against foreign trade or investment, importance of small firms
Wage–labour nexus	Low employment protection, external flexibility: easy recourse to temporary work and easy hire and fire, no active employment policy, defensive union strategies, decentralization of wage bargaining	Moderate employment protection, coordinated or centralized wage bargaining, active employment policy, strong unions, cooperative industrial relations	Employment protection within the large corporation, limited external flexibility, labour-market dualism, seniority-based wage policy, cooperative industrial relations, no active employment policy, strong firms' unions, decentralization of wage bargaining	High employment protection, limited external flexibility, job stability, conflicting industrial relations, active employment policy, moderately strong unions, coordination of wage bargaining	High employment protection (large firms) but dualism: a 'flexible' fringe of employment in temporary and part-time work, possible conflicts in industrial relations, no active employment policy, centralization of wage bargaining

Financial sector	High protection of minority shareholders, low ownership concentration, high importance of institutional investors, active market for corporate control (takeovers, mergers and acquisitions), high sophistication of financial markets, development of venture capital	High ownership concentration, high share of institutional investors, no market for corporate control (takeovers, mergers and acquisitions), no sophistication of financial markets, high degree of banking concentration	Low protection of external shareholders, high ownership concentration, involvement of banks in corporate governance, no active market for corporate control (takeovers, mergers and acquisitions), no sophistication of financial markets, limited development of venture capital, high degree of banking concentration	Low protection of external shareholders, high ownership concentration, no active market for corporate control (takeovers, mergers and acquisitions), low sophistication of financial markets, moderate development of venture capital, high banking concentration, importance of banks in firms' investment funding	Low protection of external shareholders, high ownership concentration, bank-based corporate governance, no active market for corporate control (takeovers, mergers and acquisitions), low sophistication of financial markets, limited development of venture capital, high banking concentration
Social protection	Weak social protection, low involvement of the State, emphasis on poverty alleviation (social safety net), means-tested benefits, private-funded pension system	High level of social protection, high involvement of the State, high importance of the Welfare State in public policy and society	Low levels of social protection, expenditures directed towards poverty alleviation, low share of public expenditures in welfare, low share of welfare expenditures in GDP	High degree of social protection, employment-based social protection, involvement of the State, high importance of social protection in society, contribution-financed social insurance, pay-as-you-go pension systems	Moderate level of social protection, expenditures structure oriented towards poverty alleviation and pensions, high involvement of the State

TABLE 3.2 (Cont.)

Institutional area	Market-based economies	Social-democratic economies	Asian capitalism	Continental European capitalism	South European capitalism
Education	Low public expenditures, highly competitive higher-education system, non-homogenized secondary education, weak vocational training, emphasis on general skills, lifelong learning	High level of public expenditures, high enrolment rates, emphasis on the quality of primary and secondary education, importance of vocational training, emphasis on specific skills, importance of retraining, lifelong learning	Low level of public expenditure, high enrolment rates, emphasis on the quality of secondary education, company-based training, importance of scientific and technical education, emphasis on specific skills, weak lifelong learning outside the corporation	High level of public expenditure, high enrolment rates in secondary education, emphasis on secondary-education homogeneity, developed vocational training, emphasis on specific skills	Low public expenditures, low enrolment rates in tertiary education, weak higher-education system, weak vocational training, no lifelong learning, emphasis on general skills

flexibility in the labour force. But flexibility is not simply achieved through lay-offs and market adjustments; retraining of a highly skilled workforce plays a crucial role in the adaptability of workers. Protection of specific investments of employees is realized through a mixture of moderate employment protection, a high level of social protection, and easy access to retraining thanks to active labour-market policies. A coordinated wage-bargaining system enables solidaristic wage-setting which favours innovation and productivity. A centralized financial system enables firms to develop long-term strategies.

The Asian model of capitalism hinges on the business strategies of the large corporations in collaboration with the State and a centralized financial system, which enables the development of long-term strategies. Workers' specific investments are defended by a de facto rather than *de jure* protection of employment and possibilities of retraining within the corporation. Lack of social protection and sophisticated financial markets make risk diversification difficult and render the stability provided by the large corporation crucial to the solidity of the model.

The Continental European model possesses some features in common with the social-democratic model. The latter combines a high degree of social protection with moderate employment protection, the former is based on a higher degree of employment protection and a less developed Welfare State. Here again, a centralized financial system facilitates long-term strategies and means that firms are not compelled to respect short-term profit constraints. Wage bargaining is coordinated and a solidaristic wage policy is developed, but not to the same extent as in the social-democratic model. Retraining of the workforce is not possible to the same extent as in the social-democratic model, which limits the possibilities for an 'offensive' flexibility of the workforce and fast restructuring of industries. Productivity gains are obtained by labour-shedding strategies elaborated in complementarity with social protection, as with the early-retirement policy.

The South European or Mediterranean model of capitalism is based on more employment protection and less social protection than the Continental European model. Employment protection is made possible by a relatively low level of product-market competition and the absence of short-term profit constraints as a result of the centralization of the financial system. However, a workforce with a limited skills and education level does not allow for the implementation of a high wages and high skills industrial strategy. Increased product-market competition may create pressure for an increase in the flexibility of the labour market, for instance by a marked dualism of the workforce. Established employees of

TABLE 3.3*a* Institutional complementarities: market-based capitalism

	Product markets	Labour market	Financial system	Social protection	Education system
Product markets		Intense product-market competition generates employment flexibility	Competitive market pressure means firms want quickly reacting financial markets		Fast structural change requires a labour force with flexible skills
Labour market	Decentralized labour markets favour firms' adjustment to competitive pressure and make structural change less costly		A flexible labour market allows quick adjustment of the labour force and maintenance of short-term profits	Liquid labour markets diminish unemployment risks and lower the demand for social protection	Weak employment protection and important structural change are incentives to invest in general skills
Financial system	Sophisticated financial markets enable a quick reaction to opening markets and favour industrial dynamism	Short-term constraints prevent the establishment of a high level of employment protection		A financial-markets-based system favours instantaneous risk diversification and lowers the need for a public-funded system of welfare	Shareholders' protection, not stakeholders', hence low incentives to invest in specific skills
Social protection	Minimal public-funded social protection, hence no need for high tax levels	Liberal Welfare State does not protect against unemployment, liquid labour markets are necessary, minimal safety net against poverty favours the existence of a low-wage labour market	Low degree of public-funded social protection calls for market-based means of risk diversification through private insurance, pension funds provide an institutionalized voice for shareholders in a system of corporate governance		No protection for specific-skills investment, hence incentives for individuals to acquire general skills in order to move from job to job and make retraining easier
Education system	Labour force with general skills favours structural change	Low specific-skills investment, hence no hold-up problem, less need for high employment protection	A private higher-education system requires an easy supply of credit to students	No strong demand for specific-skills protection	

TABLE 3.3*b* Institutional complementarities: social-democratic economies

	Product markets	Labour market	Financial system	Social protection	Education system
Product markets		Competitive pressure requires some labour flexibility	Firms' long-term strategies require 'patient' capital	Strong competition implies risk for wage earners, which calls for social protection in the absence of sophisticated financial markets	Foreign competitiveness requires a highly skilled workforce
Labour market	Centralization of wage bargaining and corporatism favours 'coordination' among firms		Employment protection calls for the absence of short-term constraints	Labour flexibility augments the demand for social protection	Competitive pressure and employment protection call for some skills flexibility, need for constant retraining, centralization and coordination favour the definition of useful specific skills
Financial system	'Patient' capital allows long-term strategies	No short-term constraints enables employment protection		The financial system cannot provide individual risk diversification	
Social protection	High welfare expenditures imply high tax levels and distortions in domestic markets	High levels of social protection allow workers to be flexible	A highly developed Welfare State lowers the demand for market-based means of risk diversification and social insurance		Social protection allows protection of specific-skills investment
Education system	High levels of education and skills create sophisticated consumers in the domestic market	Demand for specific-skills protection, i.e. employment protection, skill levels allow for (offensive) flexibility		Demand for specific-skills protection even with a high competitive pressure, hence the need for the Welfare State	

TABLE 3.3c Institutional complementarities: Asian capitalism

	Product markets	Labour market	Financial system	Social protection	Education system
Product markets		Long-term corporate strategies allow de facto employment stability	Protection against foreign investment does not provide incentives to develop highly sophisticated corporate governance	Corporate and competitive structure allows a certain protection for workers without a fully developed welfare system	Efficient corporate training requires a good level of secondary education
Labour market	Corporation-based labour markets favour internal structural change		Corporation-based market calls for insurance against short-term demands from financial markets	De facto employment stability lowers the need for formal social protection	De facto employment stability enables investment in specific skills
Financial system	Absence of short-term constraint enables long-term strategies and intra-corporation restructuring	No short-term constraints for the large corporation allows de facto employment stability		Lack of sophisticated financial markets will create a demand for social protection	
Social protection	Low welfare expenditures imply low taxes	Low levels of social protection make wage-earners more dependent on the corporation	Lack of public social protection implies the development of private welfare funds which provide a large volume of resources available for the supply of 'patient' capital		Lack of protection deters from investing in too specific skills
Education system	A highly educated workforce make sophisticated consumers	An efficient secondary-education system provides a homogeneous labour force ready to acquire specific skills within the corporation		A workforce with general skills does not need so high a level of welfare expenditure	

TABLE 3.3d Institutional complementarities: Continental European capitalism

	Product markets	Labour market	Financial system	Social protection	Education system
Product markets		Moderate internal competitive pressure enables a relatively high degree of employment protection, but external pressure demands important productivity gains	Moderate competitive pressure allows the establishment of stable finance–industry relations	The quest for productivity gains implies labour-shedding strategies which are politically sustainable only with social protection	Quality-based competition demands a workforce with a high level of general education, slow structural change favours the acquisition of specialized skills
Labour market	Employment protection prevents fast structural change		Employment protection limits the need for a strict short-term-profit constraint	Employment protection permits a moderately high degree of social protection	Employment protection is an incentive to invest in specific skills, centralization and coordination favour the definition of useful specific skills
Financial system	Absence of short-term constraints enables long-term strategies	Lack of short-term constraints enables employment stability		Weak individual risk-diversification possibilities, hence a need for social protection	
Social protection	Welfare expenditures imply high taxes	Social-insurance schemes linked to occupation, organized labour plays an important role in their	High welfare expenditures lower the need for individual risk diversification		A relatively high level of social protection enables specialized-skills acquisition

TABLE 3.3d (Cont.)

	Product markets	Labour market	Financial system	Social protection	Education system
		administration, social protection reinforces differentiation across social groups, a high level of social protection leads to high non-wage labour costs, which is detrimental to employment at the lower end of the skill scale			
Education system	Labour force with specialized skills allows stable industrial strategies to be followed	Demand for specific-investments protection		High demand for specific-skills protection	

TABLE 3.3e Institutional complementarities: South European capitalism

	Product markets	Labour market	Financial system	Social protection	Education system
Product markets		Low competitive pressure allows employment stability (large firms)	Low competitive pressure allows the establishment of stable finance–industry relations		Industrial specialization and structure (small firms) do not require a highly skilled workforce
Labour market	Formal employment protection prevents fast structural change (large firms)		Employment stability demands a lack of short-term constraints	De facto employment stability lowers the demand for social protection	Stability of employment prevents need for constant upgrading of the competences of the workforce
Financial system	Underdeveloped financial markets and stable bank–industry relations slow down structural change	Lack of short-term constraints enables employment stability		Weak individual risk-diversification possibility implies a higher level of social protection	
Social protection	Low welfare expenditures imply lower tax distortions on the domestic market		Low welfare expenditures increase the demand for individual risk diversification		Low levels of social protection deter from investing in specific skills
Education system	The skill level of the work force prevents the need to engage in high-tech activities	The education system does not allow a large, highly skilled workforce		Low specific investments lower the demand for protection	

large firms would still benefit from job security while young workers or employees of small firms would have more flexible labour contracts.

No single developed economy is accurately described by any of the five models of capitalism, which are ideal types. They may possess characteristics which make them close to one or the other model, without being fully identifiable with the model itself. For instance, a strict market-based economy organized according to the institutional complementarities documented in Tables 3.3a–e may never exist. It is nevertheless useful to refer to these ideal types in order to understand the institutional mechanisms upon which the coherence of the various developed economies is based. Moreover, the models of capitalism allow us to go beyond the apparent dissimilarities between two economies and identify their common structural traits.

4

Institutional Diversity: An Analysis of Five Domains

The previous chapter identified five possible models of contemporary capitalism based on specific institutional features and characteristic institutional complementarities. It remains to be seen whether it is possible to relate this classification of capitalism to actual developed economies on an empirical basis. This is the aim of the following two chapters. An empirical analysis of twenty-one developed capitalist economies will be performed in order to emphasize their similarities and dissimilarities in each of the five institutional areas considered in the previous chapter. The institutional domains are considered separately in this chapter. This is a first step in the empirical analysis of the diversity of types of capitalism, which is based on a consideration of overall institutional structure, and will be presented in the next chapter. The method chosen for the statistical analysis is presented in the appendix to this chapter. Typologies of countries will be established as follows. First, a principal-components analysis is performed, then a cluster analysis. This gives at each stage a typology of country by domain and some characterizations of the variables which are most significant in the analysis. The results are contrasted with those produced in various comparative institutional analyses of the domain under consideration. Data taken into account in the empirical work concerns the late 1990s or the second half of the decade.

4.1 Product Markets

The most fundamental dimension separating different varieties of capitalism in the area of product markets probably concerns intensity of competition. The last chapter showed that models of capitalism exhibited different features according to the type of competition prevailing on product markets. Intensity of competition is a difficult concept to express through simple indicators. We are concerned here with competition at the aggregate level, not at the disaggregate, industry level. It is possible to find data on competition in a few sectors, in the form of concentration indices, for instance. But these indicators reflect the state of competition, i.e. an 'output', whereas we are interested in an 'input' variable, i.e. the determinants of competition. For this reason, indicators of product-markets *regulation* were chosen. These indicators assess the various levels and nature of regulations bearing on economic activity. They thus help to show the institutional settings defining the state of competition.

Data on product-markets regulation comes from the OECD (Nicoletti, Scarpetta, and Bouylaud 2000). The indicators are based on expert scoring with respect to the national situation in various dimensions of product markets. Nicoletti et al. (2000) propose both detailed and synthetic indicators of product-market regulation. Only the detailed indicators are used as active variables in the factor analysis, not the summary or more synthetic indicators, which are themselves constructed through data analysis. The summary indicators will however be used as illustrative variables; although they do not contribute to the definition of the principal components, they may be projected on the axes in order to help interpret them.

Data used here applies to the end of the 1990s, and the indicators were constructed to measure the progress of market liberalization. The data is split into two parts; namely, inward-oriented and outward-oriented policies. The follow-up of these scores leads to the conclusion that while outward-oriented policies have shown an appreciable degree of reduction in regulation constraints (stemming in large part from the concerted efforts to liberalize trade and investment at an international level), the regulatory constraints within inward-oriented policies remain more widely dispersed. This nevertheless does not apply to all dimensions of regulatory controls. 'Barriers to entrepreneurship' have significantly decreased. Most of the dispersion is thus linked with the forms of State controls. This includes not only the size and scope of the public sector, definitely a quite discriminating variable, but also the forms of regulations applying to many network services, of which seven are distinguished in the data base, from competitive industries like road freight, air-passenger transport, mobile telephony, and retail distribution, to services more dependent on infrastructure networks, like electricity, railways, or fixed telephony. Table 4.1 presents the different indicators and their structure.

Principal-Components Analysis

Running a data analysis on the above-mentioned indicators gives the following results. The first three factors of the principal-components analysis account for about 60 per cent of the total variance of the data. The first five axes (which will contribute to the cluster analysis) represent about 80 per cent of initial variance. The active variables, i.e. those which contribute effectively to the determination of the factorial axes, are represented in two planes defined by axes 1 and 2 and axes 2 and 3 respectively in Figs. 4.1 and 4.2.

TABLE 4.1 Product-market-regulation variables

Policies	Category	Summary indicator	Detailed indicators
Inward-oriented policies	State control	Public ownership	Scope of public enterprise Size of public-enterprise sector Special voting rights Control of public enterprises by legislative bodies
		Involvement in business operation	Use of command and control regulation Price controls
	Barriers to entrepreneurship	Regulatory and administrative opacity	Licence and permit systems Communication and simplification of rules and procedures
		Administrative burdens on start-ups	Administrative burdens for corporations Administrative burdens for sole-proprietor firms Sector-specific administrative burdens
		Barriers to competition	Legal barriers to entry Antitrust exemptions
Outward-oriented policies	Explicit barriers to trade and investment		Ownership barriers Tariffs
	Other barriers		Discriminatory procedures Regulatory barriers

The representations of active variables in Figs. 4.1 and 4.2 confirm that product-market regulation is not merely one-dimensional. The fact that almost all variables point in the same direction in Fig. 4.1 does signal the existence of some 'size effect',[1] but the most significant variables concern which summary indicators regroup under State control; i.e. the characteristics of the public sector and of its direct involvement in business operation. An examination of the variables significantly contributing to the factorial axes provides some further explanation of the characterization of countries. Table 4.2 presents the most significant variables associated with the first three factorial axes and indicates whether these variables are

---

[1] See Escoffier and Pagès (1998).

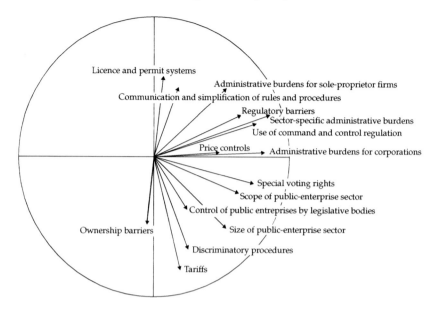

Fig. 4.1 Active variables in the first factorial plane—product markets

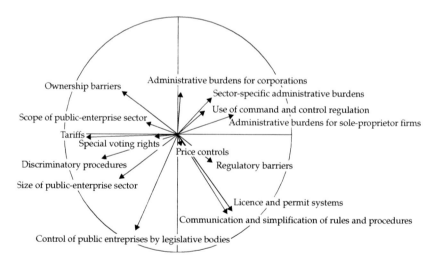

Fig. 4.2 Active variables in the second factorial plane—product markets

associated with the positive or the negative side of the axis. The 'size effect' is illustrated by the fact that variables are significantly associated with one side only of each axis. Both active and illustrative variables are mentioned in Table 4.2 in order to facilitate interpretation.

TABLE 4.2 Variables associated with the first three factorial axes

−	+
	First axis
	Inward-oriented policies
	Product-market regulation
	State control
	Regulation of economic behaviour
	Involvement in business operation
	Economic regulation
	Sector-specific administrative burdens
	Administrative burdens on start-ups
	Second axis
Tariffs	
Explicit barriers	
Barriers to trade and investment	
Outward-oriented policies	
	Third axis
Control of public enterprises by legislative bodies	
Regulatory and administrative opacity	

The interpretation of the three axes appears fairly straightforward. The first one refers to the governance of internal product markets, the second axis is more concerned with foreign trade, while the third focuses on public intervention. The first axis can be interpreted as an axis of increasing regulation on domestic product markets. This is the most obvious dimension of product-market competition. One can consider that the countries where product-market competition is more intense are on the left hand side of the first axis. It combines the importance of general regulation with the weight of the public sector. The second axis is one of explicit protection against foreign competition, with indicators for tariffs and discriminatory procedures characterizing the left-hand side of the axis. The third axis is composed of variables representing public involvement in product markets' functioning: regulatory and administrative opacity, control of public enterprises by legislative bodies. This axis represents not so much the importance of the public sector nor the role of State-owned enterprises but the kind of control exerted by the public sector.

How countries differ with respect to product-market competition can be assessed by their projections on the planes defined by the first three axes, which are presented in Figs. 4.3 and 4.4. As mentioned before, countries

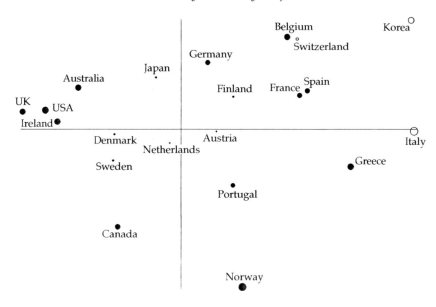

FIG. 4.3 Countries' representation in the first factorial plane—product markets

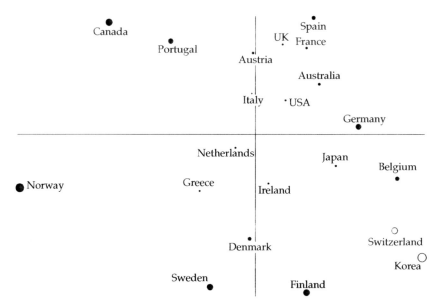

FIG. 4.4 Countries' representation in the second factorial plane—
product markets

with less-regulated product markets are on the left-hand side of the
first axis, countries with more-regulated product markets are on the
right-hand side of the first axis. This first factor thus opposes the UK,
the USA, Australia, and Ireland (i.e. the less regulated product markets)

to France, Belgium, Spain and Greece (and Italy). This characterization is compatible with previous analyses of product-market competition (Hall and Soskice 2001). Continental European countries possess on average product markets where competition is less strong than in Anglo-American markets. The second axis is largely determined by the features of Norway and Canada, where protection against foreign competition is high compared with most of the other countries. Considering the limited extent of protection against foreign trade of OECD countries, one should not deduce that Norway and Canada are 'protectionist' countries. Their relatively more restrictive regulation concerning foreign trade may thus simply stem from the importance of natural resources in their trade structure. The third axis is tied to both the existence of a legislative control over public enterprises and the weight of administrative procedures, which seem to single out Finland and Sweden as opposed to a large set of countries including the Anglo-Saxon ones such as Canada and the UK together with some Mediterranean countries such as Spain and Portugal.

Cluster Analysis

The cluster analysis performed after the principal-components analysis regroups countries that are similar to each other with respect to certain variables, when compared to the other countries in the sample. The analysis leads us to define six different clusters. The distributions of countries and the variables associated with the clusters are given in Table 4.3. The variables associated with each cluster assume either significantly lower values than average over the whole sample of countries (−) or significantly higher values (+). The 'size effect' allows the identification of clusters according to the intensity of regulation. A more aggregate clustering could have been chosen too, distinguishing three groups rather than six. For instance, countries of clusters 1 and 2 would have been grouped together if a three-cluster typology had been selected. The common characteristics of countries belonging to the same group at the three-cluster level are also indicated in Table 4.3.

Thus, the first cluster, which gathers the UK, the USA, Ireland and Australia, is characterized by significantly lower values for administrative burdens, public ownership, State control, etc. To sum up, this cluster is characterized by less product-markets regulation than all the other countries of our sample. The common factor behind this group of countries is the fact that their product markets are less regulated and hence more sensitive to competition. This grouping of countries is compatible with other results as well as received wisdom. This is the cluster of liberal market economies, where coordination is mostly achieved through the price channel. The opposition between this cluster and the others on a single

TABLE 4.3 Country clusters for product-market regulation

Clusters	Countries	Common characteristics −	Common characteristics +	Specific characteristics −	Specific characteristics +
1	UK USA Ireland Australia	Outward-oriented policies Price controls Regulation of economic behaviour Involvement in business operation		Administrative burdens on start-ups Special voting rights Public ownership Economic regulation State control Inward-oriented policies	
2	Finland Sweden Denmark	Product-market regulation Sector-specific administrative burdens			
3	Norway Canada				Tariffs Explicit barriers Barriers to trade and investment Outward-oriented policies Ownership barriers Other barriers
4	Austria Netherlands Portugal		Administrative burdens on start-ups Sector-specific administrative burdens Administrative burdens for corporations		
5	Greece Spain (Switzerland) Italy, Korea		Administrative regulation Involvement in business operation Barriers to entrepreneurship		Regulatory barriers
6	Germany France Belgium Japan		Use of command and control regulation Inward-oriented policies Regulation of economic bahaviour		Administrative burdens for sole-proprietor firms Regulatory and administrative opacity

dimension that can be interpreted as the intensity of price or market coordination would at first sight lend some support to the dichotomy between LMEs and CMEs, but the other side of the axis does not feature CMEs so much as a mix of Asian, Mediterranean, and Continental economies.

All the other clusters are characterized by more or less strong product-market regulation. The second cluster (Finland, Sweden, and Denmark) gathers countries which are close to one another in terms of product-market regulation, but which are not characterized by extremely high or extremely low values of the variables used in the analysis, when these countries are taken as a group. This does not mean that these countries are characterized by average values for all the variables, in which case they would appear in the centre of the graphs featured in Figs. 4.3 and 4.4. The three Nordic countries are similar to one another with respect to some aspects of public involvement in product-market regulation. They are however not too distant from the Anglo-Saxon countries when projected on the plane defined by factors 1 and 2, which points to the presence of less product-market regulation than in other European countries. The third cluster (Norway and Canada) is characterized by a relatively more intense outward-oriented product-market regulation, which is also reflected by the position of these two countries in Fig. 4.3. It may reflect the trade specialization of these countries, which export natural resources, products which have their own specific regulations in terms both of taxes and FDI. The fourth cluster regroups Austria and the Netherlands with Portugal. The former two countries are characterized by average values for most of the variables, as indicated by their central position in Fig. 4.3. They are intermediate between countries where product-market competition is high (the liberal market economies) and countries where product-market competition is more heavily regulated (the sixth cluster). The presence of Portugal in this group is less straightforward, as one would have expected it to have featured along with the other Mediterranean countries, as it will do in other domains. Portugal is a country in rapid transition and integration within the EU, and benefited for the period under study from relatively high employment levels and positive net flows of foreign direct investment. The fifth cluster gathers Greece and Spain, to which are added illustrative countries Switzerland, Italy, and Korea. This cluster is representative of substantial product-market regulation. The last cluster can be split between Germany, France, and Belgium on one side and Japan on the other. All these countries exhibit substantial product-market regulation, but Japan is also characterized by opacity and emphasis on outward-oriented policies, meaning that protection against competition is stronger than in the other countries of the cluster, each of them founding countries of the European Community.

To conclude: This first data analysis, which concerns a domain that experienced substantial deregulation in the 1990s, mainly separates a group of overall more liberal market economies representative of the market-based model from the other countries. However, the latter do not constitute a homogeneous group. There are significant differences regarding the degree of openness to external trade as well as the role of the State, whether it concerns the importance of public enterprises or public involvement in firms in some service businesses. Furthermore, the Anglo-Saxon liberal market economies are clearly distinguished as a group on the first axis of the principal-components analysis. But this axis does not oppose them to coordinated market economies like Germany, Japan, or Austria, but rather to Southern European countries (as well as France): All of this stresses the importance of national differences in regulatory environments in business operations.[2]

4.2 The Wage–Labour Nexus

Another important institutional context for the study of diversity is that of labour markets. It too has undergone many changes in the 1990s, driven by a widespread search for flexibility. There are several dimensions to the analysis of the wage–labour nexus. We will distinguish three of them. The first one is that of employment protection, i.e. whether the hiring and firing decisions are relatively easy and involve low costs, or whether employment is protected and hence labour markets are less 'flexible'. It has become routine to distinguish Europe and the USA with respect to this aspect of the labour market. The former has been shown to possess less flexible markets than the latter (Siebert 1997), a fact which has sometimes been at the forefront of explanations of high and persistent unemployment in Europe. But this binary opposition between US, or even Anglo-Saxon, and (Continental) European labour markets is a broad qualification that could be refined. Similarly to the analysis of product-market regulation, a richer picture of the diversity of countries with respect to employment protection would be needed. A specific data analysis of employment protection variables would help to show which institutional characteristics are more precisely responsible for the different features and properties of the labour markets under consideration.

A second aspect of labour-market institutions classically concerns the pattern of wage bargaining and industrial relations. International comparison in this area is here again often one-dimensional. Whether wage bargaining is centralized or decentralized, whether industrial relations can be characterized as corporatist or not, is the focus of all the attention. But considering more than one indicator (be it centralization, corporatism,

---

[2] Mainly in services—see Nicoletti et al. (2000), esp. 40, table 1.

or whatever) will allow for a richer representation of the diversity of countries and will lead to more relevant assessment of effective labour markets, which often combine these characteristics in different ways.

A third aspect of labour markets refers to employment policies, with all the schemes that have developed along with the contemporary drive for active labour-market policies, induced by the rise in unemployment and the constraints set on macroeconomic expansionary policies. Anglo-Saxon economies are often opposed to Scandinavian countries with respect to the importance of active labour-market policies. It might be interesting to check the validity of this classification and consider the relative position of other countries.

4.2.1 Employment Protection

The variables considered here concern what is generally seen as labour-market flexibility (or rigidity), i.e. the ability to hire and fire; their structure is described in Table 4.4. Several aspects of flexibility are taken into account: the ease of use of temporary employment, the ability to use fixed-term contracts, the period of notice, etc. As already mentioned for product-market indicators, these data have been collected by the OECD to follow the process of market liberalization recommended to many

TABLE 4.4 Employment-protection variables

Category	Summary indicator	Detailed indicators
Employment-protection legislation: regular contracts	Procedural inconvenience	Regular procedural inconveniences in case of no-fault dismissal
		Delay to start of notice
		Definition of unfair dismissal
	Direct cost of dismissal	Severance pay for no-fault dismissal
		Reinstatement in case of no-fault dismissal
	Notice and trial period	Notice for no-fault dismissal
		Trial period before conditions for unfair dismissal apply
Employment-protection legislation: temporary contracts	Definition of types of labour and procedures	Temporary work: types of work admitted
		Temporary work: restrictions on number of renewals
		Fixed-term contracts: types of work admitted
		Fixed-term contracts: maximun number of successive contracts
	Maximum cumulated duration	Temporary work: maximum cumulated duration
		Fixed-term contracts: maximum cumulated durations

countries from the early 1980s on. For obvious reasons regular contracts are distinguished from temporary ones. Labour-market liberalization over the 1990s effectively shows that the bulk of the adjustment has been borne by temporary contracts. In other words, overall indicators of regular-employment protection seem to have been fairly steady over the decade (even if the level of protection remained very different between countries), while the indicators of temporary-employment protection showed clear reductions over the same period.[3] In all the countries the number of temporary contracts noticeably increased in the 1990s, while the overall conditions of employment became more lax. A greater flexibility of labour markets, i.e. a greater ability to make short-term adjustments, has thus been achieved by means of changes in structural composition: increasing the number and flexibility of temporary contracts. The distinction between regular- and temporary-employment protection is thus a key issue.

Principal-Components Analysis

The high percentage of variance explained by the first factor and the shape of the cone defined by the active variables suggest that there is here again a 'size effect': countries in the sample are first differentiated by whether the employment relationship offers much protection or not (Fig. 4.5). The first axis is effectively defined by the intensity of restrictions to temporary employment on the left-hand side. This factor alone accounts for as much as 41 per cent of the whole variance. It sets apart Greece, Spain, France, Norway, and Japan on the employment-protection side, from the USA, the UK, Canada, Australia, and Ireland on the lack-of-employment-protection side. It looks as if here again the countries of the market-based system are clearly separated from the other developed countries. The second axis (17 per cent of the variance) is defined by the amount of severance pay on one side and the delay before start of notice on the other, separating Greece, Spain, and Canada from the Netherlands, Sweden, and Germany. This axis predominantly reflects the protection of 'regular' employment (Fig. 4.5). The third axis, which explains a signifi-cantly lower fraction of the variance of the data (12 per cent), is defined by some more specific characteristics: the length of the notice period and the maximum number of successive fixed-term contracts (FTCs) (Fig. 4.6).

Table 4.5 lists the active and illustrative variables most clearly associated with the various axes. The representation of countries in the factorial planes helps show clearly the kind of country groupings that this analy-sis leads to.

---

[3] See Nicoletti et al. (2000), 47.

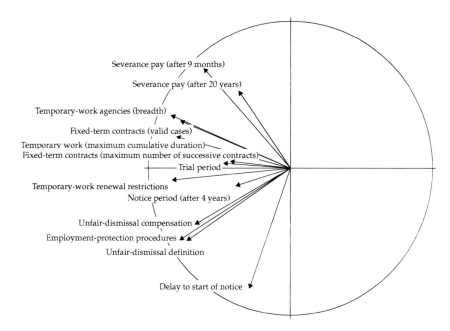

FIG. 4.5 Active variables in the first factorial plane—employment protection

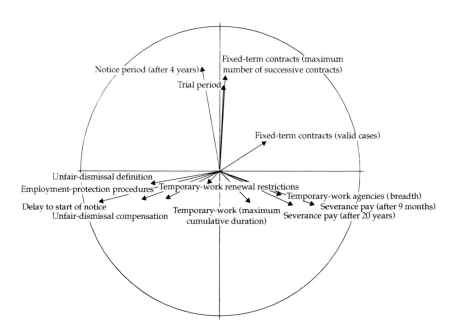

FIG. 4.6 Active variables in the second factorial plane—employment protection

TABLE 4.5 Variables defining the first three axes

−	+
First axis	
Temporary-work agencies: types of work admitted	
Temporary-work renewal restrictions	
Employment protection (synthetic indicator)	
Temporary work: maximum cumulated duration	
Fixed-term contracts: types of work admitted	
Employment-protection procedures	
Second-axis	
Delay to start of notice	Severance pay for no fault (after 9 months)

Employment-regulation rigour
  (synthetic indicator)
	Fixed-term contracts: maximum
	  number of successive contracts

Unfair-dismissal definition	
Third axis	
	Notice period (after 4 years)

The projection of countries on the first plane (factors 1 and 2) clearly suggests a partition between countries where labour markets are said to be 'flexible' (the USA, the UK, Canada, Australia, Switzerland, Denmark, and Ireland) and the others (Fig. 4.7). Liberal market economies exhibit greater labour-market flexibility, which applies to virtually all types of employment. Fixed-term contracts can be renewed more than in other countries, employment protection in general is weaker, restrictions to temporary work are lower, etc. However, as in the previous analysis on product-market regulation, the other countries do not form a homogeneous group. Some countries are very near the market-based countries in terms of the flexibility identified on the first axis: Denmark or Switzerland, for instance. These two countries are however dissimilar to the market-based countries when projected on axis 3, which represents protection of stable employment.

Cluster Analysis

The situation of the other countries is sufficiently varied to identify five clusters. The first one groups countries characterized by a high flexibility in the labour market: dismissal compensation is significantly lower than in other countries, the use of fixed-term contracts and temporary employment

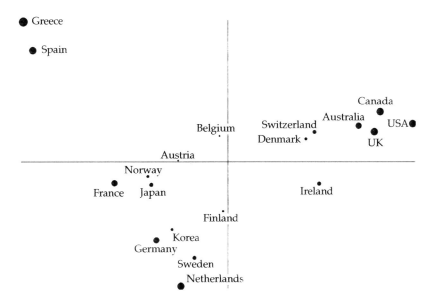

FIG. 4.7 Countries' representation in the first factorial plane—employment protection

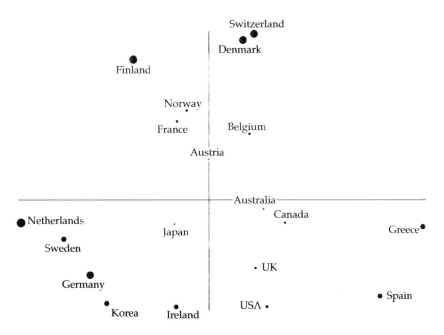

FIG. 4.8 Countries' representation in the second factorial plane—employment protection

is easier, firing is easier. Tenure seems to be significantly lower than anywhere else, as witnessed by low seniority. The countries in this group taken together show lower values than the average for variables representing employment protection. This cluster represents the archetypical Anglo-Saxon model of labour-market flexibility. The second cluster would lump some supposed CMEs along with the Anglo-Saxon economies in a three-cluster typology. Belgium, Denmark, and Switzerland exhibit significant labour-market flexibility, but regular employment seems better protected than in market-based countries, through longer notice periods. The other clusters are characterized by the presence of some 'rigidity' in the employment relationship: a more restricted use of fixed-term contracts for the third cluster (Finland, Norway, and France) and a higher-than-average seniority for Austria and Japan, which reflects a de facto stability of employment; more employment protection in general for the fourth cluster (Netherlands, Germany, Korea, and Sweden); more restrictions on the use of temporary work and more valid cases for fixed-term contracts in the fifth cluster (Greece and Spain, as well as Italy and Portugal).

Table 4.6 summarizes the characteristics of the different clusters. The picture of employment protection by countries that emerges separates the market-based system from different groups of other countries, as in the analysis of product-market regulation. These other groups are more difficult to characterize. Figure 4.7 does stress that they are effectively different, scattered in the plane, whereas the first group of countries, with relatively low protection of employment, remains compact. The characteristics explaining the existence of these other groups (Table 4.6) are not very explicit; they concern specific regulations reinforcing the protection of employment. The explanations for these groupings will have to be found in relation to other analysis of the flexibility of labour markets.

4.2.2 Industrial Relations

The type of industrial relations has often been considered crucial in the relation between labour-market institutions and macroeconomic performance. A low level of unemployment has been attributed to the existence of 'corporatism' in the relation between workers and firms, or to either low or high levels of wage bargaining. By introducing more indicators relevant to the area we will avoid resorting to a dichotomy to qualify the diversity of industrial relations. The list of variables used is in the appendix and concerns wage-bargaining coordination, centralization, and corporatism, as well as union density, disputes, and relations between managers and employees.

TABLE 4.6 Country clusters for employment protection

Clusters	Countries	Common characteristics −	Common characteristics +	Characteristics −	Characteristics +
1	USA, UK, Canada, Australia, Ireland	Delay to start of notice; Average seniority; Seniority—more than 20 years; Temporary-work agencies: types of work admitted; Fixed-term contracts: types of work admitted; Unfair-dismissal compensation; Temporary-work renewal restrictions; Employment-regulation rigour (synthetic indicator)		Trial period; Notice period (after 20 years); Fixed-term contracts (maximum number of successive contracts); Dismissal notice and pay-offs (synthetic indicator); Notice period (after 4 years); Notice period (after 9 months)	
2	Belgium, Denmark, Switzerland		Firing difficulties (synthetic indicator); Employment-protection procedures; Employment protection (synthetic indicator)	Employment protection (synthetic indicator)	Notice period (after 9 months); Notice period (after 4 years)
3	Finland, Norway, France, Austria, Japan	Unfair-dismissal definition	Unfair-dismissal definition; Employment-regulation rigour(synthetic indicator); Employment protection (synthetic indicator)		
4	Netherlands, Germany, Korea, Sweden		Delay to start of notice; Firing difficulties (synthetic indicator); Employment-protection procedures (synthenic indicators)		Fixed-term contracts (valid cases); Average seniority

TABLE 4.6 (*Cont.*)

Clusters	Countries	Common characteristics		Characteristics	
		−	+	−	+
5	Greece Spain (Italy, Portugal)		Employment-protection procedures (synthetic indicator)		Severance pay for no fault (after 9 months) Temporary work (maximum accumulated duration) Temporary work agencies (breadth) Fixed-term contracts (valid cases) Severance pay (after 20 years)

Principal-Components Analysis

As can be seen from Fig. 4.9, the analysis of industrial relations and wage bargaining does not exhibit as great a size effect as the previous data analyses. Table 4.7 presents the variables most significantly associated with the first three factorial axes.

The first factor represents unionization and corporatism. It accounts for 35 per cent of the whole variance—which is important, but less than in the previous data analysis on employment protection. The most unionized and 'corporatist' countries are thus on the right-hand side of this axis: Denmark, Norway, and Sweden. The least 'corporatist' countries are on the opposite side: the USA and Italy (Fig. 4.11). The second factor (17 per cent of the variance) represents the extent to which industrial relations are conflictual (on the negative side) and wage bargaining is centrally coordinated (on the positive side). It separates countries like Finland (and Korea) from Ireland and Germany. The third factor (16 per cent of the variance) represents manager–employee relations (on the negative side) and wage-bargaining centralization (on the positive side). It opposes the UK and Switzerland to Spain and Portugal (and Greece).

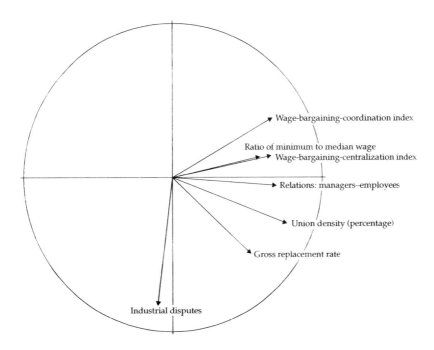

FIG. 4.9 Active and illustrative variables in the first factorial plane—industrial relations

TABLE 4.7 Variables defining the first three axes

−	+
	First axis
	Union density (percentage)
	Wage-bargaining-corporatism index
	Rate of union membership
	Relations: managers–employees
	Second axis
Industrial disputes	
	Third axis
Relations: managers–employees	Wage-bargaining-centralization index
	Collective-agreement coverage

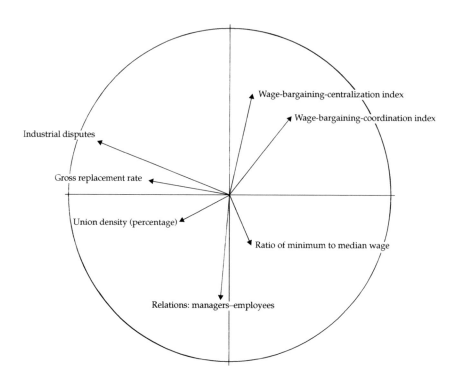

FIG. 4.10 Active and illustrative variables in the second factorial plane—
industrial relations

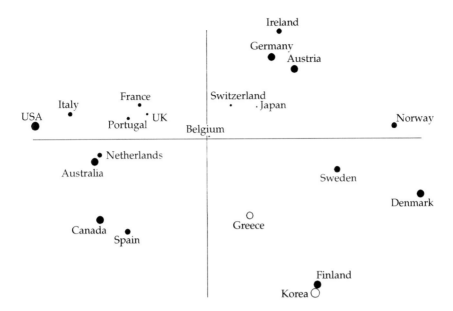

FIG. 4.11 Countries' representation in the first factorial plane—
industrial relations

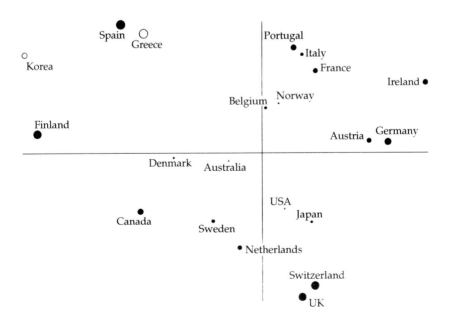

FIG. 4.12 Countries' representation in the second factorial plane—
industrial relations

The spread of countries across the plane mainly defined by union density and centralized wage bargaining (factor 1) and industrial disputes (factor 2) implies that there is little correlation between the two, although one would have expected that corporatism as evoked by union density and centralized wage bargaining would significantly reduce conflict as measured by industrial disputes. The absence of correlation may stem from the fact that the industrial-dispute indicator mixes a high number of conflicts with large conventional actions of support for centralized bargaining.

Cluster Analysis

The cluster analysis leads us to identify five groups of countries (Table 4.8). The first cluster groups again the Anglo-Saxon countries, but this time

TABLE 4.8 Country clusters for industrial relations

Clusters	Countries	Characteristics	
		−	+
1	USA Canada Netherlands Australia UK Switzerland	Coordination degree Wage-bargaining-coordination Index Centralization degree Average effective tax wedge Wage-bargaining-corporatism index Wage-bargaining-centralization index	
2	France Portugal Belgium Italy Spain	Relations: managers–employees	
3	Germany Austria Ireland		Wage-bargaining-corporatism index
4	Japan Norway (Greece)		Union density (percentage)
5	Finland Sweden Denmark (Korea)		Rate of union membership Union density (percentage) Gross replacement rate

associated with the Netherlands and Switzerland. This cluster represents countries where corporatism, coordination, and centralization of wage bargaining are low; they are also countries with a low degree of employment protection as measured by the global index of Nicoletti et al. (2000). The second cluster groups France, Portugal, Belgium, Italy, and Spain. They are countries where relations between managers and employees are conflictual and where bargaining is neither particularly centralized nor coordinated. These countries are also characterized by a high degree of employment protection, measured by the global index referred to above. The third cluster groups traditional corporatist or coordinated countries (Germany and Austria) with Ireland. The last two clusters consist of countries where unions play an important role. A high union density characterizes cluster 4 (Japan and Norway, to which one can add Greece) and union membership is high in the last cluster (Finland, Sweden, and Denmark, to which one can add Korea). These countries would be regrouped in the same cluster if they did not differ along the second factor. Industrial relations seem to be less adversarial in the fourth cluster than in the fifth, and the gross replacement rate, measuring the generosity of unemployment benefits, is relatively high.

The partition of countries obtained by this analysis differs somewhat from the previous ones. This is because market-based economies are not the only ones where wage bargaining is decentralized or uncoordinated. We can compare the results obtained above with the classification featured in Crouch (1993), where three modes of interest intermediation are distinguished: contestation, pluralist bargaining, and neo-corporatism. Contestative relations are characterized by an antagonistic conflict of interests between capital and labour; lack of cooperation blocks negotiations in zero-sum games. When conflict intensifies, State intervention provides the necessary mediation. Pluralistic bargaining arises when employers supported by the necessary political changes and legal framework change their strategy from outright conflict to the development of procedures avoiding mutually damaging action. This system still suffers from short-termism and particular-interests representation and the State is reluctant to intervene. Neo-corporatism is based on long-term, positive-sum conceptions of common interest between organized agents. This requires centralized and encompassing organization of interest and institutionalized support from the State. Crouch (1993) further distinguishes between a model of 'extensive neocorporatism', which presupposes strong and centralized unions, seemingly characterizing a large part of the history of Austria and the Scandinavian countries, and the simple model of neo-corporatism, characteristic of the German case, where unions are relatively weak but endowed with a strategic capacity.

TABLE 4.9 Four types of industrial-relations system

Labour unions	Weak power	Strong power
Short-term objectives	Contestation (France)	Pluralism (UK)
Long-term objectives	Neo-corporatism—type 1 (Germany)	Neo-corporatism—type 2 (Austria, Scandinavia)

Source: Crouch (1993).

The results of Table 4.8 can be interpreted in terms of the classification presented in Table 4.9. Cluster 1, i.e. some of the Anglo-Saxon economies, Switzerland, and the Netherlands, represents pluralism; cluster 2, i.e. France, Portugal, Belgium, Italy, and Spain, represents contestation; cluster 3, to which Germany belongs, is that of neo-corporatism of type 1; cluster 5, the Scandinavian countries, represents neo-corporatism of type 2. Cluster 4 is that of Japan, a country not included in Crouch's analysis, which focused on European states. Nevertheless, this cluster would be near to the group of type 2—corporatist countries. It is also interesting to note that Ireland does not belong to the pluralist group, as does the UK, but is nearer to the group of type 1—corporatism.

4.2.3 Employment Policy

Looking at the extent of labour-market policies is a useful complement to the analysis of the institutional dimension of the labour markets. It shows to what extent countries are committed to intervening in labour markets and which kind of programmes they favour. The number of institutional variables that have been retained to describe the employment policies is low: they reflect the share of GDP invested respectively in public employment, in programmes for handicapped persons, in unemployment allowances, in youth programmes, and in general labour-market programmes.[4]

Principal-Components Analysis

Unsurprisingly, the structure of the data analysis is very simple. The first two factors explain nearly 75 per cent of the variance. The results are therefore straightforward. The first factor represents active labour-market policies (on the negative side). The second factor represents public expenditure on youth programmes (on the negative side). The third factor represents expenditure on handicapped persons (on the positive side).

---

[4] Data come from the OECD: Employment Outook. Series are three-year averages for the period 1994–6.

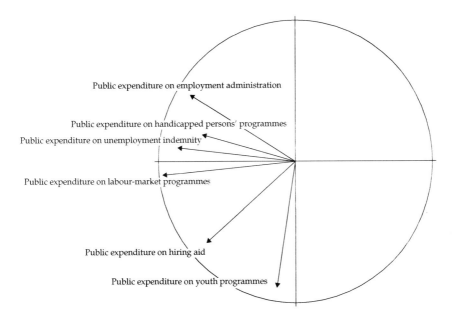

FIG. 4.13 Active variables in the first factorial plane
(as % of GDP)—employment policy

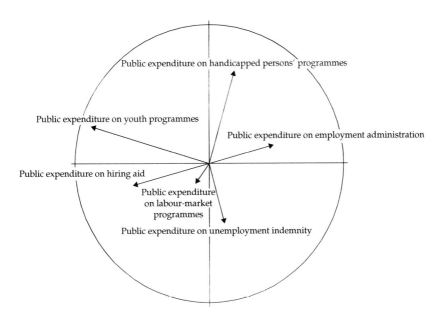

FIG. 4.14 Active variables in the second factorial plane (as % of GDP)—
employment policy

TABLE 4.10   Variables defining the first three axes (as % of GDP)

−	+
First axis	
Public expenditure on labour-market programmes	
Public expenditure on unemployment indemnity	
Second axis	
Public expenditure on youth programmes	
Third axis	
	Public expenditure on handicapped persons' programmes

The representation of countries on the first factorial plane clearly sets apart countries with very active labour-market policies (Sweden, the Netherlands, Finland) from countries where these policies are not very active (the USA, Greece, Korea). This alone explains half of the variance between countries. The other differences are clearly second-order: opposition between countries where youth programmes are important (Italy, Ireland, Portugal) and the others on the second axis, and countries where programmes for the handicapped are more important (Norway, Sweden) and the others on the third axis.

Cluster Analysis

Four clusters can be identified. The first one groups countries where employment policies are limited in every dimension: the USA, Norway, Greece, Switzerland, the UK, Canada, Australia, Korea, Austria, and Spain. The other three clusters gather countries with active employment policies. They differ from one another on the specific areas targeted by the policies: youth programmes for the second cluster (Italy, Portugal, and France), hiring policies for the third cluster (Germany, Finland, Ireland, Belgium, and Denmark), and handicapped-persons' programmes for the last cluster (Sweden and the Netherlands).

The clusters found in this analysis are less homogeneous or straightforward than in the three previous analyses. The heterogeneity of the first cluster is linked to the fact that expenditure on labour markets can be low for different reasons: a reliance on price mechanisms for labour-market adjustments; or a consequence of the level of development, as for Greece and Korea. Cluster 3 also shows that a high level of expenditure on labour

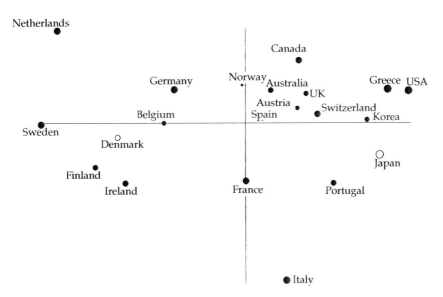

FIG. 4.15 Countries' representation in the first factorial plane—
employment policy

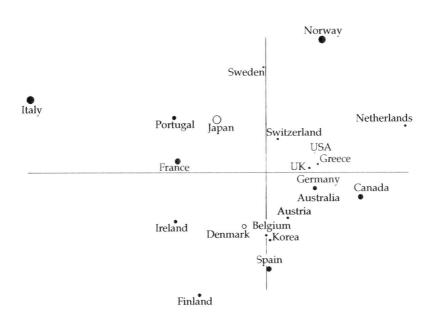

FIG. 4.16 Countries' representation in the second factorial
plane—employment policy

TABLE 4.11 Country clusters for employment policy

Clusters	Countries	Characteristics (as % of GDP)	
		−	+
1	USA Norway Greece Switzerland UK Canada Austrlia Korea Austria Spain	Public expenditure on youth programmes Public expenditure on hiring aid Public expenditure on labour-market programmes	
2	Italy Portugal France		Public expenditure on youth programmes
3	Germany Finland Ireland Belgium Denmark		Public expenditure on labour-market programmes, total Public expenditure on hiring aid
4	Sweden Netherlands		Public expenditure on handicapped-persons' programmes Public expenditure on employment administration

markets can be reached in countries with various levels of employment protection and various types of industrial relations.

4.3 Financial Systems

Financial systems present important distinctive features in a comparative analysis of the institutional context of capitalist economies. This variety goes beyond a dichotomic opposition between bank-based and finance-based systems. Moreover, this diversity seems to have maintained itself across the 1990s in spite of the globalization of some financial activities and the growing interdependence of financial markets. The inclusion of several variables reflecting various aspects of the finance–industry relationship allows us to go beyond a simple opposition between

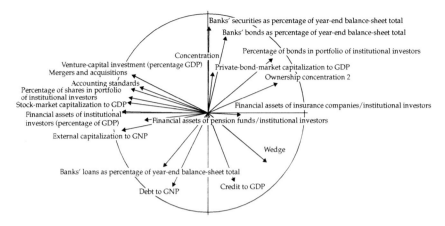

Fɪɢ. 4.17 Active variables in the first factorial plane—financial systems

financial-markets-based and bank-based finance, since actual financial systems present original combinations of these two polar cases. This accuracy is all the more necessary in that such mixed patterns have developed in the 1990s following common trends leading to the development of financial markets in all countries as well as new venture-capital schemes. Whether these trends produce some convergence among financial systems is thus a key question for a comparative institutional analysis. For these reasons the variables considered in the analysis of financial systems cover several important aspects of the financing relationship: the sources of funds, the development and dynamics of financial markets, corporate governance, and the development of venture capital.[5]

Principal-Components Analysis

Figures 4.17 and 4.18 display the active variables in the first two factorial planes. There is no 'size effect', because of the variety of indicators taken into account and the many dimensions structuring the diversity of these systems, in contrast with what we saw with product-market regulation, for instance, where one dimension prevailed over the others. The first dimension of interest is expressed on the first axis, which accounts for nearly one-third of total variance. The first factor can be understood as representing the extent to which countries depend on 'market-based' finance. Variables such as the ratio of external capitalization to GNP, financial assets of institutional investors as a percentage of GDP, the ratio

[5] Data on financial systems come from several sources. Indicators on financial intermediaries are constructed using data from the OECD financial statistics and are three-year averages 1994–6. Data on the institutional features of financial systems come from La Porta et al. (1998) and Pagano and Volpin (2001).

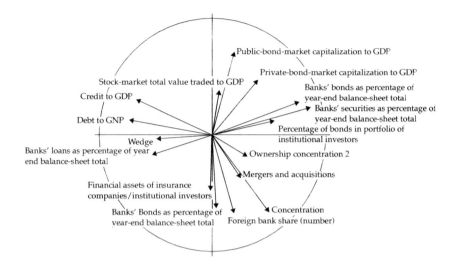

FIG. 4.18 Active variables in the second factorial plane—financial systems

of stock-market capitalization to GDP, etc all point to the negative side of
the axis. On the positive side one finds variables characterizing a more
centralized financial system: ownership concentration or the percentage
of bonds in the portfolio of institutional investors. Control variables
associated with this axis are widely held variables on the negative side,
concentration of ownership and State control on the positive side. The second factor (17 per cent of the variance) differentiates countries according
to their banking sector: the importance of bank securities in the balance
sheet on the positive side, a more 'traditional' banking sector on the
negative side, with variables such as credit to GDP or debt to GNP on the
negative side. Control variables also shed some light on the composition
of this factorial axis: one finds family control of firms on the positive side.
The third factor (12 per cent of the variance) has the relative size of the
bond market on the positive side and the share of foreign banks on the
negative side.

The first factorial plane easily sets apart the countries where market
finance plays a major role from the countries relying more on banking
finance systems. We can consider this axis as denoting the degree of centralization of financial systems (Dewatripont and Maskin 1995). It can also
be interpreted in terms of control, as will be seen below, and it would then
distinguish between outsider-dominated and insider-dominated systems
(Franks and Mayer 1997), or between portfolio-oriented and control-
oriented systems (Berglöf 1997). However, here again the analysis shows

TABLE 4.12 Variables defining the first three axes

−	+
First axis	
External capitalization to GNP	
Financial assets of institutional	
investors (percentage of GDP)	
Venture-capital investment	Ownership concentration
(country of management)	Percentage of bonds in portfolio of
(percentage of GDP)	institutional investor
Stock-market capitalization to GDP	
Percentage of shares in portfolio of	
institutional investor	
Venture-capital investment	
(percentage of GDP)	
Mergers and acquisitions	
Second axis	
Debt to GNP	Banks' securities as percentage of
	year-end balance-sheet total
	Banks' bonds as percentage of
	year-end balance-sheet total
Third axis	
Concentration	Public-bond-market capitalization to
Foreign-bank share (number)	GDP

that there is more than a simple opposition between Anglo-Saxon countries and the rest or between market finance and a unified bank-based system. Countries which cannot be characterized as relying on financial markets are not homogeneous. They differ with respect to the concentration of the banking system, the role of public bonds, or the extent of securitization. Hence, countries appear more scattered when projected on the factorial planes than might have been expected when accepting without question the simple opposition between banks and financial markets (Figs. 4.19 and 4.20).

Cluster Analysis

The cluster analysis gives a partition of countries into four groups (Table 4.13). The first cluster is clearly that of decentralized finance. The financial sectors of the USA, Canada, the Netherlands, the UK, and Australia are characterized by the importance of institutional investors and particularly pension funds, the importance of the stock market as

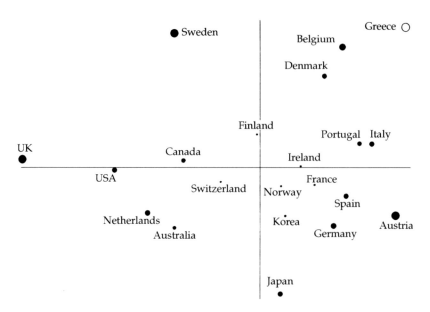

Fig. 4.19 Countries' representation in the first factorial plane—
financial systems

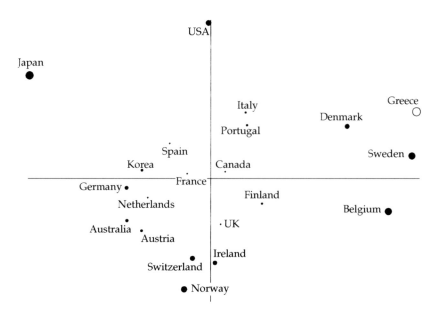

Fig. 4.20 Countries' representation in the second factorial plane—
financial systems

TABLE 4.13 Country clusters for financial systems

Clusters	Countries	Characteristics	
		−	+
1	USA Canada Netherlands UK Australia	Percentage of bonds in portfolio of institutional investors Ownership concentration	Venture-capital investment in early stage high-tech projects (country of management) (percentage of GDP) Share of financial assets in pension funds of institutional investors Venture-capital investment in early-stage projects (country of management) (percentage of GDP) Venture-capital investment in high-tech projects (country of management) (percentage of GDP) Financial assets of institutional investors (percentage of GDP) Banks' profit before tax/average balance-sheet total Control (10%) of large publicly traded firms, widely held Control (10%) of large publicly traded firms, widely held corporation Control (20%) of medium-sized publicly traded firms, widely held External capitalization to GNP Stock-market capitalization to GDP Total venture-capital investment (country of management) (percentage of GDP) Stock-market total value traded to GDP Banks' net non-interest income average balance-sheet total External capitalization to GNP Venture-capital investment (percentage of GDP) Percentage of shares in portfolio of institutional investors Mergers and acquisitions Total venture-capital investment (country of destination) (percentage of GDP)

TABLE 4.13 (*cont.*)

Clusters	Countries	Characteristics	
		−	+
2	Belgium Denmark Sweden Greece	Banks' net non-interest income average balance-sheet total Debt to GNP	Banks' bonds as percentage of year-end balance-sheet total Banks securities as percentage of year-end balance-sheet total Private-bond-market capitalization to GDP Control (20%) of large publicly traded firms, family Financial institutions controlled, share market capital Financial institutions controlled, N firms
3	Finland Korea Norway Ireland Switzerland		Foreign-bank share
4	Germany Japan Austria France Italy Portugal Spain	Control (20%) of large publicly traded firms, widely held Control (20%) of medium-sized publicly traded firms, widely held Venture-capital investment in early-stage projects (country of destination) (% of GDP) Percentage of shares in portfolio of institutional investors Total venture-capital investment (country of destination) (% of GDP) Mergers and acquisitions Accounting standards	Banks' bonds as percentage of year-end balance-sheet total Control (10%) of large publicly traded firms, State Control (20%) of large publicly traded firms, State Credit to GDP Financial assets of investment companies/institutional investors Percentage of other financial assets in portfolio of institutional investors ownership concentration 2 Banks' capital and reserves (% of year-end balance-sheet total)

indicated by a high capitalization relative to GNP, a well-developed venture-capital system, high mergers-and-acquisitions activity, and a low concentration of ownership. These countries also have a profitable banking sector. The features of this market-finance model are well known. This system relies on a particular type of corporate governance, associating a dispersed ownership with the takeover threat. The other countries are not grouped in a homogeneous ideal bank-based system. Three groups can be distinguished. The financial system of Belgium, Denmark, and Sweden (with which one can associate Greece) is certainly bank-based, but the banks have a somewhat 'passive' role: bonds and securities represent a large part of the banks' assets and the debt/GNP ratio is significantly lower than in other countries; control of firms is concentrated, with families playing an important role. The third cluster consists of small countries (Finland, Korea, Norway, and Ireland) as well as Switzerland, which is a large country in terms of banking activity. The countries of this cluster do not seem to represent the ideal bank-based system either; their common characteristic is to have many foreign banks. The fourth cluster is more representative of the ideal bank-based system, with countries like Germany and Japan, but also Austria, France, Italy, Portugal and Spain. The characteristics of this cluster are those traditionally associated with a bank-based system: a high credit/GDP ratio as well as an important share of insurance companies among institutional investors. Likewise, these countries show(ed) little mergers-and-acquisitions activity,[6] weak development of accounting standards, and a lagging venture-capital sector. Ownership is concentrated and the State plays a relatively important role in the control of some large corporations.

4.4 Social Protection

Welfare systems are characterized by the type of risks they cover and the extent to which they cover them; their features are the results of long-term conflicts and debates and are therefore strongly country-specific. The frontier between the risks that can be taken care of on a private basis and those which require public intervention is bound to change with the development of markets, demography, technologies, and the prevailing visions of society and solidarity. Social-protection systems have evolved in recent years but present much more inertia than the domains that have

---

[6] Ch. 6 will consider the most recent period and the upsurge in mergers and takeovers in European countries.

been dealt with so far. The past two decades have seen large shifts in the welfare-budget structure, with the improvement of health coverage, the rise in pensions tied to the ageing of the population, and the rise in the share of unemployment benefits forced by rising unemployment. It follows that in most countries, despite a turn towards a more restrictive vision of solidarity which aims at linking benefits more closely to personal efforts to reduce the relevant risk,[7] welfare expenditures have increased relative to GDP, most of the increase being related to the rise in health expenditures and pensions.

The structure of social-protection expenditure will be considered: old-age benefits, disability cash benefits, sickness benefits, services for the elderly and disabled people, survivors' benefits, family cash benefits, family services, unemployment benefits, health benefits, housing benefits, and 'other contingencies'.[8] The structure of expenditure should reveal the broad orientations of each type of welfare system, according to the type of risk that is most protected. Indicators are computed in the following way. First, the share of public expenditures in total (public and mandatory private) expenditures is computed for each type of expenditure. This measures the role of publicly provided social protection by type of expenditure. The second type of indicator focuses on the share of each type of publicly funded expenditure in total public expenditures and reflects the weight of welfare expenditures in the budget. Finally, for each type of expenditure, the ratio of the sum of public and mandatory private expenditures to GDP is considered and expresses the economic weight of welfare.

Principal-Components Analysis

The results of the data analysis can be summed up as follows. Figures 4.21 and 4.22 give the projection of active variables in the first two factorial planes. Table 4.14 gives the variables most significantly associated with the first three axes. The first factor (which accounts for a third of total variance) represents the size of public social expenditure, expressed relative both to all public expenditures and to GDP. On this axis countries with a well-developed public-welfare system (Finland, Sweden, Austria, and Norway) are distinguished from countries with a more limited public-welfare system (Japan, the USA, Canada, and Portugal). The second factor distinguishes expenditures on old age (the negative side) from

---

[7] Ch. 6 will deal more thoroughly with this topic.
[8] Indicators are constructed using the OECD social-expenditures database and are averages for 1994–8.

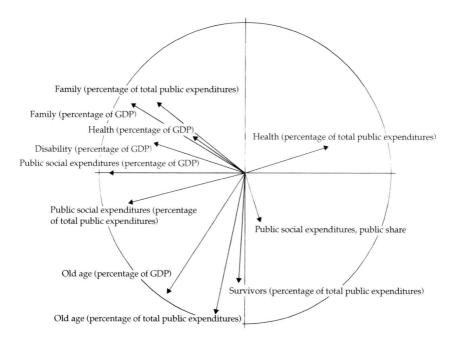

FIG. 4.21 Active variables in the first factorial plane—social protection

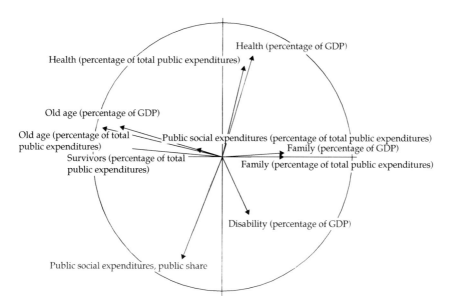

FIG. 4.22 Active variables in the second factorial plane—social protection

Table 14.14 Variables defining the first three axes

−	+
First axis	
Share of public social expenditure in GDP	
Share of public social expenditure in total public expenditure	
Share of total family benefits in GDP	
Second axis	
Share of public old-age expenditure in total public expenditures	
Share of total old-age-benefits expenditure in GDP	
Share of public survivors' expenditure in total public expenditures	
Share of total survivors' benefits expenditure in GDP	
Third axis	
Public social expenditure in total social expenditure	Share of total health expenditure in GDP

family benefits (the positive side). The third factor discriminates according to the importance of health expenditures in GDP and public expenditures (on the positive side) as well as the share of public expenditures in total social expenditures (on the negative side).

Thus, the three factors of this data analysis on social protection point to the three main facts concerning the evolution of welfare systems in the last two decades: the rise in welfare expenditures relative to GDP following rises both in old-age benefits and in health benefits.

The projection of countries on the first plane clearly sets apart those with a well developed public-welfare system, which are on the left-hand side, from countries where this public system is weak (Japan, the USA, Canada). This axis does not divide countries according to their relative level of GDP per capita, since very rich countries can be found on each side of this axis. More generally, it should be noticed that this plane (which accounts for nearly 60 per cent of the variance) does split up the usual groups of countries from the previous analyses. More precisely, the market-oriented cluster, which was conspicuous in the previous data analyses, is here dismantled. The fact that the UK has a welfare budget

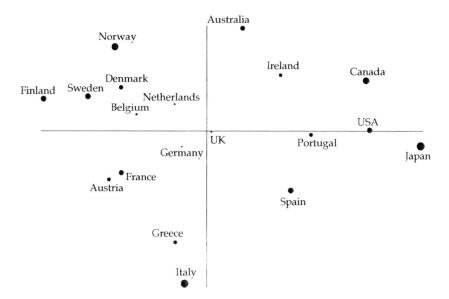

FIG. 4.23 Countries' representation in the first factorial plane—social
protection

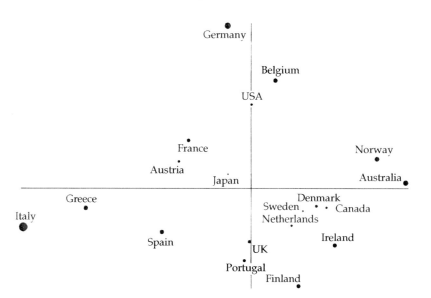

FIG. 4.24 Countries' representation in the second factorial plane—social
protection

more in line with the other European countries is a main cause for this breakup.[9]

A similar reshuffling occurs when one looks at the projection on the second factorial plane (factors 2 and 3, accounting for 40 per cent of the variance). The importance of total health expenditures in the USA (largely stemming from high private expenditures) brings this country into the club of high spenders on health, along with Germany, Belgium, and France. Old-age benefits, represented on axis 2, by contrast produce more expected groupings, with Mediterranean countries on the left-hand side and Nordic countries on the right-hand side.

Cluster Analysis

The cluster analysis confirms the above observations, leading to three or six groups as described in Table 4.15 below, depending on the level of aggregation. Cluster 4, composed of Sweden, Denmark, Norway, and Finland, represents the typical social-democratic Welfare State: high public social expenditure relative to GDP, especially for the elderly and family services. Some tax variables, included as illustrative variables, also characterize the cluster. Unsurprisingly, tax revenue is high as a percentage of GDP. The second cluster, the USA, Canada, and Japan (with Korea), exemplifies a private social-protection system and, as mentioned, does not include the UK, breaking with the usual market-based clustering. Taxes on property give a larger share of tax revenues than in other clusters, but taxes on goods and consumption taxes are lower. The first and sixth clusters are opposed on the second axis. Australia and Ireland have more common characteristics with the private welfare system of cluster 2 than with the Continental European public system of France, Germany, Austria, and Belgium, which in turn are characterized by a high level of public-support welfare expenditure, combined with a relatively small share of taxes on corporate income as a share of GDP.

How do these findings relate to the literature on comparative welfare systems? Table 4.16 summarizes various typologies found in the literature and compares them with the clustering obtained above. All typologies agree on making the social-democratic model a highly specific one, different not only from the liberal market economies, but also from the rest of the European countries. There is a fairly general agreement in the literature to classify all Scandinavian countries in this model. Titmuss (1974) is an exception in lumping Great Britain along with the Nordic countries in one specific group: the institutional-redistributive model. Our findings

---

[9] But countries like Australia and Ireland also turn out to have important welfare budgets.

TABLE 4.15 Country clusters for social protection

Clusters	Countries	Common characteristics +	Common characteristics −	Characteristics +	Characteristics −
1	Australia, Ireland		Share of total old-age expenditure in GDP		Public share in total old-age and disabled expenditures
2 (1)	USA, Canada, Japan (Korea)		Share of social expenditure in public expenditure		
3	UK, Netherlands, Spain, Portugal		Share of public social expenditure in GDP	Share of disability expenditure in public expenditure	
4 (2)	Sweden, Denmark, Norway, Finland			Share of old-age and disabled expenditure in total public expenditure; Share of total old-age and disabled expenditure in GDP; Share of total family-services expenditure in GDP; Share of family-services expenditure in total public expenditure	

TABLE 4.15 (cont.)

Clusters	Countries	Common characteristics		Characteristics	
		−	+	−	+
5 ⎤ (3) ⎦ 6	Italy Greece France Germany Austria Belgium (Switzerland)		Share of total old-age expenditure in GDP Share of old-age expenditure in total public expenditure Share of total survivors' expenditure in GDP Share of survivors' expenditure in total public expenditure		Share of public social expenditure in GDP Share of health expenditure in GDP

support the thesis of the specificity of Scandinavian countries. The characteristics of the model are, for instance, exposed in Esping-Andersen (1990). It entails relatively high levels of transfers and provides redistributive benefits and services. The system is universal, based on citizenship, promotes social equality, and implies decommodification and defamiliarization: individuals can achieve a reasonably high standard of living without market participation and independently of family support.

Most authors identify a liberal model, which could apply to our first three clusters in the six-group typology, i.e. the first cluster in the three-group partition. The characteristics of the liberal system are low and means-tested assistance, flat-rate benefits providing incentives to seek income from work, as well as the predominance of limited social-insurance plans. Benefits are designed to provide a safety net for the poorest categories of the population. No redistributive aim is given to the system. Entitlement rules are strict and often associated with social stigma; benefits are weak and the State encourages market-based protection, both by providing only minimal assistance and by subsidizing private schemes. Contrary to the universalist social-democratic system, the liberal system favours (re)commodification. Ebbinghaus (1998) introduces a distinction between the liberal residualism of the USA and the liberal-universalist model characteristic of the UK. This distinction would make the UK an intermediate case between the pure liberal model and the universalist model of Scandinavia. Flora (1986) takes a broadly similar position.

The conservative-corporatist model is committed to preserving status and providing solidarity within rather than between social groups and therefore does not redistribute as much as the social-democratic model. Welfare benefits are linked to activity and employment. The regime favours moderate decommodification and familiarization. Ebbinghaus (1998) has added a 'Latin' residual-Welfare State cluster derived from the liberal cluster. The differences between Spain and Portugal but also Italy and France and the Continental Welfare States are emphasized: fewer Welfare State benefits, more traditional intermediary institutions such as Church and family. This separation is partly found in our results. Italy and Greece are in a separate cluster, as a subgroup of the Continental Welfare States, but Spain and Portugal are in the same cluster as the UK. Ebbinghaus's classification of France and Portugal in the same category of a rudimentary Welfare State is exaggerated when one checks the extent of social protection in France.[10] The same remark could also apply to Italy.

---

[10] Ebbinghaus actually considers France as a 'borderline' case, a mix of Bismarckian social-security State and more familialist Latin welfare.

TABLE 4.16 A comparison of our results with typologies of welfare systems found in the literature

Countries	Typologies						
	Titmuss (1974)	Flora (1986)	Esping-Andersen (1990)	Bradshaw et al. (1994)	Boismenu (1994)	Théret (1997)	Ebbinghaus (1998)
Australia Ireland			Liberal model				
USA Canada Japan	USA in the residual-welfare model	USA in the non-welfare model	Liberal model	USA and Japan in the weak familiarist model	USA and Canada in the pluralist liberal-democrat model	US zero-level model of social protection	USA in liberal residualism
UK Netherlands Spain Portugal		UK in the minimal-universalist model					UK in the liberal-universalist model

			Social-democractic model		Integral Welfare State	Social-democratic universalism
Sweden Denmark Norway Finland	Scandinavian countries (with the UK) in the institutional-redistributive model	Nordic countries in the universalist-maximal model		Sweden and Norway in the strong corporatist group		
Italy Greece			Italy in the familiarist model	Italy (and France) in the weak corporatist group		Latin particularist-clientelist subsidiarism
France Germany Austria Belgium	France and Germany in the industrial-achievement model	France and Germany in the Continental statist-bureaucratic model	France and Germany in the conservative-corporatist model	Germany and Belgium in the average-corporatist group	Germany as liberal-corporatist model	Continental corporatism

Indeed, according to the decommodification measures of Esping-Andersen (based on old-age, sickness, and unemployment expenditures), these two countries belong to the same group as Germany and Austria.

4.5 Education

If knowledge accumulation leads to innovation and technological progress one would expect a close link between education systems, educational levels, and economic growth. Yet—at the time of the so-called knowledge-based economy—finding robust empirical evidence on the macroeconomic effects of education is not simple. The economic impact of education systems cannot be analysed independently from the quality of educational services and of relationships with industry. It is thus important to study the structure of educational systems and not only pay attention to the gross outcome in terms of educational levels. Education systems tend to be highly country-specific because of their historical development and the lack of a converging trend, if only because of the absence of competitive pressure. They tend to be very heterogeneous not only across countries but within countries too. Complementarity of education systems with other systems is self-evident: with labour markets because of industry-skill requirements and with social-protection systems because of the need to protect specific skills. Attempts to classify educational systems have been relatively rare, although international comparisons are quite numerous. But these comparisons are limited to a few countries (two or three at most) and conducted on a specific basis, which makes the comparison of international comparisons themselves difficult.[11] One can identify a few key dimensions that differentiate the systems: the extent and nature of standardization of curricula; the degree of differentiation or stratification (Allmendinger 1989) between 'general' and 'vocational' programmes; the degree of flexibility of the system, i.e. whether a 'second chance' is given or not; whether vocational training is mainly school-based or work-based; whether the system is mainly public-funded or private, etc. Hannan et al. have proposed a country-by-country classification along the differentiation and standardization dimensions (Table 4.17).

The typology clearly opposes Germany and the Netherlands to the USA and Canada. In the former countries standardization is very high: curricula, school-funding, teacher certification, exam procedures, etc. At the same time, a selection process at an early age orients pupils along strictly separate tracks, inducing a pronounced differentiation among

---

[11] See Hannan et al. (1996) for an attempt in this direction.

TABLE 4.17 A typology of education systems

Standardization	Differentiation		
	High	Medium	Low
High	Germany	England	Japan
	Netherlands	France	Ireland
		Italy	
Medium		Spain	
Low			USA
			Canada

Source: Hannan et al. (1996).

individuals. This type of differentiation makes perfect sense in the context of occupational and segmented labour markets and well-developed Welfare States. North-American countries are characterized by wide variations in curricula, teacher qualifications, instructional effectiveness, examination procedures, school resources, and the pattern of funding. This lack of standardization implies that employment decisions are only weakly related to a secondary-level qualification, whose value is difficult to assess. Other countries fall somewhere in between. Japan is an interesting case, where the secondary-level education is highly standardized, sending employers a reliable signal on the skills of the student. However, since vocational training is mostly company-based, differentiation is low, as careers depend on the worker's evolution within the corporation. Vocational training itself is a strong factor of differentiation across countries. Estevez-Abe, Iversen, and Soskice (2001) thus distinguish five groups of countries: (1) the UK, the USA, (New Zealand,) Australia, Ireland, and Canada, where vocational training is weak; (2) Denmark, the Netherlands, and Belgium, where it is achieved in a cooperative way at industry and company levels; (3) Switzerland, Germany, and Austria, where a system of dual apprenticeship is practised; (4) Sweden, Norway, and Finland, which resort to vocational colleges; and (5) Japan, Italy, and France, where vocational training is mainly done at the company level. The interactions between labour markets and educational systems thus depend on the features both of 'general' education and of vocational programmes.

Aventur, Campo, and Möbus (1999) propose a typology of training systems for European countries according to the involvement of the individual employee and the employer. They propose two mappings of countries, one based on combining the intensity of employers' and employees' initiative in 'continuing training', i.e. lifelong learning (Table 4.18*a*), the other on the

Table 4.18*a* Initiative in lifelong learning

Individual initiative	Employer initiative		
	Slight	Average	Strong
Limited	Italy Spain Greece Portugal	Ireland	
Moderate		Germany Austria Belgium Luxembourg	France
Widespread		Netherlands	UK
Strong			Denmark Finland Sweden

Table 4.18*b* Employer's role in training

Vocational training	Continuing training		
	Weak	Average	Strong
Little importance	Spain	Belgium	Finland Sweden
Slightly formalized	Italy Greece Portugal		UK
Minority role, institutionalized		Ireland Luxembourg Netherlands	France
Dominant, institutionalized		Germany Austria	Denmark

Source: Aventur, Campo and Möbus (1999).

employer's role in continuing and vocational training (Table 4.18*b*). Their mappings are somewhat different from the typology of Estevez-Abe et al. (2001) based on an intensity indicator mixed with institutional considerations, and even contradict them in the case of some countries. Looking at Table 4.18*a*, there seems to be a complementarity between employers' and employees' initiative, except for France, where employers play a relatively stronger role than employees. The dynamism of employer-initiated continuing training depends, among other factors, on economic activity and company size. The most training-oriented industries have a higher technological intensity and a highly skilled workforce. Continuous innovation demands that the workforce's skills be constantly upgraded. The size of the firm determines the financial constraints that training is subject to. Employer-initiated continuing training is also related to the forms taken by vocational training (Table 4.18*b*). One configuration is that of heavy company investment in continuing training as a complement to initial vocational training. For Aventur et al. (1999), this case corresponds to France, where there is school-based vocational training, or Sweden, where there is no apprenticeship and employers take care of the company- or industry-specific training of their workforce. Thus, the distinction between Sweden, which is in group (iv) in Estevez-Abe et al. (2001), and France, in group (v), is refuted by Aventur et al. (1999). Germany is a case where firms are heavily involved in initial training through apprenticeship, but less so in continuing training. Italy, Greece, Spain, and Portugal are characterized by a low-level complementarity between continuing and vocational training.

The institutional and regulatory environment of training differs across countries. Mandatory employer funding of training is found only in France, but more limited constraints exist via bipartite (Italy, Netherlands, Denmark, Belgium, and Ireland) or tripartite (Spain) agreements. More initiative is given to the employer in Germany, Austria, Finland, Sweden, Portugal, and the UK. Some government financial incentives go directly to the firm under the guise of subsidy or tax credit in France, Germany, the UK, Ireland, and the Netherlands. In some Scandinavian countries there are government aids to the hiring of a job seeker to replace an employee on training leave. Public involvement in the quality of training can take the form of direct subsidies (Denmark and Finland) or the promotion of quality standards for training supply (France, Germany, and Ireland). A system of certificates can be found in the UK, Spain, Portugal, Finland, and Denmark. A few countries have set up specific structures providing assistance to the firm for the definition of needs or training supply: the UK, France, Spain, Portugal, and Greece. Scandinavian countries have a strong tradition of lifelong learning and their training supply is diversified and efficient, but concern for lifelong learning is also important in the Netherlands and the UK. It is much less so in France or South European countries. Rights to training leave vary across Europe: they are well-established and guaranteed in Scandinavian countries, but left to negotiated agreements in the Netherlands and Spain. Government aid is present everywhere, but is much higher in Scandinavia than anywhere else. Training certification can be awarded, as in Scandinavia, in the form of vocational diplomas which are recognized by employers, or to a lesser extent in Germany. Certification is not centralized in the UK, but depends on agreements signed at the individual-company level.

It is not possible to conduct an empirical analysis involving that much precision in the institutional description for lack of comparable data. The structure of expenditure in the education system, as well as data on enrolment rates, percentages of graduates, and orientation of the education system will be considered in the principal-components analysis that follows. Lack of reliable and comprehensive data on vocational training has led to its non-inclusion in the data analysis, at least not as an active variable.

Principal-Components Analysis

The first factor (22 per cent of the variance) can be interpreted as representing the share of public expenditure in university-level education. Some countries rely on a public tertiary-education system (Austria, Finland, and Germany) and others depend on a private university system (the USA and Japan). The second factor (19 per cent of the variance) is that of the enrolment rate (on the positive side). The third factor (15 per cent of the variance) represents the relative importance of the secondary-education system, where enrolment is opposed to the percentage of graduates. It may also be noted that the indicator of lifelong learning,

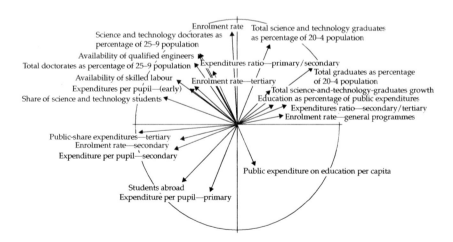

Fig. 4.25 Active variables in the first factorial plane—education

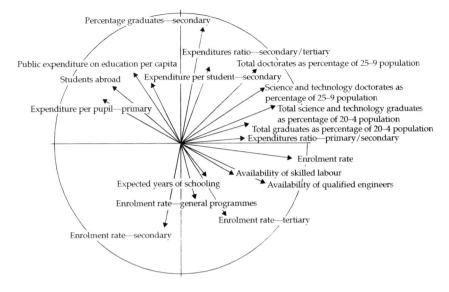

FIG. 4.26 Active variables in the second factorial plane—education

Table 4.19 Variables defining the first three axes

−	+
	First axis
Public share of expenditure in tertiary education	Total graduates as percentage 20–4 population
Share of science and technology students	Enrolment rate in general programmes—tertiary
	Second axis
Relative employment—all levels	Enrolment rate
Expenditure per pupil—primary	Total science and technology graduates as percentage of the 20–4 population
	Science and technology doctorates
	Third axis
Relative employment—upper secondary	Percentage of graduates—secondary
Percentage of labour force—primary	Expenditure per pupil—secondary
Relative employment—university	Percentage of labour force—secondary
	Employment ratios—all levels

introduced as an illustrative variable, is associated with the positive side of this axis.

Science and technology graduates and science and technology doctorates both indicate that factor 2 is tied to a standard form of science–industry relationship. Factor 1 by contrast would be linked more with the importance of general training at the tertiary level. Factor 3, which is attached to the percentage of graduates at secondary level, could also be an indicator of vocational training, which would explain the fact that factors 2 and 3 are marked by an important availability of skilled labour and qualified engineers.

Looking at the positions of countries in the two planes defined above, a familiar clustering pattern seems to emerge: the market-based group of economies appears more intact than in the analysis for social protection. The plane defined by factors 1 and 2, which may be interpreted as opposing general (north–east) to vocational (north–west) training, seems to suggest that general training is indeed more predominant in market-based economies. The second plane is less straightforward to interpret as it combines characteristics of vocational training and science–industry relations.

Cluster Analysis

The analysis allows us to distinguish five clusters (Table 4.20). Cluster 1 (Italy, Spain, Portugal, Greece, Austria) is characterized by a relatively

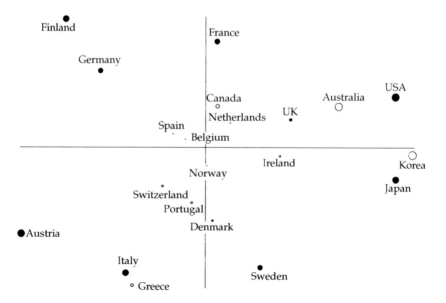

FIG. 4.27 Countries' representation in the first factorial plane—
education

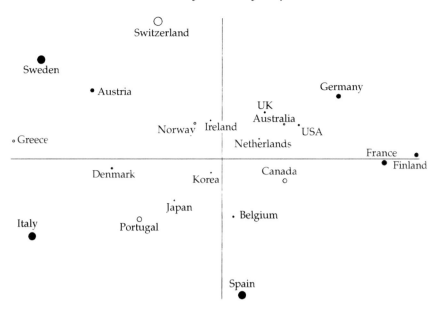

FIG. 4.28 Countries' representation in the second factorial plane—
education

small population of graduates which is however growing relatively rapidly. Spain, Italy, Portugal, and Greece are nevertheless somewhat different
from Austria. The former have all the characteristics of a lagging educational system, adapted to relatively low-tech industry requirements: a
high percentage of the labour force has a primary degree as highest
educational level, whereas a relatively low proportion of the labour force
has experienced secondary education. Unemployment for the university-
level-educated workforce is high but tertiary education still gives an
employment advantage over other education levels. The Finnish education system seems to have highly specific features. This country is nearest
to the group of countries composed of the Netherlands, Belgium, France,
Germany, and Ireland, characterized by a strong public education system
with a marked emphasis on secondary education. Denmark, Sweden, and
Norway possess a system with a high level of public expenditure, which
delivers a high quality of education, judging by the relative employment
ratios at secondary and below secondary levels. Only qualified engineers
seem to be lacking. Finally, the USA and Japan, along with the UK,
Australia, Korea, and Canada, possess a tertiary-education system where
the public financing share is lower than in other countries.

The clustering we come up with partly overlaps with Hannan et al.'s
classification. The clustering pattern associating Germany, France, the

TABLE 4.20 Country clusters for education systems

Clusters	Countries	Characteristics	
		−	+
1	Italy	Percentage of labour force—secondary	Percentage of force—primary
	Spain	Employment ratio—university	Relative employment—upper
	Portugal	Relative expected years out of	secondary
	Greece	employment—women secondary	Unemployment rate—university
	Austria		Relative employment—university
		Expected years in employment—	Enrolment rate—secondary
		women	
		Percentage of graduates—secondary	
		Employment ratios—all levels	
		Total graduates as % of 20–4	Total graduates—growth
		population	
		Total science and technology	
		graduates as percentage of	
		20–4 population	
		Percentage of labour force—tertiary	
2	Finland		
3	Netherlands	Expenditure per pupil—primary	Expenditure ratio
	Belgium		primary/secondary
	France		Expected years of schooling
	Germay		Expected years of schooling
	Ireland		
4	Denmark	Availability of qualified engineers	Public expenditure on education
	Sweden		per capita
	Norway		Employment ratio—below
			secondary
			Employment ratio—secondary
			Private payments—tertiary
5	USA	Public share of expenditure—tertiary	Relative expected years out of
	Japan		employment for men—primary
	UK		
	Australia		
	Korea		
	Canada		

Netherlands, and Ireland may be interpreted according to the standardization dimension. All these countries are characterized by a high degree
of homogeneity of primary and secondary curricula and certification procedures. Cluster 5, which groups the USA, Canada, Japan, and the UK,
could be interpreted along the differentiation dimension. Only the UK

appears in the medium differentiation category in Table 4.17, the three other countries being characterized by low differentiation. Finally, Italy and Spain, together in cluster 1, both possess systems with medium differentiation and medium to high standardization. One also finds correlations with Aventur et al.'s classification (1999). The first cluster (Italy, Spain, Portugal, and Greece) is that of limited initiative from either employer or employee in continuing training. It is also the group of countries where the employers' role is weak in continuing training and weak to moderate in vocational training. Only the presence of Austria in this group is somewhat surprising, being always associated with Germany by Aventur et al. (1999) as well as Estevez-Abe et al. (2001). But, since our results apply to educational systems and not just continuing and/or vocational training systems, one might expect supplementary factors of differentiation. The third cluster (the Netherlands, Belgium, France, Germany, and Ireland) corresponds on average to strong employer's initiative and a moderate to widespread employee's initiative in continuing training for Aventur et al. (1999), as well as on average a strong employer's role in continuing training. With Finland as an exception, Cluster 4, i.e. the Scandinavian countries, correspond to a strong initiative from both employers and employees in continuing training.

4.6 Conclusion

The analyses performed in this chapter have led us to identify the main factors of differentiation of modern capitalist economies and the partitions they imply. Since systematic analyses are seldom performed for twenty-one countries, the results presented in this chapter have shed some new light on the usual classifications of countries found in the literature. One could summarize the main findings in the following way. Most of the analyses lead us to refine the division of modern capitalism into CMEs and LMEs. Even when the picture seems relatively clear-cut, as is the case for product- and labour-market regulation, for instance, the existence of a relatively well-defined group of market-based economies does not imply that the economies of the other countries are organized according to one, opposed, principle. Besides, the archetypal coordinated economies such as Germany or Japan are not always the polar opposite of the group of LMEs. Therefore, the differentiation of modern capitalist economies takes place in more than one dimension. Furthermore, one does not always find the same partition, according to the analysis performed. The Anglo-Saxon economies are probably the ones that are the most often grouped together for a relative proximity of institutional features, but they sometimes exhibit some differentiated patterns and are distributed in different clusters. The same could be said for Scandinavian countries. This changing pattern of clustering also explains why some typologies of capitalism, such as those surveyed in the previous chapter, lead to diverging classifications. Usually, one specific institutional area (labour market, Welfare State, etc.) is privileged even when others are taken into account, and the typologies derived are partial. This is why it is necessary to take into account all the possible complementarities between the five institutional areas in order to come to an empirical classification of capitalism. This will be the task of Chapter 5.

5

The Diversity of Economic Models

For reasons exposed in the previous chapter, looking at too limited a number of institutional areas may be misleading when one is trying to grasp the institutional complementarities at the root of the diversity of modern capitalism. The whole set of institutional complementarities can be seized only when one allows for a broad interaction between institutional forms. The different varieties of capitalism are defined as specific architectures of complementary institutions, which can only be grasped by putting all the pieces together. Chapter 3 presented theoretically the five different types of capitalism and the associated institutions and complementarities. It is now time to assess the empirical content of this classification. In order to do so, a final empirical analysis will be performed, and all the (active) variables used in the preceding analyses will be taken together. The clusters of countries that are found should be interpretable in terms of the different varieties of capitalism.

5.1 The Five Models of Capitalism

Before performing the aggregate data analysis, it may be interesting to integrate all the institutional variables in several steps, adding one institutional area after another in order to check whether the links between countries belonging to the same cluster at the end appear early on. This would give an indication of the relative coherence of the country groupings and the specific mechanisms governing institutional complementarities for each model. The analysis is thus performed in five steps. We start by integrating product and labour markets, i.e. the variables considered in the analysis of product-market regulation with the variables of the employment-protection and the industrial-relations analyses. This seems natural as a first step since most of the analyses of varieties of capitalism insist on this product-market-competition–employment-relationship nexus. Variables characteristic of active labour-market policies are then added, to complete the integration of the product-market with the employment area. Variables of the financial sector are then added, then the welfare systems, and finally the education systems, to obtain a general picture of the institutional architectures of our sample of countries.

A factor analysis is performed at each step, followed by a cluster analysis. The details of the statistical analyses will not be given in what follows; only the outcomes in terms of clustering will be considered. The results of the successive steps are presented in Table 5.1. Countries appear in rows and the different cluster analyses are in columns. For each analysis, each country is given a number representing the cluster that it belongs to: for the first analysis of Table 5.1, where variables for product and labour markets are included, Australia and Canada belong to cluster 1, Japan is in cluster 3, Korea in cluster 5, Switzerland in cluster 2, etc. The same convention is adopted for the other analyses featured in the same Table. The number given to a specific cluster has no particular meaning.

The final cluster analysis gives either five or six different groups of countries, which can be linked to the five different models of capitalism presented in Chapter 3, because Switzerland and the Netherlands may either constitute a separate group in the six-cluster typology, or join France, Germany, Austria, Belgium, Ireland, and Norway in the five-cluster typology. There is thus a small subset of European countries which share some broad similarities with the bulk of other European countries but nevertheless possess some original characteristics. On the whole, the results summarized in Table 5.1 are broadly supportive of the initial typology presented in Chapter 3; the five models of capitalism can be associated with the country groupings emerging out of the cluster analysis on the basis of the variables that place the countries near one another within each group. The composition of the different clusters and the variables that make them belong to a cluster reveal the elements of both closeness and distance of country groupings with respect to the theoretical models of capitalism.

One group of countries comes out clearly as specific and homogeneous: the Anglo-Saxon economies, representing the liberal, market-based model of capitalism. As shown in the previous chapter, these countries often emerged close together in the cluster analyses performed for each institutional area. It is somehow logical that they should come out as belonging to the same group in the end. The 'coherency' of this type of capitalism can be seen in Table 5.1. The countries are grouped together from the start of our stepwise cluster analysis, i.e. the interaction between product-market regulation and labour markets, and stay together up to the final aggregate analysis. With one exception, namely Switzerland, no other country joins them in the process of successive integration of institutional domains. In a way, this type of capitalism is the most distinctive. This model also has the highest number of identified features, as is shown in Table 5.2, where the common characteristics of clusters are documented.

TABLE 5.1 The diversity of modern capitalism: five different models and five–six clusters

Capitalism model	Cluster	Product and labour markets	Product and labour markets, employment policy	Product and labour markets, employment policy, financial sector	Product and labour markets, employment policy, financial sector, welfare systems	Product and labour markets, employment policy, financial sector, welfare and education systems
Market-based capitalism	Australia	1	1	1	1	1
	Canada	1	1	1	1	1
	United Kingdom	1	1	1	1	1
	USA	1	1	1	1	1
Asian capitalism	Japan	3	3	5	6	2
	Korea	5	3	5	6	2
Continental European capitalism	Switzerland	2	1	2	2	3
	Netherlands	3	2	2	2	3
	Ireland	3	2	3	3	4
	Belgium	6	4	2	3	4
	Norway	4	5	4	4	4
	Germany	3	4	6	3	4
	France	6	4	6	3	4
	Austria	3	4	6	3	4
Social-democratic capitalism	Denmark	2	2	3	5	5
	Finland	2	2	3	5	5
	Sweden	3	2	3	5	5
Mediterranean capitalism	Greece	6	5	7	7	6
	Italy	6	6	7	7	6
	Portugal	6	6	6	7	6
	Spain	6	4	6	7	6

TABLE 5.2 The five models of capitalism: main characteristics

Product markets	Labour markets	Finance	Welfare	Education
		Market-based capitalism		
Deregulated product markets Low barriers to entrepreneurship Low administrative regulation Low State control and public ownership	**Labour-market flexibility** Few temporary-work renewal restrictions Short notice periods Trial periods Limited employment protection, even in case of unfair dismissal Limited employment protection for regular contracts Little coordination or centralization for wage bargaining Easy firing Low unfair-dismissal compensation Low average seniority Wage flexibility	**Market-based financial system and corporate governance** Dispersed ownership of large and medium-sized publicly traded companies High percentage of shares in institutional investors portfolios High number of listed firms Active financial market (IPOs) Large financial markets Importance of pension funds among institutional investors Family-controlled firms Venture capital (high share in GDP, emphasis on early stage and high-tech projects) High profitability of banks	**Liberal model of Welfare State** Residualist for the USA and Canada More universalist for the UK and Australia	**Competitive education system** Non-homogeneous secondary-education system Competitive tertiary education High enrolment rates in tertiary education
		Asian capitalism		
'Governed' rather than regulated product-market competition	**Regulated labour markets** Protection of regular employment Protection of temporary employment	**Bank-based financial system** Limited banking concentration Limited venture capital	**Low level of social protection** Low public social expenditures Limited health expenditures	**Private tertiary-education system**

	Product markets	Labour markets	Financial system	Welfare state	Education system

Continental European capitalism

	Competitive to mildly regulated product markets	Coordinated labour markets	Financial-institutions-based financial system	Corporatist model	Public education systems
	Some markets are more heavily regulated	Variance in the degree of employment protection: some countries limit temporary work	Control of firms by financial institutions Importance of insurance companies	Mostly employment-based benefits	Emphasis on secondary education High degree of standardization

Social-democratic capitalism

	Regulated product markets	Regulated labour markets	Bank-based system	Universalist model	Public education system
		Active labour-market policies High rates of union membership		Important family services	High public expenditures on tertiary education High aid to students

Mediterranean capitalism

	Regulated product markets	Regulated labour markets	Bank-based system	Limited Welfare State	Weak education system
	Administrative burdens for corporations Barriers to entrepreneurship Public sector	Limitations to temporary work Conflictual manager–employee relations	Little conformity to the standards of corporate governance Ownership concentration	Importance of old-age expenditures	Low expenditures for education, particularly tertiary education Low enrolment rates Weakness in science and technology tertiary education

Deregulated product markets combined with deregulated labour markets and a market-based financial system represent the core of the institutional complementarities shaping this model. The liberal Welfare State may have a different size according to the country concerned, minimal in the USA and Canada, more extensive in the UK and Australia, and the education system is also organized around market signals.

The distinctiveness of the market-based model explains why the dichotomous classification LME/CME can sometimes be adopted as a first approximation. Nevertheless, the other countries do not represent a homogeneous group. This can be assessed by looking at Fig. 5.1, which represents the projection of countries on the first factorial plane in the final, aggregate, analysis. Without going into detail, the first factorial axis may be interpreted as separating countries with a decentralized financial system on the left-hand side from countries with 'rigid' labour markets on the right-hand side. The second factorial axis may be interpreted as representing the extent of the Welfare State. With the help of Fig. 5.1, three other distinct groupings can be identified, located at one end of the factorial axes. The countries of the Mediterranean model are opposed to market-based economies in terms of market flexibility: 'rigid' labour market,

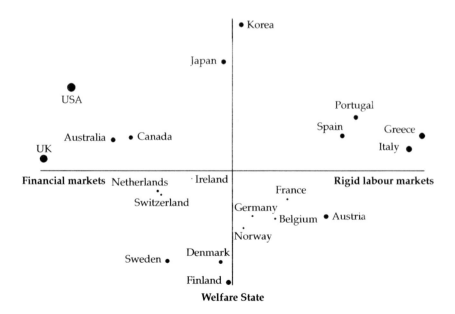

FIG. 5.1 Countries' representation in the first factorial plane—final, aggregate analysis

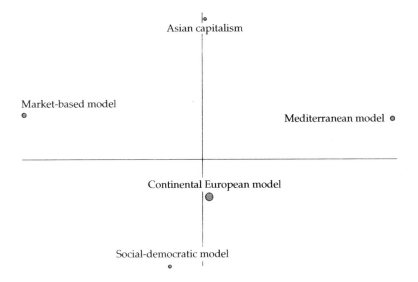

Fɪɢ. 5.2 The five types of capitalism

regulated product markets, non-developed financial markets, and 'deficient' corporate governance. Independent of this opposition on the market-regulation dimension one finds a distinct social-democratic model opposed to Asian capitalism in terms of the development of the Welfare State on the second factorial axis of Fig. 5.1. This projection allows us to measure the distance between countries in the space defined by the first two factorial axes. The countries' projection on the first factorial axis will thus serve as a measure of closeness to the market-based model. The further on the left-hand side of the axis a country is, the closer it is to the ideal market-based model of capitalism. In this respect, the UK is closer to this ideal than the USA, and Greece is the country farthest away from it. The Mediterranean model lies at the other end of the same axis. The second factorial axis serves to measure the distance vis-à-vis the ideal social-democratic model. Finland is thus the nearest country to this ideal model whereas Korea is the most distant from it. The second axis opposes the social-democratic model to Asian capitalism.

Economies of the Continental European model occupy a central place in Fig. 5.1. This would seem to point to a lack of clearly identifiable characteristics common to this group of countries. Indeed, the number of common characteristics unifying the European cluster in Table 5.2 is rather limited. The Continental European model may at first sight be considered to be an intermediate case between the market-based and the Mediterranean models (Fig. 5.2), but this is true only when one considers the market-flexibility versus rigidity axis, i.e. the first factor of the final cluster analysis. Turning to the second axis, the Continental European model could be considered as a toned-down version of the social-democratic model, i.e. with less extensive social protection, partly compensated for by more pronounced job protection. Going further in that direction, the Mediterranean model of capitalism compensates for narrower social protection with more prominent labour-market rigidity and employment protection.

The particular character of the Continental European cluster is also acknowledged by the split into two different subgroups. Switzerland and the Netherlands share some common characteristics with the rest of the Continental European economies, but they also borrow some traits from the market-based model, as can be checked by their position on Fig. 5.1 and 5.3. In Fig. 5.3 the Continental European cluster excluding Switzerland and the Netherlands is denoted 'Continental European model (A)', and these two remaining countries are the 'Continental European model (B)'. Model (A) appears as intermediate between the social-democratic and the Mediterranean models, whereas model (B) appears as intermediate between the market-based and the

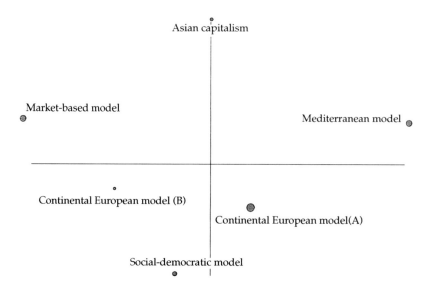

Fig. 5.3 The five types of capitalism including a differentiated Continental European model

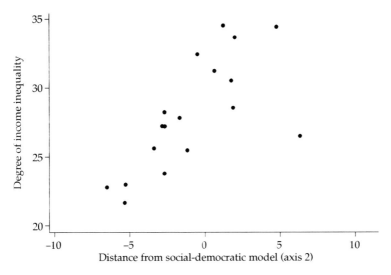

FIG. 5.4 Income inequality plotted against the distance from the social-democratic model ($r = 0.70***$). *Significance level*: $* = 10\%$; $** = 5\%$; $*** = 1\%$

social-democratic models. The same considerations could apply to some other specific countries, such as Ireland, while Norway could be seen as intermediate between Continental European capitalism and the social-democratic model. This would leave a 'core' group of Continental European capitalism, constituted by France, Germany, Belgium, and Austria, although this latter country seems close to the Mediterranean model in Fig. 5.1.

Some indicators are well correlated with the axis of the social-democratic model, such as the degree of income inequality (Fig. 5.4) measured by a gini coefficient. The correlation coefficient is 0.70, significant at the 1-per-cent level. Therefore, the second axis of the final analysis, not the first one, can be interpreted as an axis of relative income equality.[1] This is also an axis of redistribution, as shown in Fig. 5.5, where the total rate of taxation (relative to GDP) is plotted against the distance from the social-democratic model.

Thus, the aggregate data analysis and the subsequent cluster analysis have broadly confirmed the relevance of the distinction between five different models of capitalism. The clusters of countries correspond

---

[1] There is no data on income inequality for Korea. Inclusion of this country in Fig. 5.4 might have revealed an inverse-U relationship, considering that Asian countries are usually characterized by moderate income inequality.

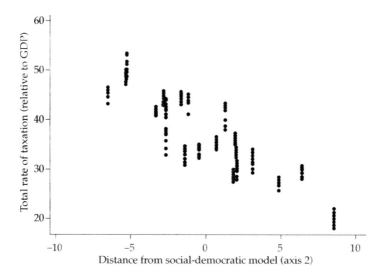

Fig. 5.5 Total rate of taxation plotted against the distance from the social-democratic model ($r = -0.88^{***}$)

to expectations in terms of common institutional characteristics and the complementarities that these imply. The identity of countries belonging to each cluster also reveals few surprises. The paragon of each cluster is the country that comes closest to the average position of the cluster as a whole; it is therefore the country that best represents the cluster. For the market-based cluster, the paragon is the USA. Since only two countries form the Asian-capitalism cluster, each can act as a 'paragon'. The paragon of the Continental European cluster is Germany, that of social-democratic countries is Denmark, and Spain plays this role for the Mediterranean cluster. The case of some individual countries is also worth noting. Although geographically a Scandinavian country, Norway belongs to the cluster of the Continental European model. In fact, Norway is a special case in most of the analyses reported in Table 5.1 and only joins Continental European countries at the end. Therefore, a partial considera-tion of institutions would lead to the conclusion that Norway is closer to the Scandinavian model than to the Continental European model. The same could be said for other countries. If one focuses on one or two insti-tutional areas, only the market-based and possibly the social-democratic and Mediterranean clusters would appear clearly. Similarly, Ireland is part of the Continental European cluster and not the market-based cluster adhered to by other English-speaking countries. It may be noted that Ireland is never associated with Anglo-Saxon economies in any of the cluster analyses in Table 5.1; it sometimes comes close to social-democratic countries, but mostly stays with Continental European countries. The example of these two countries is a further indication that the Continental European denomination is only weakly related to geography.

We can now move on and check whether these models are associated with specific characteristics in terms of political economy, comparative advantage, and economic performance.

5.2 Diversity of Capitalism and Political Equilibria

As revealed in Chapter 2 the design of institutions results from political choices. The institutional structure both reflects and affects the structure of interests, for individual as well as collective agents. We may then expect to find some correlations between the institutional structures of countries and their political choices, as well as the structure of their political systems. These two elements relate to two different aspects of the polity–institutions nexus; namely, the formation of a socio-political equilibrium and the stability of the system with respect to shifts in political support. Political choices expressed in terms of partisan politics reflect not only the structure of political supply in terms of parties and platforms, but also the constitution of political demand and how this demand is integrated into party politics in order to be implemented by a coalition in power. The most basic dimension separating partisan politics is the left–right scale opposing left-libertarian and social-democratic parties on one side to Christian Democrats and various right-wing parties on the other. The relationship between partisan politics and the diversity of capitalism is expected to be the following. A structure of interests more favourable to institutions characteristic of the market-based model of capitalism should lead to a larger representation of centre and right-wing parties. On the other hand, a stronger weight of left and left-libertarian parties would be expected to support the emergence of institutions closer to the social-democratic model.

Mediation between the expression of interests and the institutional structure is achieved by the political system. Political systems in modern democracies differ with respect to a certain number of features; in particular, the structure of interests' representation. As seen in Chapter 2, one may distinguish between two basic types of political system; namely, a majoritarian and a consensus-based system. The idealized majoritarian system is the Westminster model of democracy, defined by Lijphart (1999) as having ten characteristics: (1) The executive is concentrated in single-party cabinets. (2) Cabinets dominate the parliament. (3) There is a two-party system. (4) The electoral system is majoritarian and disproportional. It is possible for one party to win without an absolute majority in votes. (5) The interest-group system is pluralist; i.e. a multiplicity of interest groups exert pressure on the government in an uncoordinated and competitive manner. Unions and management are not integrated in the policy-making process and both sides settle their differences in a confrontational manner. (6) There is a unitary and centralized government, as opposed to federalism. (7) Legislative power is concentrated in a unicameral parliament. (8) Constitutions are flexible. (9) There is no judicial review, i.e. no written constitutional document with the status of 'higher law' against which courts can test the constitutionality of legislation. (10) The central bank is controlled by the executive. The majoritarian system is best exemplified by the United Kingdom.

The consensus model, by contrast, is based on bargaining between organized interest groups. Those affected by a decision have a chance to participate in the making of that decision. The almost perfect model of consensus democracy is given by Switzerland: (1) The executive power is shared in broad coalition cabinets. (2) There is a balance of power between the executive and the legislative. (3) There is a multi-party system, reflecting a multiplicity of divisions within the society. (4) Electoral systems are organized around proportional representation. (5) Interest representation is based on corporatism—either social corporatism, where labour unions dominate, or liberal corporatism, in which business associations are the strongest force. (6) Government is federalist and decentralized. (7) The parliament is constituted of two chambers, enabling a special representation of minorities such as the smaller states in a federal system in the second chamber. (8) Constitutions are rigid. (9) There is judicial review. (10) The central bank is independent.

There are more veto players in consensus-based democracy than in majoritarian systems, and political equilibrium is reached via a series of compromises on basic issues, where each socio-political group has the possibility of influencing, and sometimes blocking, the decision-making process. Veto players act as a safeguard against a possible questioning of the measures on which the political equilibrium rests. This implies a relatively wide diffusion of the power of decision-making, or at least some stringent consensus requirements before a decision to change is taken. On the other hand, power in majoritarian systems is concentrated in autonomous party leaders and heads of government, who have a much greater capacity to carry out an electoral mandate. In the latter case, even a small change of political majority may have tremendous consequences on the institutional structure and hence on the structure of interests, whereas voting shifts cannot easily translate into policy change in institutionalized compromise-based systems. Political strategy in majoritarian systems is ruled by the quest for the median voter, whereas the search for political compromise between interests expressed in different spheres takes precedence over the definition of political strategy in compromise-based systems. Credible commitments are more difficult in majoritarian than in compromise-based systems.

This differentiation of political systems is paralleled in the diversity of capitalism. As stressed by Iversen and Soskice (2001), certain political systems have specific abilities to make credible commitments with respect to the stability of the institutional environment; for instance, the bargaining between social agents, the regulatory framework of the financial relationship between the firm and its financiers, the type of Welfare State, etc. This institutional stability may be seen as an obstacle to adaptation and 'modernization', but it also acts as *ex ante* incentives to invest in assets whose protection is guaranteed by the presence of certain institutions.[2] Agents who invest in specific assets must be either insured against the possibility of losing their investments[3] or assured that the institutional structure will persist, by means of stable procedures that guarantee the stability of regulations, by-laws, and procedures.

5.2.1 Partisan Politics

Are there identifiable links between partisan politics and the broad features of the different economic models as identified by the analyses presented above? In order to check for possible correlations, we make use of Swank pooled time-series database on political parties and election results (2002). The data covers the period between 1950 and 1999 for all the countries of our sample except Korea and provides information on cabinet-portfolio composition, percentage of legislative seats, and percentage of votes of the major political orientations: left-libertarian, left, right, centre, Christian Democratic, and right-wing-populist parties. Only the 1989–99 period will be considered here. As mentioned above, countries will be characterized by their projection on the first axes of some of our data analyses. The type of capitalism of countries will be assessed

---

[2] See Hall and Soskice (2001); Gourevitch and Hawes (2002).
[3] Welfare benefits act as a protection of investments in specific assets (Iversen and Soskice (2001)).

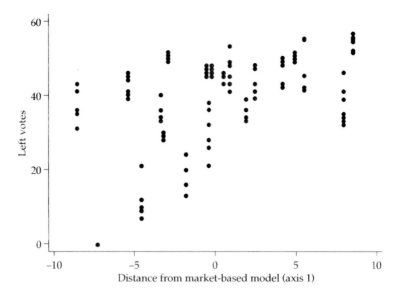

F<small>IG</small>. 5.6 Votes for left parties in lower-chamber elections plotted against the
distance from the market-based model ($r = 0.56^{***}$)

through the projection on the first two factorial axes of the aggregate data
analysis, from which clusters of countries presented in the first section are
deduced. The first axis (Fig. 5.1) divides clearly market-based economies
and Mediterranean countries and will measure the distance from the
ideal market-based model. Likewise, projection on the second factorial
axis will measure the distance from the ideal social-democratic model
(Fig. 5.1).

Figure 5.6 plots the percentage of votes for left parties in legislative
(lower-chamber) elections against countries' projection on the first factorial axis of the aggregate data analysis. It shows that the more similar a
country is to the market-based model, the less is the vote share obtained
by left parties: the correlation coefficient is 0.56, significant at the 1 per cent
level. In other words, as expected, a higher share of left parties' vote is on
average associated with an institutional structure as remote as
possible from the market-based model. This is consistent with the a-priori
expectations: left votes express a demand for specific institutional features,
such as social protection, redistributive policies, and public investments,
which are hardly strong points of the market-based model.

Proximity to the social-democratic model is associated with a higher
percentage of votes for left-libertarian parties (Fig. 5.7); the correlation

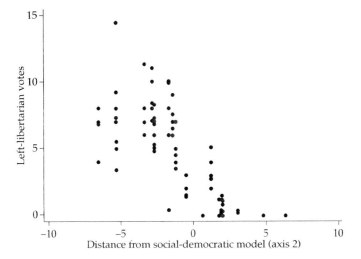

FIG. 5.7 Votes for left-libertarians plotted against the distance from the social-democratic model ($r = -0.72$)

coefficient is 0.72, significant at the 1-per-cent level. A positive correlation between votes for all left parties ('traditional' left and left-libertarian parties) might also be exhibited. A strong support for left-wing politics is thus associated with a model of capitalism closer to the ideal social-democratic one. Political preferences of voters are somehow reflected in a differentiation of institutional structures. Electoral differentiation may go beyond this simple distinction between left and 'traditional' right. A right-wing populist vote is expressed only in countries at a significant distance from the market-based model (Fig. 5.8),[4] for reasons that are partly connected to the political expression of specific interests and partly to the structure of political systems. Regarding the former point, although their political stance is very ambiguous, right-wing populist parties may be held to express a demand for protection emanating from certain groups that would be threatened by economic liberalism and competition, at least in some of the countries of the sample. This could be a demand for restriction of competition expressed by small entrepreneurs, or a demand for social protection expressed by workers who could feel that they are no longer well represented by traditional left parties. Concerning the structure of parties, most market-based economies are close to the Westminster model, at least as far as the two-party system is concerned. Such a system

---

[4] Recent election results may however have changed the picture.

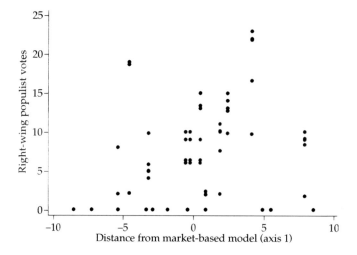

Fɪɢ. 5.8 Votes for right-wing populist parties plotted against the distance from the market-based model

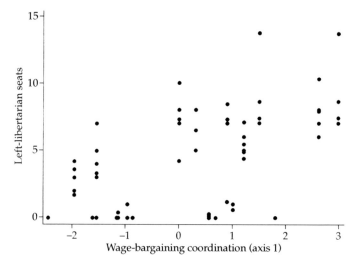

Fɪɢ. 5.9 Number of seats in the lower chamber for left-libertarian parties plotted against wage-bargaining coordination ($r = 0.56***$)

leaves very little scope for the expression of right-wing populist or left-libertarian votes.

The correlations between expressions of political preferences and specific aspects of the diversity of capitalism can be checked by using results from the study performed in Chapter 4. Figure 5.9 shows that there

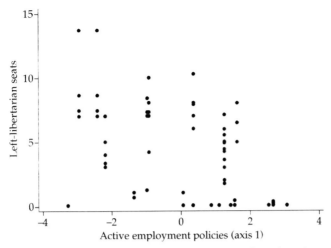

FIG. 5.10 Number of seats for left-libertarian parties plotted against active-employment policies ($r = -0.41$***)

is a strong correlation between the percentage of seats for left-libertarian parties in the lower chamber and the degree of coordination of wage bargaining (countries' projections on the first axis of the analysis of industrial relations in Ch. 4): the correlation coefficient is 0.56, significant at the 1-per-cent level. The correlation is stronger when one takes the number of seats than when taking the number of votes (where the correlation coefficient is 0.51), which suggests that the structure of the political system also matters in the representation of interests, a point that is examined below. The number of seats for left-libertarian parties is also positively correlated with the intensity of employment policies (Fig. 5.10), as shown in the projection on the first axis of the analysis of employment policies. Countries to the left-hand side of the axis have more active policies than countries on the right-hand side of the axis. The correlation coefficient is 0.41, significant at the 1-per-cent level.

As shown in Fig. 5.11, centralization of financial systems, i.e. the greatest dissimilarity from the financial-markets-based system, is positively linked to votes for left parties; the correlation coefficient is 0.46, significant at the 1-per-cent level. This result is consistent with Roe (2000), who stresses the congruence between social democracy and specific features of the financial system such as concentrated ownership. Finally, Fig. 5.12 illustrates the link between the percentage of votes for left-libertarian parties and the extent of the Welfare State (countries' projection on the first factorial axis from the data analysis on social protection). The correlation coefficient is 0.67, significant at the 1-per-cent level.

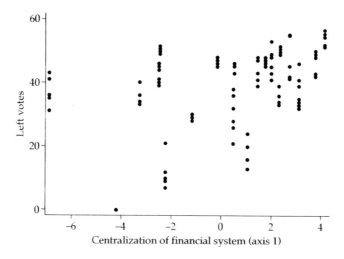

FIG. 5.11 Percentage of vote for left parties plotted against centralization of financial systems ($r = 0.46^{***}$)

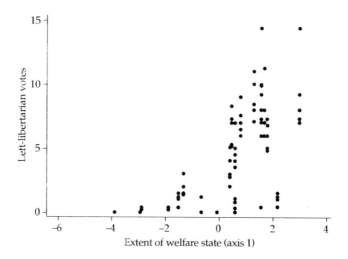

FIG. 5.12 Percentage of vote for left-libertarian parties plotted against the extent of the Welfare State ($r = -0.67$)

Summing up the results so far, partisan politics is significantly associated with some dimensions of the diversity of capitalism. The left–right axis seems to follow the social-democratic to market-based line. A higher proportion of left and left-libertarian votes would express a preference for fewer market-based mechanisms and a more universalist Welfare State.

5.2.2 Political Systems

If votes express the state of political demand, the way this demand is translated into formal institutions depends on the characteristics of the political system. Lijphart (1999) has proposed a certain number of indicators characterizing political systems. Some of them are particularly relevant for stressing the differences between the political systems underlying the different models of capitalism:

1. *The number of issue dimensions addressed by political party programmes.* A large number of political parties allows for the expression of a highly differentiated political demand, which may reflect the strong positions gained by particular socio-political groups. The dimensions of political conflict should increase with the number of parties. A two-party system must have a political platform of the 'catch-all' type, which aims at the median voter and where parties cannot afford to confront specific interest groups on well-defined issues.

2. *The degree of disproportionality of the electoral system.* The typical electoral system of majoritarian democracy is the single-member-district plurality or majority system; consensus democracy uses proportional representation. Single-member districts favour the emergence of a winner-takes-all system. The index of disproportionality gives an indication of the aggregate vote share/seat share deviation.

3. *Interest-group pluralism.* The typical interest-group system of majoritarian democracy is a competitive and uncoordinated pluralism of independent groups, in contrast with the coordinated and compromise-oriented system of corporatism. This indicator can be interpreted as anti-corporatist. One would then expect to see market-based economies associated with high values of the three indicators, whereas Continental European and social-democratic economies should exhibit low values of these indicators.

4. *Constitutional rigidity.* This concerns the presence or absence of explicit restraints on the legislative power of parliamentary majorities. Is the parliament the supreme law-maker or is there a constitution serving as a higher law? There is a distinction between flexible constitutions (changed by a majority) and rigid constitutions (changed by a supermajority). Based on the case of the UK, one would expect market-based economies to have non-rigid constitutions, but this is not so clear when one considers the USA.

Other indicators may also be taken into account. The database of political institutions of the World Bank (Beck, Clarke, Groff, Keefer, and Walsh (1999)) raises the following:

5. *An indicator of political parties' concentration, the Herfindahl index.* This is the sum of the squared seat shares of all parties in the government and

the opposition in the lower chamber. If market-based economies rest on a two-party median-voter system, they should have a higher political concentration than other types.

6. *Fractionalization of legislature.* This is the probability that two deputies picked at random from the legislature will be of different parties. Here again, this indicator should split the market-based economies from the other types, particularly the social-democratic model.

Finally, George Tsebelis' database on veto players[5] gives indicators of the number of veto players for each country as well as the government's policy-position range based on various authors' estimations of ideological positions of political parties on a left–right scale. One can thereby measure whether the government is more or less coalitional or consensual. Tsebelis (2002) and Tsebelis and Chang (2001) stress that what matters is less the number of veto players than the distance between extremes (the range). A large range implies more political stability, while a small range may or may not produce such stability. A coalition including very different parties in an ideological space cannot modify the status quo as well as a coalition with less diversified parties, let alone a majoritarian government. However, there is a clear correlation between the extent of the range of government-policy position, i.e. the diversity of political positions represented within the government, and the number of veto players in the political system, as shown in Fig. 5.13*a–b*. Figure 5.13*a* uses the Castles and Mair index of government-policy range with a left–right scale based on expert judgements.[6] Figure 5.13*b* uses Warwick's measure, generated from forty different measurements based on expert judgements, party manifestos, and survey sources.

One more or less expects that the market-based system should be associated with majoritarian two-party systems, as opposed to other types of capitalism, which aim at preserving the interests of specific socio-political groups through formal political representation and institutional influence of collective agents through the power of veto players. The latter should play an important role in the social-democratic economies and in Continental Europe. One does not expect Asian or Mediterranean capitalism to be based on a consensus democracy. Asian capitalism may exhibit some features of liberal corporatism.

Some of our findings confirm expectations. Market-based economies are characterized by a high degree of concentration of political parties; however, the relation between the distance from the market-based model and the

---

[5] http://www.polisci.ucla.edu/tsebelis/vpdata.html.
[6] See Tsebelis and Chang (2001) for details.

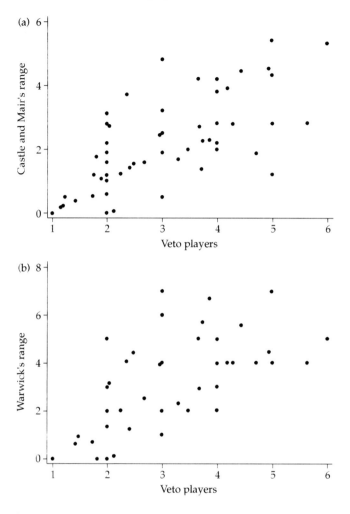

FIG. 5.13 Government policy-position range plotted against number of veto players: (a) Castles and Mair's index ($r = 0.77$***); (b) Warwick's index ($r = 0.73$***)

measure of political concentration is not monotonic, but rather U-shaped, as shown in Fig. 5.14.[7] Economies very distant from the market-based model exhibit a high degree of political concentration too. On the other hand, economies with intermediate positions on the first factorial axis, i.e. Continental Europe, social-democratic economies, and the Asian model, all exhibit a low degree of political concentration. Preservation of specific

[7] As an indication, the OLS estimate including a quadratic term gives: Concentration = 0.25*** − 0.81 distance + 0.03*** distance^2.

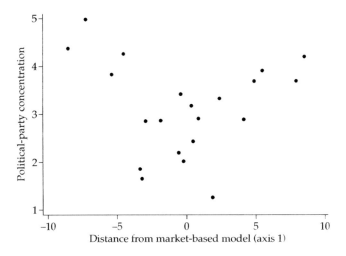

FIG. 5.14 Political-party concentration plotted against the distance from the
market-based model

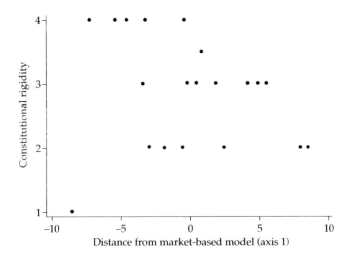

FIG. 5.15 Constitutional rigidity plotted against the distance from the
market-based system

interests is therefore characteristic of three models of capitalism, but does
not simply oppose market-based economies to all the other models as if
they were part of a single homogeneous group. Figure 5.15 shows that
market-based economies tend to have more constitutional rigidity than
other economies, but the association between the two dimensions is not
so strict. In fact, the UK is an outlier characterized by very high constitutional flexibility. To infer from this specific case that the market-based

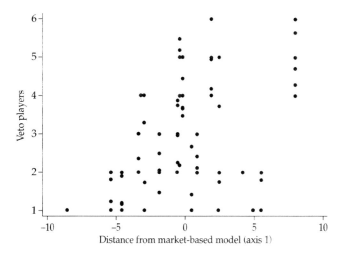

FIG. 5.16 Number of veto players plotted against the distance from the market-based model ($r = 0.23^{***}$)

model is irreconcilable with constitutional rigidity or demands a strict version of the Westminster model would be wrong. Also, market-based economies are clearly those where the number of veto players is low, in accordance with what was expected. Other models of capitalism may develop with high or low numbers of veto players, as demonstrated by the triangle-shaped scatter plot of Fig. 5.16.

Turning now to the distance from the ideal social-democratic model, Fig. 5.17 hints at the possibility of an inverse U-shaped relationship with the measure of political concentration, or simply a positive relationship. This might suggest that protection of specific assets through political-representation diversity is more a European pattern than a universal one. In Asian capitalism, where investment in specific assets is high, channels other than political-parties dispersion help represent the interests of different socio-political groups. The same features are found when one looks at the index of fractionalization (Fig. 5.18). The social-democratic model is based on consensus democracy, as shown in Fig. 5.19, where interest-group pluralism grows with distance from the social-democratic model. Unsurprisingly, disproportionality of electoral systems is antagonistic to the social-democratic model, as shown in Fig. 5.20.

We can examine some of the detailed institutional features associated with some variables characterizing political systems. Veto players are important for product-market regulation (Fig. 5.21), labour-market regulation (Fig. 5.22), and centralization of financial systems (Fig. 5.23). Highly regulated product markets require a large number and deregulated

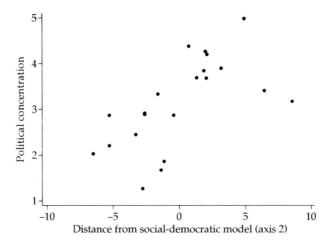

Fɪɢ. 5.17 Political concentration plotted against the distance from the
social-democratic model ($r = 0.62$***)

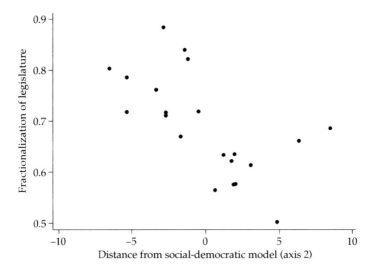

Fɪɢ. 5.18 Fractionalization of legislature plotted against the distance from the
social-democratic model ($r = -0.62$***)

markets require a small number of veto players. Intermediate situations
may accommodate small or high numbers of veto players. The same
features apply to labour-market regulation, particularly for deregulated
markets, which seem to be possible only when the number of veto players
is small. The triangular shape of the scatter plot of the number of veto

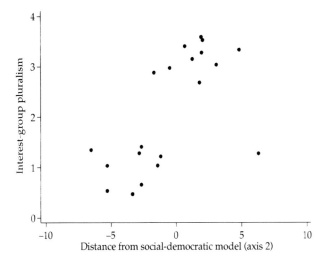

FIG. 5.19 Positive correlation between interest-group pluralism and the distance
from the social-democratic model ($r = 0.64$***)

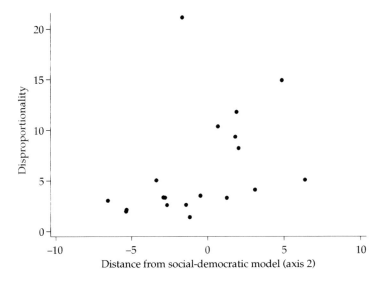

FIG. 5.20 Positive correlation between disproportionality and the distance
from the social-democratic model ($r = 0.41$***)

players against our index of financial-markets centralization hints at the
possibility that the presence of few veto players favours the emergence of
financial-markets-based systems. Finally, coordinated wage bargaining is
possible in proportional electoral systems (Fig. 5.24).

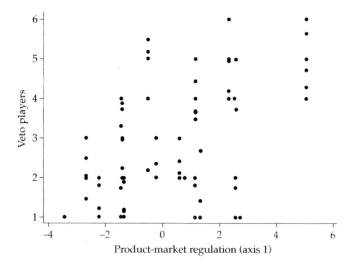

FIG. 5.21 Number of veto players and product-market regulation ($r = 0.42$***)

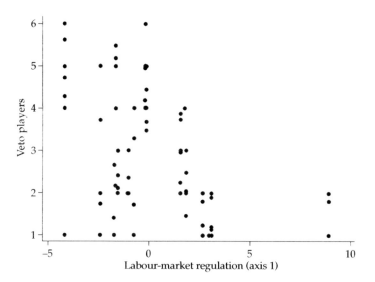

FIG. 5.22 Number of veto players and labour-market regulation

The diversity of modern capitalism, therefore, is correlated with differences in political equilibria. Both partisan politics, expressed through a left–right differentiation, and institutional features of political systems contribute to differentiating our types of capitalism. This gives broad support to the thesis that institutions are the expression of a political-economy equilibrium.

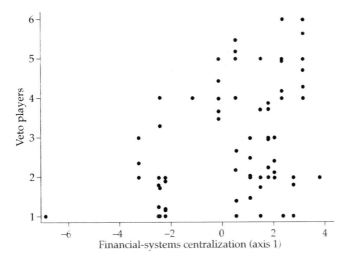

FIG. 5.23 Number of veto players and financial-systems centralization

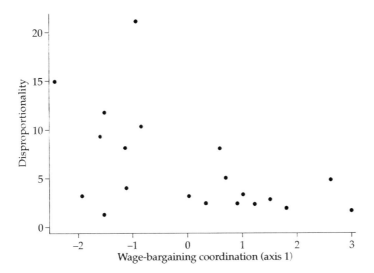

FIG. 5.24 Index of disproportionality and coordination of wage bargaining
($r = -0.52^{***}$)

5.3 Comparative Institutional Advantage?

One of the most distinctive predictions of the 'varieties of capitalism' approach is that there should be strong link between countries' institutional structure and the type of economic activities they specialize in.

Institutions define incentives to invest in certain assets, which are at the origin of competitive advantage in certain activities (Amable et al. 1997). The links between institutions and specialization in science, technology, and industry have already been presented in Chapter 3 with the concept of social systems of innovation and production. More or less detailed stories may also express the relation between competitiveness and institutions. Germany's educational and industrial institutions, such as the dual apprenticeship system, its specific management–union cooperation in the definition of required skills, together with a corporate-governance system based on close ties with banks supplying 'patient' capital, have encouraged the growth of competitiveness in industries where technology diffusion and workers' skills matter most: quality-sensitive, engineering-intensive industries such as advanced machine tools, luxury cars, specialist chemicals (Hall and Soskice 2001). The post-war French system of elite schools and tight administration–business links has facilitated the undertaking of large-scale 'mission-oriented' technological projects such as nuclear power, satellite-launching rockets, and high-speed trains (Amable and Hancké 2001). The American financial system[8] allows the financing of small, technology-intensive undertakings that make intensive use of top university graduates and scientists whose supply relies on a highly competitive university system where research departments are funded for specific research projects by powerful national agencies; the USA may therefore excel in the production of goods where drastic innovation is at the root of firms' competitiveness, such as biotechnology or computer electronics. The link between the radical character of innovation and the type of capitalism might nevertheless not be as simple as one might think. On the one hand, radical innovation often uses a large variety of sources of knowledge and the findings of scientists coming from different disciplines. This would seem to favour scientific systems where circulation of scientists is easy and the funding of research teams flexible, which is a characteristic of competitive and decentralized scientific systems such as are found in market-based economies, particularly the USA and the UK. On the other hand, following a radical innovation path also demands a coordinating capacity and an ability to fund long-term projects with uncertain returns; these capabilities can be found in Continental European systems, particularly in mission-oriented systems.

One would expect the different models of capitalism to exhibit marked differences with respect to their pattern of specialization. The intensity of

---

[8] Allen and Gale (2000) argue that financial markets allow investors to hold more diverse views about investment prospects than bank-based systems, and are thus more favourable to the emergence of new technologies and investment in high-risk activities.

competition in product markets will define incentives to innovate. A more intense price-based competition among firms would push firms towards drastic innovation. A strong quality-based competition might push firms towards incremental or radical innovation, depending on the technological capability of firms as well as the supply of scientific and technological inputs and the skill level of the workforce. Differentiated innovation patterns will define varied competitive advantages in fast-moving technological fields. Labour relations and social-protection systems will influence investment in specific skills, which will also condition competitiveness in industries where these skills are crucial determinants. Employment protection may also play a role in the protection of specific skills. Rapid labour-force adjustments lower the costs of structural change and enable redeployment of the industrial structure towards fast-growing activities. These adjustments may be facilitated by simple labour-market flexibility, defined as the ability to hire and fire at low cost, but social-protection systems may also influence the ease of labour-force adjustments. A developed education and training system coupled with an extensive Welfare State provides many opportunities for retraining the labour force and facilitates restructuring towards high-tech industries, whereas low employment protection and deficient welfare systems discourage investment in specific skills and push country specialization towards activities where skill acquisition does not matter. A recent literature has focused on the relationship between financial-system characteristics, sectoral growth, and comparative advantage. Industries where competitiveness is based on high-risk, short-term investment will thrive in countries where stock markets are well developed, whereas industries based on long-term, low-risk investment are more likely to prosper where bank-based finance is prominent. Carlin and Mayer (2002) propose econometrics-based tests of the hypothesis of a relationship between the structure of a country's financial system, the characteristics of industries, and the growth of investment of industries in different countries. There is a strong relation between information disclosure, fragmentation of the banking system, and concentration of ownership on the one hand and the growth of equity-financed and skill-intensive industries on the other. There is also a link between the institutional structure and the sectoral pattern of R&D investment. Testing for a sample of OECD countries, Svaleryd and Vlachos (2000) show that countries with 'well-functioning' financial systems specialize in industries highly dependent on external finance, and differences in financial systems are more important determinants of trade specialization than differences in human or physical capital.

These results point in the same direction as all the studies on comparative institutional advantage. A mix of institutional features in diverse areas will have far-reaching consequences for the accumulation of competencies upon which sectoral competitiveness is based. There should therefore be a clear correspondence between institutions and comparative advantage or the structure of economic production. However, other influences also determine the pattern of competitive advantage. Following the most traditional theories of international trade, natural-resource endowments should also influence the pattern of activity specialization. One would thus expect Australia and Canada to exhibit a specific pattern of comparative advantage. Some geopolitical influences are present too. A high share of defence expenditures is likely to orient the activity structure towards some high-tech industries, such as aerospace and electronics. This factor is likely to play an important role for the USA, and also for the UK and France.

The links between types of capitalism and activity structure will be assessed by looking simultaneously at the specialization of countries in scientific, technological, and industrial activities. This does not mean that the independence between each domain is neglected. The dynamics of science is partly autonomous from technological demand, for instance, and the tightness of the links between technology and industry depends on the type of specialization: stricter in countries specializing in high technology, looser in low-tech countries. But it seems interesting to consider the whole science–technology–industry nexus in order not to miss the complementarities between each area, and to allow a better comparison with the previously accepted typology of capitalism.

5.3.1 An Analysis of Science/Technology/Industry Specialization

The following analysis will concern patterns of specialization of scientific, technological, and industrial activity at three different dates: 1985, 1989, and 1995. Three-year averages for 1983–5, 1987–9, and 1993–5 respectively are taken into account in order to correct for the effect of short-term fluctuations. The availability of data at different dates will enable us to compare the evolution of countries over time and assess possible convergence or divergence in this respect. The indicator of scientific specialization is defined as the share of a country in the publications of a given scientific discipline relative to the share of this country in all scientific publications; it is thus the relative world share of a country in a scientific field. Thirty-two scientific disciplines will be taken into account: astronomy/astrophysics; molecular biology; general biology; vegetal biology; cancerology; general chemistry; analytical chemistry; medical chemistry; the environment; animals; endocrinology; surgery; genetic engineering; chemical engineering; mechanical engineering; immunology; computer science; biomedical engineering; materials; mathematics;

general medicine; microbiology; multidisciplinary studies; neurology; optics; general physics; applied physics; chemical physics; health; nutrition; other medicine; the earth. Technological specialization will be appreciated with the help of European patent data, i.e. on patents issued by the European Patent Office. The same specialization indicator as for scientific publications will be used: the relative world share. Data is available at a twenty-four-industry disaggregation level: aerospace; radio, television, telecommunications; computers; pharmaceuticals; instruments; electrical machines; non-electrical machines; cars; other transport; chemical products; plastics and rubber; refined-oil products; agriculture; non-mineral products; iron and steel; non-ferrous metals; wood and furniture; paper and printing; metallurgy; shipbuilding; textiles, clothing, leather; services; construction; other industries.[9]

Finally, industrial specialization will be appreciated through trade data, using the same sectoral classification as for patent data. The specialization index used will be the relative contribution to the trade balance. This indicator is based on both exports and imports and avoids the pitfalls associated with export-specialization indices. The relative contribution to the trade balance is defined as:

$$L_{i,j} = \frac{X_{i,j} - M_{ij}}{Y_j} - \frac{X_{i,j} + M_{i,j}}{X_{.,j} + M_{.,j}} \cdot \frac{X_{.,j} - M_{.,j}}{Y_j},$$

with $X_{i,j}$ ($M_{i,j}$) defined as the exports (imports) of country j for industry i. $X_{.,j}$ ($M_{.,j}$) is total exports of country j. $L_{i,j}$ increases with the relative trade surplus of industry i. Twenty-two different industries will be considered: aerospace; computers; electronics; pharmaceuticals; instruments; electrical machines; non-electrical machines; cars; other transport; chemical products; plastics and rubber; refined-oil products; food; non-mineral products; iron and steel; non ferrous metals; wood and furniture; paper and printing; metallurgy; shipbuilding; textiles, clothing and leather; other industries.

The method used for statistical treatment is slightly different from the principal-components analysis (PCA) previously used. Since the same data structure is available for three different periods, it is possible to exploit this data availability and adopt a multiple-factor-analysis (MFA) technique. The data will be split into three different groups with the same structure, each group corresponding to a different date. The MFA weighs differently each group of variables in order to obtain a balanced representation of each group in a common space. No single group of variables (i.e. particular period) can have too large an influence on the final

---

[9] Data for scientific and technological specialization come from the Observatoire des Sciences et des Techniques (Paris). Industry data are taken from the OECD STAN database.

TABLE 5.3 Variables associated with the first three factorial axes

Area	−	+
First axis		
Science	Optics (1985, 1989)	Surgery (1985)
	Applied physics	Medicine (1989)
	Chemistry (1995)	Health (1995)
		Environment (1995)
Technology	Electronics (1985, 1989)	Non-electrical machines (1985)
	Electrical machines (1995)	Metal products (1985)
		Construction (1985, 1995)
		Non-mineral products (1989, 1995)
		Services (1989)
Industry	Computers (1985, 1989)	Shipbuilding (1985,1989)
	Non-electrical machines	Non-ferrous metals (1989, 1995)
Second axis		
Science	Chemistry (1985)	Environment (1985)
	General physics (1995)	Earth (1989, 1995)
Technology	Textiles (1985, 1995)	Refined-oil products (1985, 1995)
	Other transport (1989)	Electronics (1985)
		Computers (1989)
Industry	Non-mineral products	Chemical products
	Textiles (1985)	
Third axis		
Science	Health (1985, 1989)	Earth (1989)
	Other medicine (1985, 1989)	Mathematics (1995)
	Endocrinology (1995)	
Technology	Instruments (1985)	Iron and steel (1989)
	Electronics (1995)	Other industries (1995)
		Other transport (1995)
Industry	Shipbuilding (1989)	Non-ferrous metals (1985)

common representation. The MFA starts with three principal-component analyses (one for each date). The inverse of the largest eigenvalue of each PCA is the weighing coefficient which will be applied to each data group. The countries will be represented in a common space. We have both the average position of each individual country taking into account the three dates, and the position of each country at each separate date. Therefore, it is possible to represent the trajectories of countries in this common space.

Results of the MFA can now be presented. Only the first factorial plane (defined by the first two factors) will be shown. Table 5.3 summarizes which variables are most strongly correlated with the first three factorial axes. The first axis (33 per cent of the variance) is characterized by the opposition between a scientific specialization based on physics and chemistry and a specialization based on health, medicine, and the environment. The technological specialization along this axis separates electronics and electrical machinery from construction, non-mineral products, and services. The trade specialization along this axis separates computers and non-electrical machinery from shipbuilding and non-ferrous metals. A first interpretation of this axis is that it splits countries apart according to the relative importance of natural resources (on the positive side) versus that of manufacturing industry (on the negative side). It would be erroneous to interpret it in simple terms of low-tech versus high-tech specialization, if only because of the position of Finland and Sweden on Fig. 5.25. It also represents a separation between physics on the one side and medicine and the environment on the other. The second axis (15 per cent of the variance) separates traditional manufacturing (light industry) from more technology-intensive industries such as electronics and chemicals. The negative side of the axis is associated with resource- and labour-intensive industries, the positive side with scale-intensive, specialized suppliers and some science-based industries such as aerospace. The third axis (11 per cent of the variance) separates a specialization in

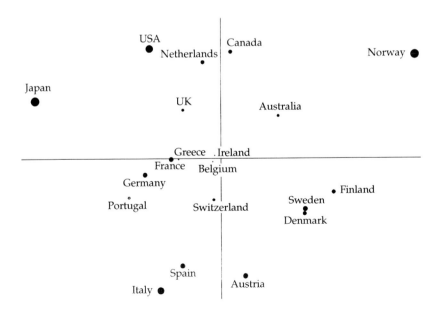

FIG. 5.25 Countries' representation on the first factorial plane

electronics and instruments from a technological specialization in light industry (other transport other industries).

The projection of countries on the first factorial plane (Fig. 5.25) does not exhibit a clear differentiation of clusters. Countries are spread over the plane, reflecting substantial difference with respect to their scientific, technological, and industrial specialization. The cluster analysis identifies five groups of countries (Table 5.4), which partly overlap with the differentiation of models of capitalism. The first group gathers the market-based economies and the Netherlands; among this cluster, one can distinguish the USA, the UK, and the Netherlands from Australia and Canada. The second group draws together Continental European economies and Mediterranean countries. The third group is that of Asian economies, the fourth is Norway, and the fifth is that of the social-democratic model.

The specializations described in Table 5.4 below confirm the results of Amable et al. (1997) and Amable and Petit (2002). The Anglo-Saxon group has a comparative advantage in technologically dynamic activities such as biology and computer science and weaknesses in mechanical industry. This is consistent with expectations; market-based systems have a comparative advantage in new technologies and industries where technological entrepreneurship is likely to matter, and a comparative disadvantage in more mature industries where patient accumulation of competence requires the implementation of patient cooperative strategies. Australia and Canada have a more natural-resources-oriented technological and industrial specialization than the other Anglo-Saxon countries. European countries specialized in more 'traditional' scientific and technological domains (physics, chemistry and mathematics) and electrical machinery. Nordic countries exhibit a scientific and technological specialization oriented towards health and electronics and an industry specialization based on wood natural resources.

Results from the multifactor analysis are broadly consistent with the differentiation of countries into five models of capitalism. However, the characterization of each model in terms of scientific, technological, or industrial comparative advantage is not complete because some countries appear highly idiosyncratic. In order better to understand the specializations characteristic of each model, one can check what the specialization indicators significantly associated with each type of capitalism are, using the cluster analysis of the first section as a basis and projecting data on scientific, technological, and trade specialization using the principal components of that analysis. In addition to the three specialization indicators used above, one can also consider data concerning the structure of industrial production.[10] We take into account the relative share of each industry in each country's

---

[10] Data on industrial production at a disaggregate level come from the OECD STAN database.

TABLE 5.4 Country clusters for scientific, technological, and trade specialization

Clusters	Countries	Common characteristics		Characteristics	
		−	+	−	+
1	USA UK Netherlands		Science: biology, computer science Technology: refined-oil products		Science: computer science Technology: electronics, refined-oil products Industry: chemical products
	Canada Australia			Industry: instruments	Science: vegetal biology, the environment, earth sciences Technology: refined-oil products Science: general physics
2	France Germany Switzerland		Science: physics, chemistry, mathematics		
	Belgium, Ireland Italy, Spain, Austria (Greece, Portugal)	Science: neurology, the environment	Technology: textiles, electrical machines Industry: non-mineral products	Technology: instruments	Science: analytical chemistry Technology: textiles, plastics and rubber Industry: textiles, non-mineral products
3	Japan (Korea)				
4	Norway				
5	Finland Sweden Denmark	Industry: plastics and rubber	Science: health, medicine, surgery Technology: paper and printing, non-electrical machines Industry: wood products	Industry: chemical products	Science: medicine, health Technology: paper and printing, non-electrical machines, electronics Industry: paper and printing

manufacturing sector. Finally, two indicators of performance are also considered. One indicator reflects scientific activity and is the number of scientific articles relative to the GDP level; the other relates to technological activity and is the number of invented patents over GDP. Finally, some indicators of R&D expenditures are also taken into account. The supplementary variables indicate the scientific and technological levels of countries associated with the different types of capitalism. The results are presented in Table 5.5 below and apply to data for the latest period, i.e. 1995.[11]

The scientific, technological, and industrial specializations of each type of capitalism do not differ much from the findings summarized in Table 5.4. Market-based economies have a strong comparative advantage in biology; Asian economies specialize in electronics and machinery; social-democratic economies are strong in health-related science and wood-based industries; Mediterranean countries specialize in 'traditional' scientific activities such as physics and mathematics, and have a trade specialization oriented towards low-tech industries. The Mediterranean model contrasts sharply with the social-democratic model in terms of technological intensity and performance. The good performance of the latter in terms of 'inventiveness' is consistent with the high level of education of its workforce.

The most salient feature of Table 5.5 is probably that the countries of Continental European capitalism are not characterized by a specific pattern of scientific, technological, or trade specialization. This is not surprising if one considers the lack of distinct institutional characteristics of that type of capitalism. The analysis in Section 5.1 hinted at the fact that Continental European capitalism is somehow intermediate between other better-defined varieties of capitalism, which possess much more marked specificities. This has consequences for the pattern of specialization too. Whereas the other types of capitalism can be identified by a few strong points in certain industries, the orientation of Continental European countries in science, technology, or industry is less easy to recognize. The institutions of Continental European capitalism as such do not seem to provide a sufficient basis upon which a clear pattern of specialization can be built.

One could think that this lack of common characteristics stems from the fact that European countries might be similar in terms of institutions but very different in terms of specialization, so that it would be impossible to match the institutional classification with that derived from an analysis of the scientific, technological, and industrial sectors. This however is not the

---

[11] As before, three-year moving averages are taken into account.

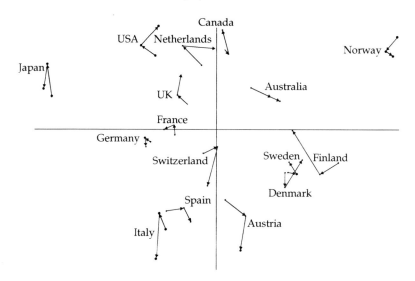

FIG. 5.26 Countries' trajectories on the first factorial plane

correct interpretation. The two 'core countries' of Continental European capitalism, France and Germany, belong to the same cluster, as shown in Table 5.4, and are actually close to one another in the hierarchical classification underlying the whole cluster analysis. Most of the other countries of the Continental European model also belong to the same group, a notable exception being the Netherlands. Therefore, the lack of distinctive specialization does not so much derive from a lack of *common* characteristics among countries as from a lack of distinctive features pertaining to the model altogether. Some pattern of increasing divergence within the group of countries may also be noticed when looking at Fig. 5.26. France and Germany (and Belgium, which is not represented in Fig. 5.26) are remarkable for the stability of their specialization pattern, but other countries, such as Austria and Switzerland, have experienced significant evolutions in the direction of a more pronounced specialization oriented towards labour-intensive or traditional industries. The relative stability of specialization of France and Germany confirms expectations.

One may also note that the UK and the USA follow parallel evolutions in the direction of more technology-intensive activities, but this pattern is not exclusive to market-based economies. It also corresponds to the trajectory followed by Finland (Fig. 5.26). On the other hand, Australia seems to follow a specialization path which diverges from the other Anglo-Saxon countries. A similar path is characteristic of Italy, Austria, Spain, and Switzerland.

TABLE 5.5 The comparative institutional advantage of the five types of capitalism

		Market-based capitalism	Asian capitalism	Continental-European capitalism		Social-democratic capitalism	Mediterranean capitalism
				Switzerland Netherlands	France Germany Austria		
Scientific specialization	+	General biology	Materials, applied physics, chemistry, chemical engineering, optics			Other medicine, health, endocrinology	Analytical chemistry, chemical physics, mathematics
	−		Health, surgery, genetic engineering				
Technological specialization	+		Computers, electronics			Wood and furniture, paper and printing	Other industries
	−	Instruments	Non-electrical machines, metal products				Non-mineral products, textiles, clothing, and leather
Trade specialization	+		Electronics			Computers	
	−						
Industrial specialization	+		Electronics, iron and steel, other industries			Paper and printing, non-electrical machines	Non-mineral products, agriculture, other transport
	−						

Indicator	Sign		
Scientific publication/GDP	+		Mechanical engineering, vegetal biology, the Earth, the Environment
	−	Computer science, mechanical engineering, optics	
Invented patents/GDP	+	Textiles, agriculture, electrical machines	
	−		Paper and printing, non-mineral products, wood and furniture, electronics, non-electrical machines, total patents, agriculture, construction, plastics and rubber, metallurgy, instruments, other industries
R&D	+	Public R&D (execution and financing)	
	−		Total patents, instruments, other industries, chemical products, pharmaceuticals Public financing of R&D R&D expenditures per capita, R&D/GDP ratio

5.3.2 The New Economy

The flexibility and adaptability of the market-based model of capitalism is expected to facilitate rapid technological change. The emphasis on market signals and the generalized market flexibility may be detrimental to long-term, patient technological strategies, but they should ease the transition from one technological paradigm to another through investment in radical technological innovation. On this point, the market-based model is generally expected to be superior to all the other types of capitalism. Financial-market-based systems are considered more liable to supply financing to high-technology start-ups, since these activities require specialized intermediaries, i.e. venture capitalists, which are less developed in financial systems where stock markets are not very active. Also, technology-based firms need to provide sufficient incentives to their managers, and these incentives usually take the form of benefits-related bonuses and stock options, i.e. the types of high-powered incentives upon which market-based capitalism is built. The competitive science systems of most Anglo-Saxon countries also seem to favour the emergence of new ideas likely to be transformed into new-technological enterprises thanks to the institutional environment mentioned above.

A crucial test of the proposition that market-based capitalism favours the exploration of new-technological trajectories can be performed when one looks at countries' relative positions vis-à-vis the new information and communication technologies (ICT), i.e. the 'New Economy'. The term 'New Economy' is sometimes taken as synonymous with the 'weightless economy', i.e. a mix of ICT, the Internet, and biotechnologies, but this latter element will not be considered in what follows. Figures 5.27–5.29 illustrate that ICT seems to be more diffused in market-based economies. A large distance from the market-based model is associated with less value added per capita in ICT, a narrower diffusion of personal computers (PCs) in the population, and a smaller number of connections to the Internet.[12] The correlations in the three figures are quite clear, and they persist even when controlling for the level of GDP per capita. It seems then that market-based economies have a clear lead in at least some aspects of the exploration of the technological paradigm associated to ICT.

This can be checked in a more systematic way by looking at whether variables reflecting the production and diffusion of ICT can be associated with the various models of capitalism. Table 5.6 summarizes the findings. Market-based economies are indeed characterized by a higher production

---

[12] Data on ICT come from Eurostat (2001) and concern the year 1999 or 2000.

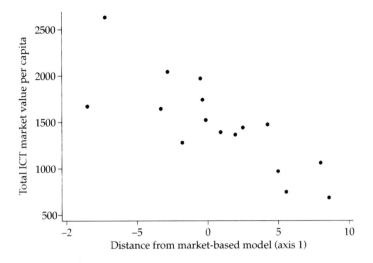

FIG. 5.27 Total ICT market value per capita plotted against the distance from the market-based model ($r = -0.80$***)

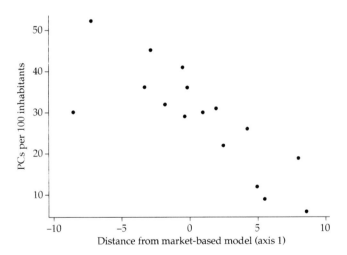

FIG. 5.28 Number of PCs per 100 inhabitants plotted against the distance from the market-based model ($r = -0.80$***)

and diffusion of ICT. By contrast, Mediterranean economies seem to suffer from a significant lag in the 'New Economy', at least in its ICT section. Neither firms nor households seem particularly advanced with respect to Internet or PC diffusion. But another type of capitalism exhibits a lead in ICT diffusion. Social-democratic economies are in fact very specific in their pattern of diffusion of these technologies: in the education sector, for

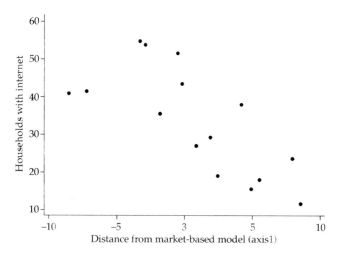

Fig. 5.29 Percentage of households with an Internet connection plotted against the distance from the market-based model ($r = -0.73$***)

Table 5.6 ICT and the models of capitalism

Market-based capitalism	Social-democratic economies	South-European capitalism
+ Total ICT market value as percentage of GDP Internet hosts per 100 inhabitants	Computers connected at secondary-school level Computers per 100 pupils at secondary level GPs communicating with patients over the Internet Web sites of municipalities with e-mail addresses of officers Households using an Internet connection (percentage) Internet users per 100 inhabitants	
−		Enterprises with Internet access (percentage) Internet users per 100 inhabitants Households having an Internet connection (percentage) Total ICT market value per capita (euros) PCs per 100 inhabitants

TABLE 5.7 Correlations between ICT diffusion in SMEs and distance from the social-democratic model (%)

	SMEs with Internet access	SMEs with a website	SMEs with Internet access for business to consumer (B2C)
Distance from the social-democratic model	−3.7***	−2.5***	−1.2**
GDP per capita (log)	18.9	24.8**	−4.6
Adj. R^2	0.59	0.66	0.21

Significance level: * = 10%; ** = 5%; *** = 1%.

health-related matters, and in communication between the population and local administrations, i.e. a pattern broadly consistent with the major features of the social-democratic model and its focus on education, the Welfare State, and democracy. Also, SMEs are more often connected to the Internet or have a web-site when their distance from the social-democratic model is short, as shown by the simple OLS regressions of Table 5.7. This effect is independent of the level of economic development of the country. Therefore, if a large ICT diffusion characterizes market-based economies, it is not exclusive to this model.

5.4 Economic Performance

The debate on the possible convergence between economic systems is often focused on the issue of economic performance. A simple evolutionary argument would predict the elimination of institutional forms that lead to inferior macroeconomic performance and the adoption of those institutions that prove to be efficient; dissatisfied agents would press for institutional change and adoption of the best-practice institutions. The problems with this view have already been analysed, and the political pressures for institutional change will be more precisely analysed in the next chapter. It may nevertheless be interesting to take a look at the comparative macroeconomic performance of the different types of capitalism. The 1990s were dominated by the outstanding growth performance of the United States and the macroeconomic difficulties of Japan and other Asian countries. In Europe, the United Kingdom experienced a decline in unemployment that few countries on the Continent could match, leading to the conclusion that market-based mechanisms were better at ensuring full employment than employment protection. Such macroeconomic performance differentials have fuelled the debate on the responsibility usually attributed to Continental European institutions in prolonged 'Euro-sclerosis'.

The most common thesis is that market-based economies possess superior institutions in times of major economic and technological changes. The all-out superiority of market-based economies needs to be qualified. Using comparative data on manufacturing productivity,[13] one can check the relative position of countries vis-à-vis the United States. Figures 5.30*a–e* display levels of value added per hour worked in manufacturing relative to the US level (=100). There is no overall productivity superiority of market-based economies over other models of capitalism. Variance in manufacturing-productivity levels seems larger across than within models; homogeneity is particularly high in social-democratic and European models, but would probably be lower in the Mediterranean model if data for Italy were available. In any case, the Anglo-Saxon economies do not show clear signs of superiority, and only Spain and Portugal seem to have a serious productivity problem.

Figures on GDP per capita are less favourable for Continental European countries.[14] Figure 5.31 shows a relative decline for Continental European

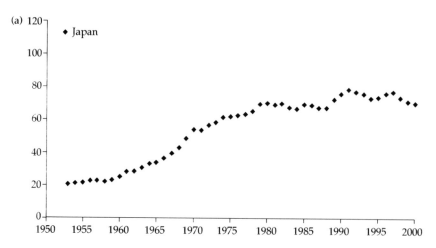

FIG. 5.30 Relative value added per hour worked in manufacturing (USA = 100)

---

[13] Data come from the ICOP industry database summary tables (http://www.eco.rug.nl/ggdc/icop.html).
[14] Data from the University of Groningen and the Conference Board, GGDC total-economy database, 2002 (http://www.eco.rug.nl/ggdc).

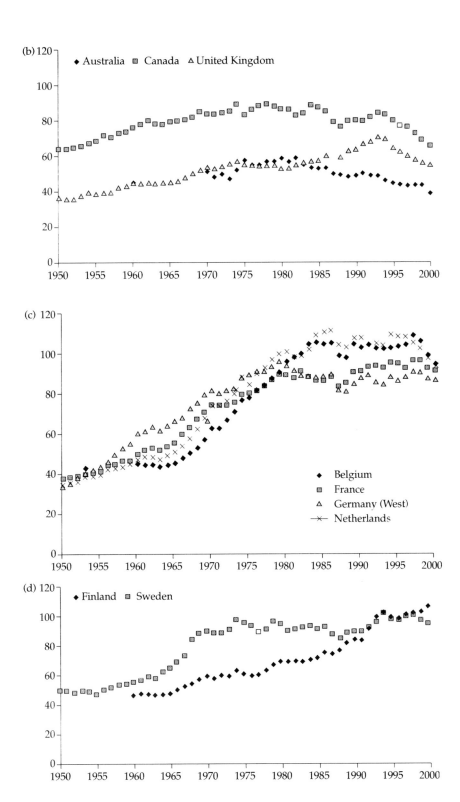

Fig. 5.30 (*Cont.*)

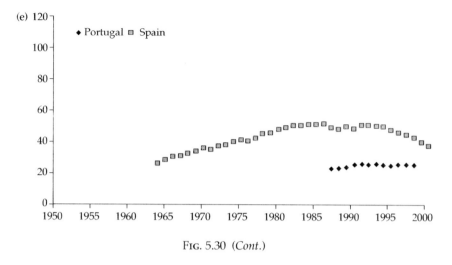

Fig. 5.30 (*Cont.*)

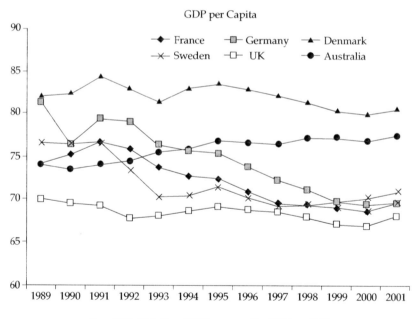

Fig. 5.31 Relative GDP per capita (USA = 100)

countries such as France and Germany. However, if Australia seems to catch up slowly with the USA, one should not generalize this pattern to all market-based economies. The UK level of GDP per capita relative to the USA stays more or less constant throughout the period considered. Besides, the lag of European countries disappears when one looks at a

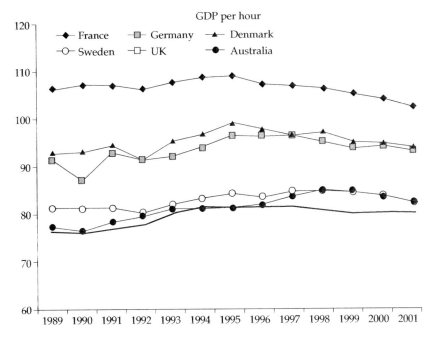

FIG. 5.32 Relative GDP per hour (USA = 100)

more precise indicator of productivity, taking into account the differences in the number of hours worked. Figure 5.32 shows the evolution of the relative GDP per hour worked for the same countries as in Fig. 5.31. The levels are substantially different; the lag of European countries relative to the USA is much more limited, and in fact non-existent for some countries, such as France. Therefore, the differences in levels of GDP per capita should not be interpreted as productivity lags so much as differences in preferences. Europeans seem to favour shorter working hours, even at the expense of a diminished standard of living. However, the relatively high rates of unemployment prevailing on the Continent hint at the fact that this 'preference for leisure' may be imposed by the competitive pressure that makes redundant a large part of the workforce in order to improve productivity.

We can check more precisely the relations between some indicators of macroeconomic performance and institutional variables. As before, the distances from the market-based and social-democratic models will be used, as well as other projections of countries on the first factorial axes of the various data analyses performed in Chapter 4. One can check for systematic relationships between macroeconomic performance and institutional characteristics using regression analyses. Considering data for the period 1989–2001 several models are estimated for a sample of twenty-one countries, testing the impact of institutions both by themselves and in complementarity with other institutions, with the help of interaction effects. If there is, for instance, a complementarity between product-market regulation and labour-market regulation, one expects that good macroeconomic performance should be associated with either a low or a high level of regulation in both product and labour markets. The institutional variables constructed with countries' projections on factorial axes can take both positive and negative signs, so that a low or high value of the interaction term reflecting complementarity between regulation in product and labour markets can be obtained, with positive as well as negative values for both indicators.

We start by looking at the rate of growth of GDP and specify a simple model where growth is influenced by monetary policy through the real rate of interest, private agents' consumption decisions through the saving rate, and possibly the balance of payments through the ratio of net private transfers to GDP.[15] Table 5.8 presents the regression results. Regression (2) shows the effect of institutional complementarity between product-market regulation and coordination of industrial relations. When controlling for the (negative) effects of the real interest rate and the saving rate, product-market regulation has a barely significant positive effect on growth, and coordination in industrial relations has no effect. However, both institutional variables have a significant effect when interacting with each other. Therefore, high growth is possible either with uncoordinated industrial relations and deregulated product markets, or with coordinated industrial relations and regulated product markets. Regression (3) shows that this effect makes the consideration of the distance from either the ideal market-based model or the social-democratic model irrelevant. Regressions (4), (5), and (6) show the effects of multiple interactions. Regulated product markets appear complementary to financial-sector centralization and labour-market regulation. Besides, centralization of the financial system reinforces the complementarity between product and labour markets. This alone would act as a disadvantage for the market-based model of capitalism. However, distance from this model significantly lowers growth in regression (6). To sum up, there does not seem to be a clear growth advantage unconditionally attached to the specific features of the market-based model. Regulated markets and centralized financial systems can deliver good growth performance too.

Another indicator of performance is the productivity level. Data on levels of GDP per hour worked is available from the University of

---

[15] OECD data are used.

TABLE 5.8 Regressions for the growth rate of GDP

	(1)	(2) $	(3) $	(4)	(5)	(6)
Real interest rate	−0.0010429**	−0.0011461***	−0.0011504***	−0.0011696***	−0.0010205**	−0.001703***
	(−2.3)	(−2.66)	(−2.59)	(−2.55)	(−2.25)	(−3.3)
Savings rate	−0.0009778***	−0.0010457***	−0.0010932***	−0.0009355**	−0.0013725***	−0.0010832***
	(−31)	(−2.77)	(−2.96)	(−2.44)	(−3.8)	(−2.62)
Product-market regulation		0.0014904	0.0015198	−0.0000339		0.0015919
		(1.56)	(1.15)	(0.02)		(0.93)
Labour-market regulation				0.0009668	0.0011444*	0.0034503***
				(1.13)	(1.69)	(2.86)
Financial-sector centralization				−0.0000952	0.0001402	−0.005804**
				(−0.12)	(0.21)	(−1.96)
Coordination of industrial relations		−0.000643	0.0013178			
		(−0.77)	(0.88)			
Product- and labour-markets interaction				0.0016329**		0.0014293**
				(2.4)		(2.04)
Product-market and financial-sector interaction				0.0006589		−0.0006528
				(1.31)		(−0.77)
Labour-market and financial-sector interaction				0.0009866***	0.0004249**	0.001484**
				(2.58)	(1.95)	(2.41)
Product- and labour-markets and financial-sector interaction				0.0002463*		0.0001469
				(1.62)		(0.93)
Product-market regulation and coordination interaction		0.001113***	0.0011606***			
		(2.79)	(2.59)			
Distance from the market-based model			0.0002791			−0.0060597**
			(0.37)			(−2.17)
Distance from the social-democratic model			0.0011446		0.0014334**	
			(1.49)		(2.51)	
Net private transfers/GDP						0.0007233***
						(3.44)

Regressions are FGLS with AR1 and panel heteroscedasticity.

$ Panel-specific AR1.

Groningen Growth and Development Centre.[16] The simplest productivity-growth model is probably a straightforward convergence model, where growth is negatively related to the initial productivity level. In order to control for possible positive effects of investment, the saving rate is also added to the model. Regression results are presented in Table 5.9. Regression (2) shows that coordinated industrial relations have a positive effect on productivity growth, and there are positive interaction effects between coordination and product-market regulation. Coordination also positively interacts with centralization of the financial system (regression (3)) and the Welfare State (regression (5)), but not with labour-market regulation (regression (4)). Therefore, these results also suggest that both coordinated and uncoordinated industrial relations can deliver good productivity-growth performance, but in association with specific institutional arrangements.

Table 5.10 presents results for the unemployment rate. A simple Phillips curve relating the rate of unemployment to inflation is specified. A large part of the debate on institutional reform in Europe focuses on labour-market characteristics. The persistence of a high level of unemployment in Europe is attributed to rigid labour markets (Siebert 1997), and the decrease in unemployment in the USA and the UK is held to be the consequence of labour-market flexibility. Regression (1) in Table 5.10 confirms the superiority of the market-based economies in terms of unemployment, and regression (2) substantiates the claim that labour-market institutions have an effect on unemployment. More regulated labour markets are associated with a higher rate of unemployment. However, coordination in industrial relations significantly decreases unemployment, and when this variable is added the effect of labour-market regulation vanishes, either alone or in interaction with coordination. The extent of the Welfare State and public education positively interact with coordinated industrial relations, i.e. contribute to a decrease in unemployment. Finally, regulated product markets alone would have an unemployment-increasing effect, but this effect is reversed by complementarity with a centralized financial system. The results of Table 5.10 suggest therefore that the market-based system is able to deliver good employment performance through a combination of deregulated product and labour markets, a limited Welfare State, a competitive private-funded higher-education system, and decentralized financial markets. However, other institutional complementarities should also be associated with a

---

[16] University of Groningen and the Conference Board, GGDC total-economy database, 2002 (http://www.eco.rug.nl/ggdc).

TABLE 5.9 Regressions for the growth rate of GDP per hour

	(1)	(2)	(3)	(4)	(5)
Lagged level of GDP per hour	−0.0265831***	−0.0202302***	−0.0252693***	−0.0231971***	−0.0278476***
	(−7.4)	(−5.0)	(−6.5)	(−5.6)	(−4.8)
Savings rate	−0.0000705	0.0000119	−0.0000531	0.0000531	−0.0000354
	(−0.4)	(0.0)	(−0.2)	(−0.2)	(−0.1)
Product-market regulation		0.0005168			−0.0000461
		(1.0)			(−0.1)
Labour-market regulation				0.0006331	0.001049*
				(1.1)	(1.6)
Financial-sector centralization			0.0008481*		
			(−1.9)		
Coordination in industrial relations		0.0015138***	0.0014274**	0.0013806**	0.0017691**
		(2.5)	(2.1)	(2.1)	(2.3)
Welfare					0.0002382
					(0.3)
Coordination and labour-market interaction				0.0006597**	
				(2.1)	
Labour-market and welfare interaction					0.0005442**
					(2.0)
Corporatism and financial-sector interaction			0.0007006***		
			(−2.8)		

Regressions are FGLS with AR1 and panel heteroscedasticity.

TABLE 5.10 Unemployment regressions

	(1)	(2)	(3)	(4)	(5)	(6)
Inflation rate	-1.925763***	-1.842482***	-1.703783***	-1.728926***	-1.732079***	-2.175501***
	(-3.71)	(-3.39)	(-3.21)	(-3.19)	(-3.50)	(-4.46)
Distance from the market-based model	0.0385217***					
	(3.83)					
Labour-market regulation		0.0536007**	0.0322166			
		(3.10)	(1.38)			
Coordination in industrial relations			-0.1098233***	-0.134421***	0.0047872	
			(-3.40)	(-4.46)	(0.09)	
Coordination and labour-market interaction			-0.0248491			
			(-1.70)			
Education (public funds)				0.0803202***		
				(3.71)		
Coordination and education interaction				-0.0266873**		
				(-2.03)		
Welfare					-0.1004302	
					(-1.60)	
Coordination and welfare interaction					-0.1052747***	
					(-3.33)	
Financial system						-0.0185222
						(-0.72)
Product market						0.0477623
						(1.57)
Product-market and financial interaction						-0.0181654**
						(-2.66)

Regressions are FGLS with AR1 and panel heteroscedasticity.

TABLE 5.11 Inventiveness regressions

	(1)	(2)	(3)	(4)
R&D/GDP	0.4207656***	0.6040248***	0.5520171***	0.3512235***
	(5.85)	(8.76)	(7.08)	(4.34)
Product-market regulation		−0.020093	−0.0297776	−0.108166***
		(−1.48)	(−1.00)	(−5.14)
Labour-market regulation				0.16097***
				(5.63)
Financial-sector centralization			0.0159064	0.0709569***
			(0.51)	(3.13)
Corporatism		0.1334307***	0.1380573***	
		(5.61)	(4.12)	
Product- and labour-market interaction				−0.0610981***
				(−5.94)
Product-market and financial-sector interaction				0.1085713***
				(9.80)
Labour-market and financial-sector interaction				−0.089308***
				(−8.63)
Product- and labour-markets and financial-sector interaction			0.0184656***	0.0114584***
			(2.50)	(4.38)
Product-market and corporatism interaction		0.0622486***		0.0847713***
		(4.77)		(3.81)
Corporatism and financial-sector interaction			0.0478328**	
			(2.37)	
Product-market and corporatism and financial-sector interaction			0.0231214***	
			(3.71)	
Dissimilarity from the market-based model	−0.0567688***			
	(−9.99)			
Dissimilarity from the social-democratic model	−0.0784494***			
	(−6.14)			

Regressions are FGLS with AR1 and panel-specific heteroscedasticity.

low rate of unemployment; namely, coordinated wage bargaining, regulated labour and product markets, and a centralized financial system.

Last, since the 1990s was the decade of the New Economy and fast innovation in technology-intensive sectors such as computers, electronics, and biotechnologies, it seems natural to consider an indicator of technological performance. Considering the emphasis put on innovation during that decade, a patent-based indicator seems the best choice. The inventiveness ratio, i.e. the number of patents divided by total population, is therefore taken as the dependent variable. The basic model specifies that inventiveness is a function of the ratio of R&D expenditures to GDP.[17] Regression results are reported in Table 5.11. It appears from regression (1)

---

[17] OECD data.

that the market-based model has a clear advantage in inventiveness, but this is also the case for the social-democratic model. These results confirm the findings of Section 5.3 about the scientific performance of the latter model and the wide diffusion of ICT in countries of both types of capitalism. Adding institutional variables reveals that product-market regulation may be detrimental to innovation when taken alone, but not in conjunction with other institutional features such as a non-flexible labour market or centralized financial system. The coefficients for the interaction terms reveal that product-market regulation is unfavourable to innovation even when combined with labour-market regulation, unless there is centralization in the financial sector. This could be interpreted as the existence of at least two ways to obtain a high-innovative performance. The first one is the liberal market way, with product market deregulation combined with labour 'flexibility'. The other way would combine coordination with product-market regulation provided a centralized financial system is present in order to secure long-term financing. This model would come near to the ideal-typical social-democratic model but also to some of the features of the Continental European model.

6

Whither Continental European Capitalism?

The aim of this chapter is to assess the viability of the Continental European model of capitalism in a context of institutional change at both the national and the EU level, and political restructuring affecting particularly the forces most associated with the defence of a specific European model different from Anglo-Saxon society and market-based capitalism, i.e. the social-democratic parties. The previous chapters have shown that European economies do not for the most part adhere to the institutional framework characterizing the market-based model of capitalism. Among EU countries, only the United Kingdom unambiguously belongs to this model. The other EU economies do not follow a homogeneous pattern; one can distinguish the group of Nordic economies, which represent the social-democratic model, the South European countries, which follow the principles of Mediterranean capitalism, and a group of countries characterized as the Continental European model of capitalism. The latter model can be defined in theoretical terms as in Chapter 3. It possesses some of the features of the social-democratic model in a more modest form, such as a less extensive Welfare State, for instance, and less active labour-market policies. Product-market competition is more regulated than in market-based economies and employment protection is not as strong as in the Mediterranean model. The empirical characterization of the Continental model proved more problematic though; if indeed the Continental model appears as a specific group, there is less homogeneity among countries of this group than in other clusters. Since our empirical analysis concerns the late 1990s, a relative lack of clearly identifiable common elements among these countries could be interpreted as a sign of the demise of the Continental European model, under the pressure of market liberalization and globalization. This raises the question of the path that European countries might follow, and the model towards which they might converge.

In fact, the institutions of the Continental European model came under pressure during the 1990s because of their alleged inferiority compared to those of the market-based system. The main criticism of the Continental European model can be summed up as follows. Labour-market rigidity prevents labour-force adjustments and structural change and is at the root of mass unemployment. A dwindling employed labour force endangers social-protection systems, which in themselves are unable to prevent an increase in social exclusion and impose too high levels of taxation detrimental to the competitiveness of European territories. Bank-based financial systems are too rigid to allow the financing of small, technology-intensive firms upon which the dynamism of the new technological paradigm is based. The combination of these deficiencies produces sluggish growth and high unemployment in the European Union, particularly in comparison to the United States. The only European countries that have enjoyed relatively good economic performance are those that were able to break from the institutional constraints characteristic of the European model and move towards more market-based institutional forms.

Two institutional areas have had a crucial importance in the questioning of the European model: the enlarged wage–labour nexus, including both labour-market and social-protection institutions, and the financial system. These two areas have experienced significant change during the last decade, and their transformations are at the heart of the viability of the European model. This chapter will look at the transformations that have taken place in these domains. But, as Chapter 2 stressed, institutional change is a political process, and any large-scale institutional transformation must be borne by a political project. The neo-liberal project in Europe was heralded by Margaret Thatcher and was implemented with considerable effect in the UK in the 1980s, but left very few marks on the Continent, where timid attempts at putting it into practice were met with considerable political opposition.[1] Market-oriented institutional change did take place in Europe, but as the result of piecemeal modifications sometimes driven at the supranational, EU level. In the 1990s the most significant political project involving substantial institutional change in a market-oriented direction was on the left. It was called the 'Third Way' and seems hardly to exist under that name at the moment, but is nevertheless present under various appellations in most European social-democratic parties.[2] The transformation of the European model is also taking place in a context of globalization and European integration, where the various political projects are also opposed to one another, in a supranational context.

6.1 The European Context

A widespread thesis is that the globalization of markets increases the competitive pressure on economic systems and implies the homogenization of

---

[1] As, for instance, in France between 1986 and 1988.

[2] Opponents name this current 'Social-libéralisme' in France, 'la sinistra liberista' in Italy.

institutions; this homogenization should be made along the lines of the market-based model. Globalization is a process that involves many dimensions. It is sometimes assumed that the diffusion of new ICT technologies will 'kill distance' and induce a massive wave of relocation and transformation of the product chain (Cairncross 2001). This gives new opportunities for multinational corporations (MNCs) to shift part of their production to low-cost areas—all the more so that the institutional process of trade and financial-services liberalization facilitates the mobility of factors and goods. These transformations question the role of the nation-state as a regulator of economic activity. It is no longer possible to defend national producers against foreign competition or to prevent domestic firms from relocating abroad. Any national factor that contributes to increasing production costs relative to other countries is therefore a potential cause of economic decline: tax policy, restrictive employment, product-market legislation, etc. Global firms are able to relocate where the production possibilities are the most profitable, and this considerably raises the competitive pressure on territories. In this context, the chances of survival of the Continental European model, but also of the social-democratic model, appear pretty slim. Skill-biased technological progress, having increased the demand for high skills, has induced a widening of the income range, putting wage regulation and solidaristic arrangements under pressure and eroding political support for redistributive policies, taking account of the fact that the impact of these regulations in combination with increasing intra- and extra-European competition is to price low-skilled workers out of employment, limiting employment growth at the lower end of the income range and augmenting the social burden shouldered by the employed. Wren (2001) presents the trilemma related to wage regulation, employment, and social spending as follows. Only two of the following three elements can be simultaneously maintained: employment creation, income equality, and budgetary restraint. There are three different policy options related to this trilemma. The social-democratic response keeps equality and employment creation at the expense of budgetary restraint. The Christian Democratic option maintains equality and budgetary restraint but gives up employment creation. The neo-liberal solution accepts inequality and keeps a balanced budget while enabling employment growth. The viability of both the Christian Democratic and social-democratic solutions in Europe seems problematic. Most Continental European countries adopted the former solution during the 1990s; unemployment soared and stayed at high levels during the whole decade. But sustained low employment growth is most probably not a political solution for the long run.

Implementing the social-democratic response could also come up against some problems at the European level. A lax budget policy is ruled out by the Maastricht and Amsterdam Treaties, strictly limiting budget deficits to 3 per cent of the GDP under the Stability and Growth Pact. Augmenting welfare expenditures while respecting the budget-deficit constraints would imply a rise in taxes that is commonly held as a non-serious option in an era of globalization and tax competition, particularly in the absence of tax harmonization in Europe. This would leave the neo-liberal solution as the only available option. Besides, this solution, which would amount to adopting the market-based model, is often held to possess advantages in its own right, since globalization and an increasing pace of technological progress require a capacity in countries to realize fast adjustments of prices and quantities, which is precisely one of the main characteristics of the market-based model.

The alleged convergence towards a market-based system can also be traced at the supranational level. The process of European integration since the Rome Treaty has been mostly dominated by a move towards market liberalization. In this sense, it was a neo-liberal project from the outset (Pollack 1998), and was met by more or less sporadic political opposition on the left for that reason. In competitive product markets, economic integration led to the completion of the single market in the early 1990s and the pursuit of liberalization and State retrenchment throughout the decade. Surveys of regulatory reform (Gonenc, Maher, and Nicoletti 2000) show that substantial change has occurred in Europe with the elimination of entry barriers to some markets, and some activities previously run by the government have been handed over or returned to the private sector. An increase in product-market competition in already competitive segments is likely to alter the functioning of the Continental European model, but not destabilize it altogether. As seen in the previous chapters, moderate competition in product markets in complement-arity with a certain degree of labour-market regulation contributes to stabilizing the environment of firms and facilitates the implementation of long-term strategies. The completion of the single market is not a revolutionary change in this respect, and the Continental European model of capitalism has blossomed in times of increasing openness to competition, since the late 1950s at least. One should not expect that further increases in product-market competition alone will radically transform this model. Transformations with more wide-ranging consequences concern the liberalization of financial services and increasing capital mobility, as well as the liberalization and privatization of network industries such as electricity, telecommunications, and railways, which were previously shielded from competition and were run within national boundaries, with general-interest goals of service provision. This move triggered concerns over the possibility of maintaining the standards of availability, equality, and affordability of these services after their privatization and restructuring. The separation between the network infrastructure, which should have one owner in order to benefit from scale economies, and the provision of services, which should be open to competition in order to lower prices and increase consumer choice, raises the question of equality of access. A pure competitive mechanism could lead to such a large increase in the access price charged to some customers that it would represent a de facto denial of access.[3] More generally, strictly competitive pricing prevents cross-subsidization and price equalization and destabilizes the mechanisms upon which equality of access rests. Therefore, maintaining access equality as a principle requires a departure from strict competitive pricing and should be assured through a political process of market-correcting regulation in order to compel private operators to provide services at a 'reasonable' cost for all consumers even if this contradicts firms' efficient pricing rules. Whether such a process of re-regulation will take place in all circumstances is a matter of European politics. The notion of general-interest services has been acknowledged as a key element of the European model of society on several occasions, particularly in the Treaty of Amsterdam, but as a result of political action and against some resistance within Europe.

One could portray the situation in Europe in the following terms. Hooghe and Marks (1999) argue that two different political projects regarding European integration are opposed, and this conflict can in large part be interpreted on a left–right axis. The neo-liberal project seeks to preserve markets from political interference by combining European-wide market integration with minimal European regulation. Any European-level institutions aiming at regulating markets are rejected in favour of the promotion of a principle of competition among national governments to provide a regulatory environment that mobile factors of production would find attractive. By contrast, the project for regulated capitalism would implement a variety of market-enhancing and market-supporting legislation to create a social-democratic dimension to European governance. This project attempts to increase the capacity of European-level institutions for regulation. The two European-integration projects can be interpreted in our framework of the diversity of capitalism as an opposition between the promotion of market-based capitalism and

---

[3] For instance, for customers located in remote areas.

the effort to find a new version of Continental European capitalism no longer resting on national political institutions but on European-level institutions. In a way, this strategy would be an attempt at creating a social market economy at the European level. Several efforts were made to apply this strategy during the 1990s. The most significant is probably the Delors White Paper on 'Growth, Competitiveness, and Employment', which proposed a strategy for reducing unemployment based on a large investment programme in infrastructure (energy, transport, and telecommunications) financed by both private and public investors, a European social pact trading off job creation against wage restraint, and reform of the labour market with the aim of increasing the intensity of growth of employment; this last point would involve a reform of the Welfare State. In parallel, a working group of the Party of European Socialists published a report presenting a two-pillar strategy to preserve the European social model: an investment-led strategy and a labour-market approach combining a reduction in working time, flexibility in work organization, an active labour-market approach, and skills formation. The report also advocated the use of active monetary policy (Aust 2001). This type of strategy would also imply a certain degree of coordination at the European level, among governments as well as between governments and the ECB regarding fiscal policy, but also between social agents, aiming at some type of European collective bargaining. This would create the institutional conditions for a sustainable mix of supply and demand policies favourable to long-term growth (Vandenbroucke 2001).

However, putting this strategy into practice proved to be extremely difficult, for lack of political support. The Delors strategy was never implemented, facing opposition from most conservative European governments. Besides, 'traditional' social-democratic parties were faced with the prospect of increasingly uncertain electoral results at the beginning of the 1990s. This was generally perceived as a sign of the generalized failure of the social-democratic strategy, and particularly its inability to solve the problems of the Welfare State (Kitschelt 1999). In short, the Continental European model was a dead end, as acknowledged by its inferior economic performance and the impossibility of building political alliances to support it at either the national or the EU level. The reversal of electoral fortunes of left parties after the mid-1990s seemed to prefigure important institutional change in European societies, but hardly constituted a return to the promotion of a social-democratic or Continental European model. Social-democratic parties won elections again in the largest European countries after 1995. The victory of Romano

Prodi's centre-left Olive Tree Coalition in 1996 was a first step, but the real landmark was Tony Blair's landslide election in 1997, which put an end to eighteen years of Conservative government in Britain. After the victory of the socialist–communist–green party coalition in France the same year and that of the social-democrat–green party coalition in Germany in 1998, which came after sixteen years of conservative ruling under Helmut Kohl, most European governments were dominated by social-democratic parties. But this comeback of the left parties was made on programmes that differed substantially from the 'traditional' social-democratic position. The vanguard of the new European left was the UK, with Prime Minister Tony Blair, leader of 'New Labour' and active promoter of the 'Third Way', not only in his own country, but also right across Europe. This particular strategy was presented as a means of overcoming the pitfalls of traditional social democracy without taking the neo-liberal route, and implied significant institutional change. Its influence on European politics, and not only on the left, was very significant, and it still represents one of the most important references for the construction of a left party platform in European countries.[4] I argue that the political programme of the Third Way and the institutional change that it implies represent a dramatic departure from the Continental European model of capitalism by altering its key components and undermining the core complementarities upon which it is built. In order to investigate this matter more closely, it is worth presenting the political project the Third Way embodies.

6.2 The Third Way and the Continental European Model

6.2.1 A Crash Course on the Third Way[5]

It is difficult to give a simple or even a comprehensive picture of the Third Way, for it is a theoretical object whose contours are not clearly defined. The aim of what follows is merely to give a broad overview of the main themes behind this political strategy, in so far as they relate to the questions of the diversity and evolution of modern capitalist economies. If there is a *third* way, this means that it aims to represent an alternative to two other ways. What are they? The most common answer to that question is that the Third Way is located beyond left and right

---

[4] In fact, the Third Way's influence extends over the centre-left and towards the centre-right.

[5] For presentations and analyses of the Third Way, see Powell (2001) and Bonoli (2001).

(Giddens 1994)[6] being neither neo-liberalism nor social democracy, or in other words neither new right nor old left. A slightly different presentation would locate the Third Way more clearly within the (centre-)left,[7] being neither old European-style social democracy nor American-style 'new left' (Blair 1998). From another, related, point of view, the Third Way can be held to represent a middle ground between the American economic model and the Continental European social model.

The Third Way is often presented as a 'modernization' of social democracy, or as the 'modern left', and the rhetoric of modernization plays a tremendously important role in the opposition between the social-democratic values and the 'new left'. Indeed, the very notion of modernization is crucial for the social theory of Anthony Giddens, the most prominent theorist of the Third Way (Giddens 1994, 1998, 2000). Giddens analyses the transformation of modernization throughout history and distinguishes between the current era of 'reflexive modernization' and the period of 'simple modernization' which preceded it. Modernization is defined with reference to scientific knowledge and its applications to production, and in particular to the diffusion of new forms of transport and communications technology. The development of capitalist economic relations is one of the aspects of simple modernization, along with the diffusion of political democracy. Simple modernization has deeply affected societies, but some of their aspects nevertheless remain influenced by tradition; for instance, the family and gender roles. What distinguishes simple modernization from reflexive modernization is precisely the way these traditional aspects are affected.

At this stage globalization enters the picture, characterized not only by an increase in factor mobility, with its resulting risks and opportunities for individuals and governments, but also by a transformation of the relation that the individual entertains with time and space. Globalization affects traditional social ties through the consequences of the invention and diffusion of new transport and communication technologies. These new technologies allow a delocation of social relations and their redeployment across time and space. The accelerated process of globalization has, through its 'distanciation' of social relations, allowed for the emergence of a post-traditional society. Individuals now have access to a much wider choice not only of goods but more fundamentally of lifestyles and

---

[6] See also McCullen and Harris (2000). Pollack (1999) cites Philip Gould's political agenda for modernizers of the Labour Party as a combination of the right and the left, right on crime, welfare, immigration, discipline, tax, and individualism, left on NHS, investment, social integration, opposition to privatization, and unemployment.

[7] 'The Renewal of Social Democracy' is the subtitle of Giddens (1998).

types of work; they are no longer constrained by traditional roles. In fact, they are constantly faced with a much wider range of choices concerning their lifestyle and have entered an era of 'self-construction'; self-identity is thus a crucial issue in modern societies. This growing reflexivity in all aspects of society characterizes the current phase of modernization. Individuals are more dependent on using information in an active way to construct their life. They must be more receptive to information to decide what they want to do, how they want to live, and who they want to be. This has obvious consequences for the family and gender equality but also increases the importance of education.

Communitarianism is another important aspect of the Third Way and distinguishes it from simple neo-liberalism. A commitment to the community can act as a substitute for the pursuit of self-interest that characterizes individualism and neo-liberalism. Communitarianism considers that individuals are socially embedded. In the words of Raymond Plant, 'the self is at least in part constituted by the values of the community within which the person finds him or herself' (Plant 1991). This appeal to the community can serve as a foundation for developing a political project regarding matters of welfare. 'Communitarianists'[8] blame individualism and neo-liberalism for the emergence of a culture of dependency. Etzioni (1995) proposed to reconsider the link between rights and responsibilities and stressed that some responsibilities do not entail rights. The community should be such that individual autonomy and the common good should be made compatible. From an economic point of view, this means making the free market 'friendlier' and ensuring that social exclusion is prevented, by allowing individuals access to paid work as well as favouring local communities and the voluntary sector. One may deduce that institutions that generate a strong opposition between 'insiders' and 'outsiders' are part of the problem; this introduces the issue of labour-market deregulation, which is so important for the economics of the Third Way. This appeal to community is sometimes held to be a rebuttal of traditional neo-liberal individualism, exemplified by the famous quote from Margaret Thatcher: 'There is no such thing as society'. However, as pointed out by Pollack (1999), this quote is often taken out of context, since it continues as follows:

There are individual men and women, and there are families. And no government can do anything except through people, and people must look to themselves first. It's our duty to look after ourselves and then, also, to look after our neighbour. People have got the entitlements much in mind, without the obligations. There is no such thing as entitlement, unless someone has first met an obligation.

---

[3] In particular Amitai Etzioni (see Etzioni (1995)).

This statement could be integrated into a communitarian manifesto without too much difficulty. The only difference would stem from the priorities set in the Thatcherian discourse: look after ourselves *first* and *then, also,* after our neighbour. Communitarianism would not put the individual first in such a blatant way.

The communitarian vision may be distant from neo-liberal individualism, but it is predominantly very different from 'old' social-democratic ideas. The latter in particular are blamed for spreading egalitarianism and the culture of dependency through their defence of the Welfare State. In fact, egalitarianism and redistribution are often associated with individualism by Third Way politicians such as Tony Blair (Goes 2000). The welfare politics of communitarianism, and, one may say, of the Third Way, is organized around the notion of welfare to work, understood as a way to promote reciprocity between the individual and the State. It is related to the notion of 'supply-side citizenship', which stresses that citizenship is an achievement and not a status; it is achieved by participating in the labour market and being rewarded for this (Plant 1998). In this perspective, equality of opportunity plays an essential role; equality of outcomes on the other hand is not an aim in itself. It is up to the State to ensure that the conditions are provided for citizens to have a fair chance and to take on their responsibilities. This primarily concerns people's ability to acquire marketable skills. Investment in skills is part of equal opportunity as a right of citizenship. For Giddens (1994) the aim of good government is to promote the pursuit of happiness. Therefore, both individual and social 'welfare' should be defined with respect to happiness, not material wealth. Happiness is promoted by security of mind and body, self-respect, and the opportunity for self-actualization. Giddens (1998) insists on the rise of 'post-materialist' values, among which one counts issues such as the environment, new gender roles, and a new type of family, and of course self-identity. New production and managerial techniques[9] allow the development of self-actualization and self-esteem; they make more intensive use of the most intrinsic human qualities. Therefore, the goals of social welfare in a modern society are to allow individuals access to work, through which happiness and self-actualization can be pursued. A welfare system that only provided material wealth would thus miss the point. As a policy consequence, the Welfare State needs reforming in order to encourage work and to rebuild society on an ethic of mutual responsibility, where people have to 'take out what they have put in', in Tony Blair's own words.[10]

---

[9] Explicit reference is made to 'lean production' in Giddens (1994).

[10] Tony Blair in a 1997 speech quoted in Goes (2000).

6.2.2 The Economics and Economic Policy of the Third Way

The presentation of the Third Way so far hints at a major questioning of the basis on which European Welfare States are built, which is an indication of the direction a Third Way economic policy can take. It is nevertheless rather difficult to define what the economics of the Third Way really is, even if one limits oneself to Great Britain, since 'Gordon Brown, the architect of Labour's policy has seldom uttered the words third and way in the same sentence. Anthony Giddens, Labour's favourite intellectual, is not an economist and restricts his analysis of such matters to some propositions about why command economies don't work anymore' (Arnold (2000)). In fact, Arestis and Sawyer (2001) argue that the economics of New Labour and of the Third Way differ substantially, which is hardly surprising, since the economic policy followed by any government is the result of political compromises rather than strict adherence to a theoretical framework.[11] In any case, the main elements of what could be 'Third Way economics' are a mixture of (chiefly) new classical and (sometimes) new Keynesian economics and can be summarized as follows (Arestis and Sawyer 2001):

1. The market economy is governed by the mechanisms analysed in endogenous-growth theory, most notably human-capital accumulation.
2. The market economy is essentially stable; macroeconomic policy such as discretionary fiscal interventions may destabilize it. Rational expectations govern financial and other markets, so that prices are crucial information carriers. Financial markets are essential in providing a well-informed judgement on the sustainability and credibility of policies.
3. Monetary policy can be used for inflation targeting, not for lowering unemployment; it should be left in the hands of experts, not politicians.
4. There is a NAIRU.[12] Inflation is a monetary phenomenon.
5. Say's Law holds, at least in the long run. Fiscal policy has at best a passive role; the budget should be balanced over the course of the business cycle.
6. The market involves market failures because of externalities, public goods, imperfect competition, etc.

---

[11] See also Glyn and Wood (2000).
[12] Non-accelerating inflation rate of unemployment.

7. Inequality of opportunity should be erased; inequality of outcomes is not bad in itself, since it provides incentives to work and acquire skills. This standpoint implies a shift in the focus of economic policy from the implementation of a progressive tax system and a redistributive social-security system to employability policies encouraging education and human-capital accumulation. The market outcomes have a 'winner takes all' element, but this is the price to be paid for an efficient incentive mechanism.

8. Globalization has eliminated possibilities for industrial, fiscal, and monetary policies. Targeted policies should be dropped in favour of 'economic environment' policies, i.e. those that foster the competitiveness of firms.

The first and seventh points are coherent with reflexive modernization and emphasize the importance of education (i.e. human-capital accumulation) in the supply-side policy of the Third Way. The second, third, fourth, and fifth points represent a farewell to Keynesianism. Giddens accepts the victory of neo-liberal supply-side economics over Keynesian demand management, and likewise the victory of free markets over a command economy.[13] The last point, about the ineffectiveness of industrial policies, can be put within a broader context of the effects of globalization. What is needed is a wave of supply-side policies favouring education, infrastructures, and the competitiveness of territories, thus more a general economic environment than a set of targets. More generally, it is held that globalization imposes new constraints on governments, limiting the action of the State and implying that its missions need to be redefined.

This also leads to considering favourably attempts to make the labour market more flexible. Any divide between insiders and outsiders is a limit to social inclusion—which is defined with respect to paid work—and circumscribes the possibilities for self-actualization of individuals. Rather than protect employment and jobs, a 'modern' employment policy should foster the employability of individuals through training and inclusion. Point 6 represents the 'new Keynesian' aspect of Third Way economics. However, recognizing the existence of market failures gives no indication of how they should be corrected. Points 7 and 8 probably represent the most significant contribution of the Third Way to an original economic policy, and the most direct attack on the Continental European model of capitalism. Combined with the other points (particularly 1, 2, 3, and 4),

---

[13] 'Keynesianism worked tolerably well in a world of simple modernisation; but it could not survive in a world of reflexive modernisation' (Giddens (1994), 42).

they define an economic-policy agenda consisting of the abandonment of redistributive policies, the favouring of orthodox restrictive macroeconomic policies, generalized welfare retrenchment, and a substantial flexibilization of the labour market—i.e. a major break from the Continental European model of capitalism and an orientation towards the market-based model.

From a Third Way standpoint, neo-liberal supply-siders are right in their criticism of the Welfare State. The Third Way is however opposed to the individualism and social disintegration characteristic of neo-liberalism. New solidarities must be found, with reference to some communitarian ideal. Welfare institutions are in crisis because they are based on a society transformed by 'simple' modernization. For example, they assume their recipients will be drawn from a relatively homogeneous working-class family where patriarchy is the norm. In other words, the 'male bread winner' base of the Bismarckian welfare regimes has waned and the current era of reflexive modernization calls for a different type of welfare.

The Third Way challenges the 'traditional' positions of social democracy on several counts. For Third Way analysts, more social expenditure will not automatically lead to a reduction in socio-economic inequality; this could be tagged the 'social-policy ineffectiveness' thesis of the Third Way. As a consequence, spending effectiveness should be looked for. Besides, welfare entitlements have a passive quality and thus contribute actively to the spread of the culture of dependency. A Third Way policy would be to 'transform the safety net of social entitlements into a springboard to personal responsibility' (Blair and Schröder 1999). More generally, some major socio-economic transformations must be taken into account in the definition of economic policy. Labour-market demand-changes in favour of the highly skilled and the ongoing changes in family structure—with a more active role for women as well as increases in life expectancy—are not sufficiently taken into account in the traditional social-democratic version of the Welfare State.[14] The 'social-democratic' European Welfare State should thus be replaced by a 'social-investment State' that would ensure equality of opportunities rather than equality of outcomes, and employability, based on welfare to work, and would grant no rights without responsibility. Social justice would mean social inclusion, fundamentally through participation in active and paid work.

This has several consequences in terms of the politics of the Third Way. Whereas traditional social democracy, i.e. the 'old left', was positioned

---

[14] No difference is made between 'Bismarckian' and 'social-democratic' or universalist Welfare States at this stage.

according to the divisions in industrial society, i.e. mostly the capital–labour conflict, the new left must seek to adopt a position with respect to the divisions found in a post-industrial or post-traditional society: man–woman, young–old, socially excluded–socially included, etc. The traditional social basis of the old left, i.e. industry workers and civil servants, has substantially declined, or is bound to, following the new conditions imposed by globalization. Therefore, the decline of the traditional working class would explain the failures of social-democratic parties in the elections of the early 1990s. The new left must thus find a new social basis, particularly in populations that were neglected by the social-democratic Welfare State: women, young people, the socially excluded, etc.

6.2.3 A Battle of Systems?

An interpretation of the Third Way which is especially relevant for the topic of this book is that it represents a middle ground between the neo-liberalism of the United States and the social model of Continental Europe. In terms of varieties of capitalism, the Third Way stands then for an alternative to the market-based model that countries of Continental Europe could follow in order to avoid the difficulties of their own out-dated model. In this perspective, the United Kingdom would be the van-guard of this movement in the EU. It can be considered as a 'sparking point for creative interaction between the US and continental Europe' (Giddens 1998), combining the economic efficiency of the US model with the European social model, marrying Anglo-Saxon shareholding with European stakeholding.[15] The Third Way would thus be the natural evo-lution for European social democracy, not an alternative political project.

On the other hand, Great Britain could also be seen as the Trojan horse of market-based capitalism in the European Union, and the Third Way would in fact represent a 'soft' transition to a market-based system for Continental European countries. Tony Blair has tried to export the Third Way to the Continent on many occasions. These efforts have met with both success and failure. Tony Blair was successful in influencing the final Treaty of Amsterdam. Abandoning the tactics of the former Conservative British government, the new Prime Minister accepted the Employment Chapter as well as the inclusion of a Social Chapter, but ensured that there

---

[15] Interestingly enough, the term 'stakeholder' was once used by New Labour, in an effort to promote a 'stakeholder society'. Probably having too many connotations with 'old' Continental European social democracy, it was subsequently discarded to avoid frightening the business community with which New Labour sought a political alliance (Goes (2000)).

was no harmonization of national employment laws nor any funds dedicated to increasing employment. The Employment Chapter called for the annual adoption of employment guidelines which would serve as a basis for national action plans to reduce unemployment. The procedure is voluntaristic and in fact served as a means to push for labour-market flexibility and promote the notion of employability. The most significant contribution to the diffusion of the Third Way in Europe took place in 1999. Gerhard Schröder had been elected with a programme based on a German version of the Third Way, the 'Neue Mitte', i.e. the 'new centre'. This mention of the centre was the most blatant signal of an effort to go beyond the divide between 'new right' and 'old left'. However, the new German government was not strictly third way, first because it was a coalition with the Green Party, and second because a significant part of the SPD was strongly opposed to the Third Way. The principal opponent was the SPD Chairman and Minister of Finance, Oskar Lafontaine, who tried to push for the implementation of a Keynesian policy at the European level, against the economic stance of the Bundesbank and the European Central Bank. Lafontaine's initiatives were perceived on the Continent as a potential threat to the euro, and his push for tax harmonization had him dubbed the most dangerous man in Europe by the British press. He soon met with opposition from business and finance circles, failed to receive substantial support at the EU level or at home, and resigned in somewhat mysterious circumstances in March 1999, from both the government and the SPD leadership. This was the occasion for Gerhard Schröder to engage Germany further in the Third Way, and this move was ratified with the publication of a joint document with Tony Blair (Blair and Schröder 1999).

The Blair–Schröder manifesto was important because the recently elected heads of government of two large European countries stated their adherence to the new values of the left. The document reaffirmed the basic principles of the Third Way and why they would represent a solution for Europe. A new fiscal policy oriented towards lowering taxes, particularly corporate taxes, should be implemented. The search for market flexibility, one of the goals of 'modern social democracy', would make the European economy more dynamic. Non-wage-labour costs should be decreased; labour markets should be deregulated, which would enable small firms to develop. The importance of investment in human and social capital was also stressed. The document concluded with a call to European social democrats to follow the path thus defined, and not bypass such a historic opportunity. However, the release of this document did not have the expected political consequences, and far from being the first step in the general conversion of the left to the new values, it marked the stalling of the Third Way on the Continent.

The conversion of other European social democrats to the Third Way was far from general. New Labour had failed to exert significant influence on the manifesto of the Party of European Socialists before the European elections in 1999, reflecting the lack of popularity of the Third Way among social democrats. As mentioned above, opposition to the Third Way had existed within the German government from day one. Oskar Lafontaine later described the 'Dritte Weg' as a 'Holzweg'.[16] One could argue that the German adherence to the Third Way was short lived anyway. The left wing of the SPD was never enthralled by the concept, and transformation of the German model into what appeared as Anglo-Saxon capitalism was rejected by a sizeable part of the German public, particularly in the light of the Philip Holzman bankruptcy and the takeover of Mannesman by Vodafone. The release of the Blair–Schröder manifesto was followed by electoral defeats for both the SPD and New Labour in the following European elections, whereas the French socialist party, supposedly the most prominent representative of the 'old left', enjoyed a comfortable success. Moreover, the beginning of Gerhard Schröder's term in office was marked by a series of defeats in local (*Länder*) elections, leading to loss of control over the upper chamber, the Bundesrat, and triggering a downward spiral in the government's popularity which was only stopped by the revelations about the CDU's possibly fraudulent financing and the related damage done to the image of former Chancellor Helmut Kohl and his party. Not long after the publication of the Blair–Schröder paper, the 'Grundwertekommission beim Parteivorstand der SPD'[17] released a document critically analysing the Third Way concepts as well as the politics of several left-wing governments in Europe. What came out of the document was that there existed not one but several approaches to the modernization of the left wing;[18] the British-style Third Way was merely one of them, with its pros and cons, and did not seem to fit with Continental European societies. Therefore the Third Way was not the universal model to follow.

The Blair–Schröder axis had left one major social-democratic leader out, French premier Lionel Jospin. His attitude towards the Third Way was

---

[16] 'Der dritte Weg ist ein Holzweg' is the title of a chapter of Oskar Lafontaine's (1999) book. This can be roughly translated as 'the third way is the wrong way'.

[17] The Commission for Fundamental Values of the German Social Democratic Party.

[18] 'Es gibt nicht *den* "dritten Weg," der die Sozialdemokratie in das nächste Jahrhundert führt'. This could be translated as: 'There is not *one* third way that leads social democracy into the next century' (Grundwertekommission beim Parteivorstand der SPD (1999), 24).

somewhat ambiguous, declaring that 'after the period of monopoly and that of deregulation, we are moving toward a third, more balanced, way between the two',[19] as well as commenting: '*The Third Way? I do not belong to it*'.[20] In fact, probably more than the German Chancellor, Jospin tried to take a 'fourth way', somewhere between the Third Way and 'old' social democracy, mixing a traditional left-wing discourse about the role of the State, the prominence of politics over the economy, and an insistence on national specificities, while launching the largest privatization pro-gramme in France ever, actively searching out new socio-political alliances beyond the traditional electoral base of the left wing[21] and adopting many of the stances of the Third Way. For Jospin (2000), the State must adopt a 'Schumpeterian' role in order to promote innovation and growth, which is close to point 1 in the 'Third Way' economic programme presented above; also, social classes can be brought together through equality of opportunity and it is better to prevent rather than cure in the field of inequalities, which is open support for the priority of equality of opportunity over redistributive policies. A not insignificant part of Jospin's government programme was in fact compatible with the core of Third Way supply-side economics. Indeed, a formula of Jospin's that is often mistaken for a critique of the Third Way—'Yes to the market eco-nomy, no to the market society'—is also included in the Blair–Schröder manifesto.[22] Nevertheless, France was not an ally in Tony Blair's ambition for the Third Way in Europe.

After the failed alliance with Germany, Tony Blair looked for other opportunities in Europe. What may seem surprising at first sight is that he turned toward non-social-democratic leaders in order to promote a series of economic institutional reforms at the European Union level. But this comes as a surprise only if one neglects the structural economic factors behind the diversity of European economies. The failure of an alliance with social-democratic leaders in Europe is best interpreted in terms of the diversity of capitalism. As seen before, the reforms advocated by the Third Way clash with the Continental European model rather than

---

[19] Speech before the Parliament, June 1997. My translation.

[20] Speech before the National Council of the Socialist Party, 2001.

[21] 'Our sociological base is neither homogeneous nor narrow; it has been renewed and extended. This is why we must find the best trade-off between social classes: those who are rather satisfied with the current state of society and do not want to incur the "cost" of increas-ing equality [and] those for whom the notion of equality and its concrete deepening are fundamental' (Jospin (2000), 50). My translation.

[22] Jospin (2000), 24; Blair and Schröder (1999), 16. Jospin accepts the market economy provided it is 'regulated'. No such provision is present in Blair and Schröder's text.

accommodating it.[23] There is still strong political support for some degree of employment protection, collective bargaining, and the Welfare State in most Continental European countries. If there is scope for a political alliance over the Third Way in Europe, it should rather be sought with the Mediterranean countries. These economies are also very different from the market-based model, as shown in the previous chapters; however, a political alliance could be reached on specific measures when one takes two points into account. Mediterranean economies are characterized by a high level of labour-market protection, as shown in Chapter 4, but this 'rigidity' may not be sustainable against increased competition. Indeed, employment protection does not protect high levels of investment in specific skills, as is the case for other European countries, since the skill level of the workforce is lower than the European average. Industrial specialization in Mediterranean countries is not so much based on skill-intensity, technological content, and quality competition as on price competition and the fast responsiveness of firms to changes in demand.[24] Therefore, the Mediterranean productive model could very well accommodate more labour-market flexibility. It actually does to some extent, since, for instance, small Italian firms are exempted from some of the labour laws, and can therefore base their competitiveness on flexibility much more than large firms. In any case, the high-skill-level job-security route seems mostly out of reach for Mediterranean capitalism,[25] and a competitive model based on flexibility is much more in order. Implementing this model potentially means meeting some considerable opposition from 'insiders'. Leaders of these countries would therefore welcome any political support at the supranational level. It would be easier to overcome domestic opposition if the labour-flexibility measures appeared to come from a European initiative. The low unemployment rate of the UK compared to Spain and (Southern) Italy could also represent a tempting objective favouring a domestic political alliance based on 'outsiders'. Another factor uniting these countries to the UK is that the level of social protection is much lower there than in Continental Europe. Therefore, the extent

---

[23] Bonoli (2001) puts forward a similar point.

[24] The small firms in the north-east of Italy can be said to base their competitiveness on their flexibility and adaptability, and the clothing chain Zara, probably world champion in flexibility of the design and manufacturing supply chain, is a Spanish (Galician) company (see Amable, Askenazy, Goldstein, and O'Connor (2002)).

[25] Put simply, there are three different productive models in Italy alone: the small firms-based model of the north-east; the large corporations-based model of the north-west; and the south. A Continental European model could probably only be supported without difficulty by the large firms-based model.

of the Welfare State would not represent so much of an obstacle to the promotion of the Third Way as in Continental European countries. Indeed, the UK and the Mediterranean economies also have in common that social charges on labour costs are rather weak, particularly on low labour costs. This element would reinforce a specialization based on labour-intensive activities.

After the call of the Blair–Schröder manifesto had fallen on deaf ears, the new initiatives for the promotion of the Third Way in Europe were supported by a political alliance between Tony Blair, Jose Maria Aznar, and Massimo d'Alema, later replaced by Silvio Berlusconi. Before the 2000 Lisbon European summit an offensive was launched to promote radical labour-market reforms in Europe. Tony Blair, along with the Italian leader Massimo d'Alema, wrote to the other European leaders calling for structural reform and implicitly criticizing French and German labour-market policies. He co-authored an article with Spanish leader Jose Maria Aznar stating that the UK and Spain were partners in the economic reform in the direction of more market flexibility. There was also a joint British–Spanish contribution to the Council of Ministers asserting that there was no need for harmonization of corporate taxes across Europe, and emphasizing the need for more flexibility, liberalization, and modernization of Welfare States. Tax and welfare issues are deeply related. Shifting the social tax burden from labour to energy consumption or other polluting activity requires coordination at the European level. More generally, tax competition would seriously threaten the stability of the most generous Welfares States. In 1998 a working group of the European Socialists called for a regulation and harmonization of tax policies at the European level. The British government refused to sign the document (Aust 2001). It is a constant of UK policy to refuse any attempt at tax coordination. The Blair–Berlusconi paper published in the run up to the Barcelona summit proposed a reform programme that was a significant step toward the adoption of the market-based model of capitalism: liberalization of the energy market, financial liberalization in favour of takeovers as well as mergers and acquisitions, a fight against 'over-regulation', a decrease in State aid, emphasis on the dynamism of SMEs, and of course labour-market flexibility. Nevertheless, if the alliance over a comprehensive market-based programme can only be achieved with Mediterranean countries for the moment, some alliances on specific points have been made beyond the original base. Some Continental European countries are less hostile than others to market liberalization, as seen at the Barcelona meeting in the case of energy, for instance. This was interpreted by Nobel Prize winner Gary Becker as a significant and welcome step towards the adoption of a market-based Anglo-Saxon system in the EU (Becker 2002). Therefore, the most active strategies in Europe at the start of the twenty-first century remain either the neo-liberal project or the Third Way, i.e. a significant rupture from the Continental model of capitalism.

6.3 The Continental European Welfare–Labour Nexus

Since the European social model is based on a socially regulated capitalism associating coordinated wage bargaining, labour-market regulation, a certain degree of solidaristic wage policy, and a redistributive Welfare State, it is necessary to assess the transformations that have taken place so far to check whether there has been a demise of the model or merely some adjustments within a maintained model. The 1990s have witnessed important changes in the welfare–labour nexus. The process of European Monetary Unification (EMU) demanded among other things a convergence across European countries in inflation rates and budget deficits. For some countries the implied drastic reduction in both inflation and budget deficits could only be achieved through social pacts, i.e. tripartite cooperation between unions, employers, and the State. This revival of cooperation ran counter to the common idea of an increasing 'Americanization' of social relations and the outmoded character of social cooperation. For Fajertag and Pochet (1997), the prospect of monetary union acted as a catalyst for the signing of social pacts, and mostly in countries where the difficulty of keeping inflation and budget deficits under control was the greatest, i.e. countries for which monetary unification would entail large social costs. This external pressure for bargaining explains why it suddenly appeared in countries which most lacked the structures to implement social bargaining, such as Italy, for instance. In fact, this could be explained by the fact that the incentives to achieve a social pact were higher in countries where public debt and inflation problems were the most severe, irrespective of the initial degree of corporatism in industrial relations (Hassel 2001).

The focus of social pacts was combating inflation through wage restraint, but also most aspects of welfare reform: new labour-market policies, social transfers, and labour legislation. This process contrasted with the Anglo-Saxon approach to welfare reform, where unilateral action prevailed (Rhodes 1999). On the Continent, the structure of governance of social protection explains why cooperation is an important factor in the success of reform (Ebbinghaus and Hassel 1999). Unions and employers generally have self-regulatory competencies in social-protection systems;

therefore governments need their consent for reform. Their formal agreement for changing the social-insurance conditions or implementing reform is necessary. But social pacts were also seen by unions as a way to reaffirm their prominent role, and they supported social cooperation. They were ready to exchange welfare retrenchment and pay moderation for a central role in a context of increased pressure towards the decentralization of wage bargaining.

The success of these pacts varied across Europe. As stressed by Ebbinghaus and Hassel (1999) in their four-country comparison, the success or failure of the reforms depended on the incentives for and ability of social agents to come to an agreement. Tripartite cooperation was a success in the Netherlands, where there is a long tradition of statutory wage policy, bargaining is centralized, and unions saw cooperation as a way to regain some influence over wage policy. The involvement of government in wage policy is also a long-standing French characteristic, but trade unions have a weak base there and have no common objectives; French employers are also split, between large and small firms, to name one of the many divisions, and their main interest seems to be to exert pressure for bargaining decentralization. In fact, the spread of firm-level bargaining was facilitated by the Auroux laws of the 1980s. France was in a situation where social partners were too weak to regulate the labour market or decide upon welfare reform, yet powerful enough to block unilateral moves by the government. The government does not interfere with wage bargaining in Germany (*Tarifautonomie*) and unions are stronger than in the Netherlands, having fewer incentives to make cooperation a success.

6.3.1 A Limited Welfare State Retrenchment

Social-protection systems are under stress in most European countries because of the growth in expenditures related to various welfare commitments and the seemingly increasing resistance of the population to higher levels of taxation. The structural reasons behind the growth in expenditures are varied: the ageing of the population increases the pensions burden, particularly in Pay As You Go (PAYG) systems; the growth slowdown and de-industrialization (Iversen and Cusack 2000) increased unemployment and hence the amount of related benefits; household structures were transformed, with the growth of one-person households making it difficult to internalize social protection within the 'family' (Pierson 2001). These pressures have led to calls for substantial reforms of welfare programmes. However, although the 1990s were characterized by worries about the future of the European Welfare States, there has been no major dismantling of social protection in Continental European countries (Rhodes 2001). The major attacks on Welfare States have in fact taken place in a country where social protection was already very limited (Iversen and Soskice 2001), namely the UK. Limited changes have concerned some attempts to associate more 'responsibilities' with 'rights', notably for unemployment benefits. One may also add a limited introduction of additional private schemes and some additional control of expenditures. In any case, there is no convergence to the Welfare State of the market-based model of capitalism. The general background in Continental Europe is that of a limited retrenchment in a context of 'permanent austerity'.

Why is such a limited change taking place? The 'path dependence' story would insist on the fact that welfare systems are embedded in national regulations which are difficult to change without substantial transformation in the structure of interest groups. This would also probably imply a political representation with few veto players, since, as we saw in the previous chapter, a strong Welfare State is associated with social corporatism, or more generally with 'proportional representation', rather than with a majoritarian system. Systems where power is concentrated have more scope for welfare reforms, whereas systems where power is shared more widely must in general establish compromises. Also, reforms of PAYG systems are bound to hurt important vested interests, which limits the scope for radical change. The benefits of welfare reforms are also held to be more difficult to assess than the costs (Pierson 2001). Even globalization, usually mentioned as a factor of Welfare State dismantling, could have had counter-influences. As suggested by Ganghof (2001), if globalization increases income inequality and risks, it may create incentives for increasing rather than reducing welfare efforts. Capital mobility may render this effort difficult, implying tax reforms and the sacrifice of some objectives of the Welfare State, but the dismantling of social protection is certainly not in order. Basically, there are systemic institutional-complementarity-based reasons for the existence of a strong Welfare State in Continental Europe, as we saw above.

This does not mean that there are no problems. Continental welfare systems have specific weaknesses. The predominantly wage-based financing imposes a cost on labour which prices low-productivity workers out and slows down employment growth, generating a vicious circle of increasing unemployment and increasing welfare burden on labour costs. The lack of active labour-market policies produces a bias towards early retirement, which depresses the participation rate and increases welfare expenditures. Besides, if pension entitlements are based entirely on length and level of previous contributions, workers will be reluctant to engage in part-time work and fixed-term employment. This hinders the development of non-standard forms of employment and job creation in the service sector (Hemerijck and Manow 2001). This welfare-without-work strategy pushes Continental economies toward a high-wages and high-productivity industrial strategy through increasing labour productivity. This requires a high effort in R&D and workforce training, which calls for a constant upgrading of the European productive structure; this strategy runs the risk of creating a new division between unemployed, low-skilled, welfare-dependent workers and employed, high-skilled, tax-paying workers. The uneven distribution of costs and benefits of welfare systems fuels a dualism in the workforce that could in the long run erode the political support of the Welfare State.

Continental European systems have been modified during the 1990s (Table 6.1), but at a differing pace and with varying success. Considering the structure of interest-group representation characteristic of the Continental model of capitalism, one would have expected a generalization of the negotiated path to Welfare State reform. Yet, only some countries went through a negotiated reform; among the countries of the Continental European model, the Netherlands are the most prominent example that there can be a way out of the welfare-without-work equilibrium. More generally, as argued in Palier (2002), the reforms that passed (the German pension reform of 1992, the French reform of 1993) were obtained after having gained the support of at least some social partners. On the other hand, reforms without negotiations (France and Italy in 1995, Germany in 1997) failed to be implemented, facing strong opposition from the trade unions. Even the German Old-Age Provision Act of 2001, which represents a non-negligible break with the previously existing system by reducing benefits and introducing a private scheme, was passed with the support of the trade unions, and even of the left-wing of the SPD—in spite of the pronounced 'Neue Mitte' flavour of the Act.

In all countries Welfare-State reform is necessarily limited because of the role that the Welfare State plays in this model, reflected in the interest structure of social groups and the political influence of socio-political groups. The common trends of reform can be taken from Schludi (2001): a strengthening of the link between contributions and benefits (towards a lifetime principle); a lowering or a suppression of non-contributory benefits; a rise in the retirement age; less generous indexation mechanisms. One may add that supplementary private and/or funded schemes will probably be generalized, but their scope is bound to be limited.

TABLE 6.1 Institutional reforms in the welfare–labour nexus in Europe during the 1990s

Countries	Social protection	Wage bargaining	Employment
France	Failure of reform plan without negotiation; moderate retrenchment. Implementation of universal health protection. New distribution of power between the State and social partners	Growth of company-level and individual bargaining. Limited agreement between unions and employers on collective-bargaining procedures	Increased use of atypical contracts; but increased constraints on collective dismissals (social plans). Working-time reduction (35-hour week)
Germany	Pension reform: attempts without negotiation (Kohl) and with union support (Schröder). Gradual introduction of subsidies/tax advantages to private/occupational schemes. Introduction of a less generous pension-indexation mechanism	Employers' pressure for decentralization	Reduced protection against dismissal for white-collar and small-firm workers
Netherlands	Reform without negotiation. Reform of invalidity benefit, compromise reached in 2002	Decentralization after the Wassenaar agreement (1982) but coordination reinforced at the top (bipartite or tripartite)	Obstacles to part-time work largely eliminated
Italy	Pension reform negotiated with unions; switch toward a (notional) defined contribution scheme. Harmonization between private- and public-sector pensions	Coordination and decentralization through a two-tier system: national-industry bargaining confined to inflation matters; decentralized bargaining deals with productivity and	Liberalization of collective dismissals. Implementation of work and training contracts labour-market reform: alteration of

	non-wage matters	workers' dismissal regulation
Introduction of a less generous pension-indexation mechanism		
Spain Unions–government agreement on pensions	No coordination; failure to come to an agreement on collective bargaining	Flexible contracts for under-thirties. No agreement on labour-market reform
Denmark Welfare cuts negotiated with unions	Spread of company-level bargaining without coordination	Reform of unemployment benefits. Increase in atypical forms of employment
Sweden Unions' opposition to welfare cuts; moderate cuts in monetary social transfers; reduction in pensions; introduction of employee contributions Switch toward a (notional) defined contribution scheme Introduction of a fully funded private mandatory pension scheme Introduction of a less generous pension-indexation mechanism	Unions defend industry-level bargaining, employers company-level bargaining; government's attempt to coordinate	Pro-reemployment active labour-market policy Weakening of unions' veto right over firms' outsourcing Lift of ban on private employment agencies
Norway Social pact for the maintenance of various welfare benefits	Incomes policy and central coordination Employers' pressure for decentralization	
UK Unemployment-benefits reform without negotiation with unions	Encouragement for individual bargaining	

Sources: Regini (2000); Grundwertekommission beim Parteivorstand der SPD (1999); Schludi (2001); Ebbinghaus (2002); Palier (2002).

6.3.2 New Bargaining Patterns

If there is no 'Americanization' of industrial relations in Europe, it remains the case that the 'revival of corporatism' manifested by the phenomenon of social pacts is a change towards a new type of corporatism, a competitive corporatism. The objective of cooperation is no longer the implementation of labour-market regulation but an increase in flexibility; they have switched from redistribution and distribution of productivity gains to wage restraint and escaping competitive pressure from foreign partner countries. Indeed, many social pacts of the 1990s have a certain 'beggar thy neighbour' aspect, adopting binding wage-policy guidelines aimed at undercutting the average wage trend in partner countries.

Besides, the general trend is one of wage-bargaining decentralization, even if it is 'organized' decentralization.[26] But the evolution so far is more in the direction of a moderate dose of deregulation instilled into existing systems rather than a complete change, with even some attempts at re-regulating certain types of occupation (atypical work) in some countries, such as France and the Netherlands. Some countries have implemented a strategy of limited flexibility, differentiating between types of labour contract (fixed-term versus open-ended contracts), while other countries have followed flexibility as a guiding principle. Similarly, even if a general trend toward wage-bargaining decentralization across Europe can be observed, some countries have instigated a greater central coordination whilst others have not. Taking account of the two criteria gives a partition of countries as shown in Table 6.2, where countries belonging to the Continental European model are featured in bold. Among the Continental European countries, those that experienced the most disappointing employment performance, i.e. France and Germany, are also those where central coordination has not increased. Other countries of the same model have seen an increase in central coordination, with or without an adherence to labour-market-flexibility principles.

Some limited labour-market flexibility does not threaten the Continental European model as such. It is possible to increase work sharing or part-time work, and even to increase incentives for growth in low-wage service-sector employment through tax decreases without fundamentally altering the set of institutional complementarities underlying the model. There is however a possibility of an increasing divide in the

---

[26] Regini (2000). With organized decentralization, company bargaining occurs within the framework of the sector agreement. By contrast, disorganized decentralization occurs when sector agreements are replaced by company-level bargaining (Traxler (1995)).

TABLE 6.2 Wage-bargaining and labour-market evolutions

	No increase in central coordination	Increase in central coordination
Limited or controlled increase in flexibility	**Germany** **France** Spain	Italy **Norway**
All-out increase in flexibility	UK Denmark Sweden	**Ireland** **Netherlands**

Source: Regini (2000).

labour force, which should be limited by Welfare State programmes, preventing a too significant growth in income inequality. Selective labour-market deregulation, leading to an expansion in part-time employment, has been achieved in the Netherlands, while the social pact maintained coordinated wage bargaining, and in a maintained system of social protection (Ebbinghaus and Hassel 1999). But maintaining the model demands cooperation among social agents, hence sufficiently strong unions. This could be a problem in some European countries, such as France, where, as mentioned before, social partners are involved in the administration of social-security funds but unable to take a responsible role in the regulation of labour markets and wage policy.

6.3.3 No European Level Wage Bargaining

The project of regulated capitalism supposed that some degree of integration of European-level industrial relations could be achieved. The social protocol of the Maastricht Treaty reassessed the role of a 'European social dialogue' at the macroeconomic level, and a social dialogue between partners at the sectoral level was introduced in the social chapter of the Treaty of Amsterdam. A new arena for industrial relations was created at the European-firm level with the European Works Councils (EWCs) directive of 1994. EWCs should be set up to provide for the information and consultation of workers in European (transnational) firms. EWCs thus concern company-level negotiations. How much progress this directive represents depends on the country considered. From a British point of view, the directive might be seen as a way to reinitiate a social dialogue that had suffered from two decades of labour-market deregulation. From a Continental European point of view, however, the directive fails to grant workers the rights of industrial citizenship, i.e. rights to collective bargaining and collective participation in decision-making, since informing and consulting is different from taking views into consideration (Streeck 1997*b*). Indeed, the directive bypasses the union-representation level and is based on voluntarism and subsidiarity, which is bound to reinforce regime competition, since the national representation system is left unchanged except for the extra layer of EWCs. Since the implementation of the directive is left to national legislation, the directive even allows employers to choose the country with the least demanding implementation legislation for the location of their headquarters. Far from promoting the establishment of industrial rights at the European level it promotes the emergence of a competition between nationally fragmented European systems of industrial relations.

Schulten (2002) argues that this social dialogue is not leading to the elaboration of European-level wage bargaining; it concentrates on 'soft' issues of social policy or minimum labour standards, whereas the 'hard' issues of distributional conflict stay at the national level. Moreover, as mentioned before, the social pacts of the 1990s had a strong 'beggar thy neighbour' flavour. This would induce a type of 'negative' market coordination based on downward competition between locations. The counter tendency would be to build the equivalent of a coordinated bargaining system at the European level. There is no supranational European collective wage bargaining as such at the moment, but some cross-border-coordination mechanisms exist. Unions try to counter negative coordination with positive action aimed at wage coordination and a collective wage-bargaining policy at the European level. This is done in three main directions (Dufresne and Mermet 2002):

(1) at the inter-regional level, as with the Doorn initiative between Belgium, the Netherlands, Luxembourg, and Germany;
(2) at the sectoral level, with the European Industry Federations;
(3) at the cross-sectoral level, supported by the European Trade Unions Confederation (ETUC).

This coordination approach does not aim at establishing supranational wage bargaining, which would, of course, be out of reach for lack of a second party. However, it seeks to interconnect national wage-bargaining systems in order to prevent or limit wage competition and 'market-based', negative coordination. In this respect, the ETUC guidelines for nominal wage increases are that they should cover inflation (real-wage maintenance) and incorporate a part of the productivity gains; the remaining productivity increases should be used for 'qualitative' improvements, such as training (lifelong learning) and gender equality, and there should be parallel evolutions between pay rises in the public and the private sectors. But implementing this strategy runs up against the institutional limitations of European-level bargaining coordination. The ETUC has no power over its national union members and must rely on their voluntarism and their active participation, with the risk of realizing more a generalized information exchange than an actual bargaining coordination. Voluntarism is in fact a more general problem for Continental Europe. Its generalization leads to the spread of the 'contract culture' and a shift from hard to soft regulation such as framework agreements (Supiot 1999). Collective bargaining then runs the risk of turning into a social dialogue rather than a vehicle for making agreements. In parallel to this loss in means, it incorporates new objectives: taking over some of the legislative functions of the State, being given a greater responsibility for implementing legal provisions (regulatory function), and also becoming an instrument of adaptability at sector and company levels (flexibility function) and a vehicle for involving employees in economic decision-making (management function). The risk is that, instead of achieving new European-level coordination, it would merely be a vehicle for market coordination and competition across countries, adding more pressure to the decentralization of wage bargaining.

6.4 The Financial Sector

An important pillar of the Continental European model of capitalism is its financial system, based on intermediation rather than markets, with a supposedly active involvement of intermediaries in firms' monitoring and strategy making, diminishing uncertainty and allowing for the realization of long-term investment strategies by supplying 'patient' capital, stabilizing the firm, and enabling the elaboration of social compromises and cooperative industrial relations. In the context of a hypothetical convergence towards the market-based model, a weakening of the role of financial intermediaries in this set of institutional complementarities would hasten the demise of the Continental European model. These complementarities are in part understood at the EU level: the Green Paper of 1997 on 'Supplementary Pensions in the Single Market' mentioned a virtuous circle of increasing funding of supplementary pensions in European capital markets which would in turn set in motion an increased securitization leading to a deepening of financial markets. The dynamics would thus link a scheme for increasing the share of private social insurance to a rise in the role of financial markets. There are strong reasons to believe that the 'virtuous' circle would not stop there but affect other interconnections with other European institutional forms. The role of political factors in the shape of the financial structure of a country has been emphasized by Rajan and Zingales (2000). They show that in the twentieth century some European countries classified today as 'bank-based' systems, such as France and Germany, had important capital markets before the Second World War, whereas the USA once had all the necessary characteristics to become a bank-based system. Why these countries took certain directions is the direct consequence of political choices. In the case of the United States, Roe (2000) links the emergence of the 'Berle and Means' corporation to the rise of concerns about the concentration of control in the hands of a small number of financial intermediaries (such as J. P. Morgan) and the translation of these concerns into a populist politics-inspired wave of regulation restricting the involvement of banks in corporate activities. Regarding the present evolution of European economies, there are reasons to believe that the evolution taking place in financial systems is the result of political choices too. Indeed, political forces at the EU level are very active either in pushing financial systems toward the market-based paradigm or strongly opposing it.

There are no signs of a complete conversion of Continental financial systems to a market-based system, but there are signs that the systems are changing. Rather than a transformation of European systems into a financial-markets-based system, there are hypotheses of a move towards a hybrid system (Deeg 2001), in particular in Germany. Schmidt, Hackethal, and Tyrell (1998) have insisted on the lack of a general pattern of disintermediation among developed economies, except for France. There is also a general trend toward securitization, and this move is more pronounced in the case of France. Both France and Germany experienced changes in the regulative framework of the banking industry, and the soar of financial markets. The main reforms affecting French banks were undertaken in the 1980s, with the 1984 Banking Act putting an end to the regime of different interest rates; the creation of a futures market in 1986; and the liberalization of the Stock Exchange in 1988. After 1986 most public banks were privatized, in several waves. By contrast, public banks still represent over a third of the market share in Germany and local *Landesbanks* are backed by public guarantee. The Stock Exchange was reorganized during the 1990s and transformed into a publicly traded company (Deutsche Börse AG). Some additional transformations were necessary to harmonize German law with international norms as well as EU directives. A series of financial-market-promotion acts were passed, introducing a secondary capital market, increasing transparency, protecting small investors and allowing more types of investment funds, and making gains from risk capital tax-free after one year instead of six. An independent authority for securities-trading supervision was established. A new stock market for fast growing firms, *the Neue Markt*, was created at the Frankfurt Stock Exchange.

One of the main forces for change in the French financial sector was the privatization of a substantial amount of French industry through the 1980s and 1990s, which mechanically 'deepened' existing financial markets. Moreover, in order to obtain better conditions for its public debt, the State initiated a process of financial liberalization that led to a surge of direct instead of intermediated finance. In both countries, the development of financial markets contributed to loosening the ties between firms and banks. The former tried to diversify their investor base while the latter aimed at redirecting their activities away from direct participation and towards financial services such as securities trading and business consultancy, or tightening their links with the insurance sector. The evolution of bank-asset structures clearly shows the rise of these activities at the expense of more traditional loan activity in France. This evolution also takes the form of creation of subsidiaries dedicated to investment banking and/or insurance.

Firms internationalized their investor base and had to comply with international accounting rules in order to be listed on foreign stock exchanges such as the NYSE. A consequence of investor diversification was the growing importance of market finance in the guise of institutional investors, particularly foreign Anglo-Saxon institutional investors who had special requirements in terms of corporate governance. In both countries new laws were passed in 1998 to authorize firms' shares buyback up to a limit of 10 per cent. This enabled firms to put into practice stock-option plans in order to supply high-powered incentives to the top management as well as boost share prices, making them more attractive on the Stock Market. In general, managerial behaviour had to reorient towards a policy of shareholder value: improving the informational quality of annual reports, which involves among other things a change in the accounting rules to international or American standards. Höpner (2001) reports that the orientation of large German companies toward a policy of shareholder value since the mid-1990s is indeed linked to the rise of institutional investors as shareholders. Nevertheless, German company law explicitly denies the role of shareholders' agent to the management. Fiduciary duties are due to the firm itself, not to any particular group.[27]

---

[27] See Pistor et al. (2001) for a comparison of company laws. The supervisory board must act independently from any specific stakeholder in the Netherlands.

TABLE 6.3 Country scores on conformity to
the principles of corporate governance

Country	1989	1994	1999
France	3	4	5
Germany	1	1	3
Netherlands	1	3	3

Source: Shinn (2001).

The transformation of Continental European countries may be assessed using an indicator of conformity to corporate governance practices proposed by Shinn (2001). Seven points are taken into account: accounting, audit, the presence of non-executive directors on board, the existence of fiduciary duty, voting-rights rules (i.e. 'one share one vote' or not), anti-takeover provisions (lack of), and (management) incentives. Table 6.3 shows that France, Germany, and the Netherlands have significantly raised their degree of conformity to corporate-governance practices—in the second half of the 1990s in Germany, most of the decade in the Netherlands, and the whole decade in France, which is actually scoring 'best' on this issue, missing only conformity to the 'one-share-one-vote' rule and still allowing for takeover defences.

This deeper transformation of France with respect to the principles of market-based finance is confirmed by Goyer (2002), who compares the process of refocusing on core competencies by large French and German firms. Such refocusing is a standard requirement of Anglo-Saxon institutional investors, who criticize the conglomerate form of corporations on several grounds: the cross-subsidization from profitable division to unprofitable units is a denial of market incentive mechanisms and makes outsiders' investment more difficult to assess; a company with a diversified portfolio of activities should focus on a limited number of core competencies for fear of becoming a 'jack of all trades'; (financial) markets are held to be far better at risk diversification than internal company procedures. Goyer (2002) shows that French and German companies have changed their corporate strategies of diversification in differentiated ways. French companies have reduced their degree of diversification to a greater extent than their German counterparts. Restructuring was more radical in France than in Germany. Therefore, France, more than Germany, has made significant steps towards market-based principles of corporate governance.

The turn towards more market-based finance principles also concerns the market for corporate control, which can only be active if ownership is diffuse enough. Continental firms exhibit a higher degree of cross-shareholding than their Anglo-Saxon counterparts. This pattern was initially preserved in France even after the second privatization wave, in the mid-1990s. The so-called 'hard cores', i.e. a specific pattern of cross-ownership linking large industrial firms, banks, and insurance companies aimed at preserving ownership stability and the capacity to implement long-term industrial strategies. Of course, the presence of hard cores was particularly unattractive to foreign institutional investors, and was thus an impediment to the development of market-based finance in France. The hard-core structure soon began to be dismantled after the merger between insurance companies AXA and UAP in 1996 (Morin 1998). The disappearance of the hard cores subsequently encouraged foreign investors to enter the French share market. In Germany, the tax-reform law of July 2000 (*Steuerreform*) abolished capital-gains taxes on the liquidation of cross-shareholdings. This was a deliberate policy to dissolve the cross-shareholding pattern characteristic of the long-term relationships between corporations and banks. Neither party seemed that interested in keeping the close relationship going; as mentioned above, firms were eager to obtain cheap capital from financial markets, and universal banks wanted to reorient towards the investment-banking business. The tax measure was also thought of as an instrument to boost the German securities markets and force German companies to restructure and adapt to a changing economic environment. The consequences for the ability of German corporations to resist hostile takeovers—without a solid pattern of cross-shareholding—were however underestimated, as will be seen below.

The dynamism of the market for corporate control is probably best appreciated through hostile-takeover activity. Table 6.4 shows that it has noticeably gathered pace in Continental European countries during the 1990s. Hostile takeovers used to be very rare in Germany before that decade, but they are now quite possible, as shown by the impressive increase in both target and acquirer takeovers. An important event in this respect was Krupp's attempt at a hostile takeover of its competitor Thyssen in 1997. As a symbol of the demise of the close-relationship bank-based system in Germany, the hostile takeover attempt was prepared by subsidiaries of the *Hausbank* of both Krupp and Thyssen (Lütz 2000). For the first time German banks not only let a hostile takeover take place but actually sided with the attacker. As with the case of company restructuring, France seems more involved in the practices characteristic of market-based finance than Germany, and the end of the

TABLE 6.4 Announced hostile corporate takeovers

Country	Transaction value (% of world total)			
	Target		Acquirer	
	1980–9	1990–8	1980–9	1990–8
France	1.9	5.4	2.9	3.6
Austria	0.0	0.1	0.0	0.1
Germany	0.2	1.8	0.2	1.8
Norway	0.0	0.6	0.0	0.4
Ireland	0.0	0.1	0.0	0.1

Source: Guillen (2000).

decade was marked by large-scale hostile takeovers in banking (BNP, Paribas, and Société Générale) and the oil industry (Elf and Total-Fina).

It is now time to summarize and consider the broader picture. Takeovers and institutional-investor-induced restructuring are threats to specific investments. Some other transformations of financial systems may not be that much of a threat to stakeholders. The increased transparency demanded by outside investors may actually be welcomed by non-managing stakeholders such as workers and unions. German firms have a two-tier board structure:[28] the management board (*Vorstand*) and the supervisory board (*Aufsichtsrat*), where workers' representatives have a 50 per cent representation when the firm has more than 2000 employees. In France, the presence of workers' representatives on the board is mandatory only in formerly State-owned enterprises. An alternative form of stakeholder representation is in fact to turn them into shareholders. Employee share ownership is increasingly devised as a protection against hostile takeovers. In Germany, the dominance of the management board in the auditing function is no guarantee of transparency towards the supervisory board, and the risk was that of collusion between management and bank, bypassing other stakeholders, most notably workers. Increased transparency may thus benefit the supervisory board members, i.e. shareholders and workers, over management. Other aspects of corporate governance, such as stock-option plans, may nevertheless be detrimental to workers or favourable to the management.

---

[28] The two-tier structure is optional in France but tends to be diffuse among large firms.

The German control and transparency law (*KontraG*) of 1998 was part of a financial-markets-promotion strategy aimed at reinforcing the protection of small owners and more generally adapting Germany to Anglo-Saxon corporate governance. It prohibited banks holding more than 5 per cent of a corporation's shares from voting with their equity *and* the proxies deposited with them, and was thus an incentive to reduce their stakes in German firms. In the desire to protect minority shareholders, the law prohibited unequal voting rights; it abolished voting ceilings and forbade the voting of cross-shareholding stakes of over 25 per cent in the supervisory board. In conjunction with the tax reform which created incentives to unravel cross-shareholdings, this law increased the vulnerability of German firms to hostile takeovers. The takeover of Mannesman by British company Vodafone was a signal to German management that the defence mechanisms of the German system were weak. As Höpner and Jackson (2001) recall, Mannesman was unable to resist the takeover because its ownership was fragmented and neither banks nor the supervisory board were in a position to withstand. The former were increasingly unable to provide protection and the latter proved incapable of mobilizing resistance against the bid. It suddenly dawned on German management that the most efficient defence against hostile takeovers was cross-shareholding, and this would not exist for long after the tax reform had produced its full effects. Whereas the politics of corporate governance were part of the *Neue Mitte*'s strategy to modernize the economy in an Anglo-Saxon way with the support of business, the latter changed views with the sudden perception of German corporations' vulnerability. The change was manifested by an all-out opposition to the draft takeover directive pushed forward by the European Commission Cioffi (2002). The EU had been unsuccessful at developing a takeover directive since an initial draft in 1989. An attempt at harmonizing rules regarding takeover bids was made. The draft was influenced by British law, requiring an equal treatment of the shareholders of the target company and establishing rules for the actions of the bidder prior to the bid announcement. The draft met with opposition, particularly on the question of defence against takeovers, and a long process of redrafting and discussions ended after ten years when a special mediation committee reached an agreement. The directive was submitted to the European Parliament in 2001. The general objective of the draft directive was to introduce the principles of market-based finance in Europe by making takeovers easier. It required the neutrality of managers and senior directors in response to a hostile takeover bid. Besides denying the possible existence of 'stakes' and imposing a norm of shareholder supremacy in takeover situations when the interests of shareholders and employees come into conflict, this neutrality requirement would have prevented the use of defensive measures without shareholders' approval and would also have prevented solicitation of this approval in advance, which is still possible in Continental European countries such as Germany.

The fight against this draft directive reunited unions and managers in an effort to oppose changes that would have made German firms vulnerable to takeovers and more generally more sensitive to shareholders', i.e. non-stakeholders', pressure, presumably in the 'restructuring' direction of plant closure and job losses. Management particularly feared a wave of takeovers since the *KontraG* had eliminated anti-takeover defences that the draft directive itself did not forbid. In fact, the directive plus the *KontraG* would have denied German firms access to defence measures which American firms can use.[29] Therefore, German firms were in an asymmetrical position with respect to extra- and intra-European firms. This prompted a 180-degree change in the German government's position, from a strong proponent to the most declared opponent. As a result, all the German deputies at the European Parliament voted against the draft directive. Opposition to the directive was not as strong on the French side. Reflecting the broad influence of the Third Way on the Socialist Party, a high percentage of socialist deputies voted in favour of the project, and so did most of the Conservatives. The communists voted against the proposition, but more surprising is the fact that a centre-right pro-European integration party, the UDF,[30] joined the opponents to the directive. Their leader François Bayrou was very explicit about the motivations behind this position in a newspaper interview.[31] Bayrou rejected the directive because it would have represented a significant blow to the 'economic model of Europe' and would have led the EU in a direction that would have been condemned by public opinion and a majority of entrepreneurs not only in France but also in other European countries. The defence of a specific European model, distinguished from Anglo-Saxon capitalism by its focus on manufacturing industry's dynamism and social cohesion and not just financial constraints, and the will to preserve Franco-German solidarity as the basis of European construction were the main reasons for the UDF's position. The final results were 273 for the directive, 273 against, and 22 abstentions. The directive failed because the President of the European Parliament, Nicole Fontaine, abstained.

---

[29] American company law (Delaware) allows the board of directors to fight against a hostile takeover.

[30] 'Union pour la Démocratie Française'. This party was founded by former President Valéry Giscard d'Estaing.   [31] F. Bayrou interview with *Les Echos*, 12 July 2001.

The story of the anti-takeover directive is not over yet. In 2002 a high-level working group was appointed by the Commission under the direction of a Dutch law professor. The working group published the so-called Winter Report, which requires that shareholders, not management or unions, approve any defensive measures once a bid has been launched. It also requires among other things the application of the 'one share one vote' rule in votes on takeover defences. The recommendations are thus basically in favour of shareholders against the defence of stakeholders. One may thus expect the same type of opposition again when a new attempt is made to pass the directive at the EP.

6.5 Conclusion

The Continental European model of capitalism still exists and will do so in forthcoming years. Its features have nevertheless been altered: bank-based finance has not vanished altogether, but it no longer plays the role it used to; the labour market has been made more 'flexible' and the prospects for an increase in job security are uncertain; the social-protection system has experienced a limited adjustment to times of austerity and will have to face the challenges of the ageing population and social exclusion. New challenges will come up for countries of the European Union with the enlargement and the inclusion of countries with lower levels of economic development and labour costs. As always, one can expect increased pressure for real-wage moderation and a wave of relocation of the most labour-intensive activities to the new EU member states. This is likely to augment unemployment problems in segments of the labour force where they are already serious, i.e. for low-paid and low-skilled workers.

A move towards a generalization of the market-based model on the Continent is not foreseeable, for structural reasons first, because competitiveness in European countries is based on specific institutional features and the complementarities associated with them, and for political reasons, because no socio-political bloc would be found to support such a radical change. The most successful political strategies behind the diffusion of the neo-liberal project were adopted by the Conservative parties in the 1980s and by the left in the 1990s. In both cases inspiration for Continental European parties came from the UK, a country whose institutional characteristics are markedly different from those of the other EU countries, and which can be unambiguously classified as a market-based economy. Both strategies were proposed in the same way; i.e. as the only alternative. One may indeed compare the TINA[32] rhetoric of

---

[32] There Is No Alternative.

Margaret Thatcher to the style of the Third Way: 'the old left cannot exist in new times' (Giddens 2000). If successful in their home base, these strategies have both failed on the Continent. One may come back to the fate of the Third Way. Its initial success in Europe was largely based on the belief that it represented the key to new electoral victories for social-democratic parties. If the Third Way was strong enough to defeat the British Conservatives, it could succeed anywhere. The late 1990s seemed at first to confirm this impression, when the new left dominated most EU governments. However, the winning formula soon turned into a recipe for electoral disasters—in Italy, Denmark, Norway, the Netherlands, and France. The third-way orientation of the social-democratic platforms left considerable scope for right-wing populist parties to take advantage of the worries of a fraction of the electorate that might have voted for the left. The case of France can be mentioned in this respect. Although presented as the figurehead of the 'old' left, Lionel Jospin geared his presidential campaign of April 2002 towards the centre, in an attempt to capture the median voter.[33] This strategy was perfectly logical from a third-way perspective, with the decline of the left/right division and the alleged waning of the social base of traditional socialist parties. It was nevertheless a failure, with Jospin unable to pass the first round, leaving a second round opposing right-wing populist Jean-Marie Le Pen and conservative candidate Jacques Chirac. Disorganized after the shock of the first round, the left lost the legislative elections that followed and control of the Lower Chamber. The failure of the median-voter strategy and the inability either to obtain votes from the traditional social base or to gather new support from 'outsiders' can be read in the participation rates: 59 per cent of the unemployed and 44 per cent of workers abstained, compared to a national average of 28 per cent. Jospin obtained 13 per cent of workers' votes, i.e. as much as conservative candidate Chirac. Finally, the Trotskyite candidates alone gathered an unprecedented 11 per cent of the vote, which, in addition to the votes for the Green Party candidate, make a total of 20 per cent for left-libertarian parties, i.e. as more than the percentage obtained by the socialist candidate.

On the other hand, the September 2002 social-democratic victory in Sweden followed a deliberately left-oriented campaign[34] hingeing upon

---

[33] L. Jospin opened his presidential campaign with the declaration that his programme was not socialist.

[34] Whilst paying lip-service to some of the third way themes, the party programme of the Social Democratic Party of Sweden is basically pure unadulterated 'old-school' social democracy (party programme of the Social Democratic Party adopted by the Party Congress in Västerås, 6 November 2001). The election manifesto 2002–6 insists on security and

the defence of the Welfare State and a willingness to pay the necessary price for it in the form of high tax rates, in opposition to the third-way logic of tax competition following on from globalization. In fact, the Conservative Party lost voter support even within its own electorate when it proposed tax cuts perceived as non-credible in a context of a maintained Welfare State. Even the German campaign of September 2002 was marked by a return of more 'traditional' social-democratic rhetoric based on State intervention in cases of emergency[35] and the defence of 'Modell Deutschland', with no reference to the *Neue Mitte*. Therefore, the electoral results in Europe seem to point towards a rejection of the market-based solution and a quest for a renewal of the Continental and social-democratic models.

What direction could such a renewal take? The social-democratic and Continental models—one may add the Mediterranean model—differ on the trade-off between job security and social protection. Job security protects workers and their specific investments without the need for a fully-developed system of social protection. Also, active labour-market policies are far less developed than in the social-democratic model. Labour-force adjustments are either prevented when firms retain jobs, or their burden falls on the social-protection system. The shortcomings of job protection concern structural change. If employment protection prevents excessive labour-force flexibility, it also slows down structural change. An alternative exists, which is considered to be at the root of the 'Danish miracle',[36] combining relative flexibility in the labour market with extended social protection coupled with active labour-market policies. The so-called 'flexicurity' triangle is represented in Fig. 6.1, where arrows' sizes are proportional to transitions. Relative labour-market flexibility induces a higher possible labour-force turnover than in the Continental European model. Generous welfare systems prevent a drop in living standards and act as protection for specific investments, and active labour-market policies allow for the retraining of the workforce. Direct transitions between

---

development: 'Welfare policies must cover everyone... the proportion of our common resources destined for health care will be increased... Labour law must be developed and not dismantled... we want to see full-time jobs as a right and part-time jobs as an option... we intend to spend more on the elderly'.

[35] Severe floods took place in the eastern part of the country during the summer preceding the elections. G. Schröder was quick to step in and assure the population that the federal State would intervene.   [36] See Madsen (2002).

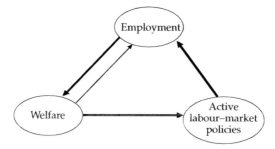

FIG. 6.1 The flexicurity triangle

employments or from unemployment to employment are thus more limited than in either the market-based or the Continental model. Flexicurity
enables structural change and career progression, at the cost of a fully-
fledged social-protection system and an extensive programme of active
labour-market policies, which imply a high level of taxation. This would
be a social-protection-based alternative to the market-based employability strategy developed by the UK. Since retraining plays a central role, the
implementation of the flexicurity strategy demands a highly efficient education and training system that favours lifelong learning. In this respect,
Continental European systems appear somewhat deficient. According to
Eurostat data, lifelong learning affects around 20 per cent of the workforce
in Scandinavian countries and in the UK, but only 5.8 per cent in
Germany or Ireland and 2.8 per cent in France. Taking the flexicurity route
would then demand a sizeable effort towards improving education and
training systems, all the more because general education, which is often
complementary to training, may not be a strong point of Continental
European countries according to the controversial results of the PISA
study.[37] It would also probably require that limits be placed on the spread
of the principles of market-based corporate governance and more generally market-based finance, which more or less impose a preference for
'flexibility' and reversibility of arrangements, and downward competition
between industrial locations. Attractive locations not based on low wages
and diminished social protection should be built on skilled labour pools
and efficient infrastructures.

---

[37] OECD (2001).

Which socio-political alliance would be liable to support such a reform of the Continental European model? As shown by the episode of the takeover directive, there is among large European manufacturing employers a certain reluctance to let the principles of market-based finance become too prominent, whereas banks and insurance companies welcome the transition to the market-based model. Since wage earners would have an interest in the maintenance of the Welfare State and protection assured by a mechanism akin to flexicurity, there is scope for the formation of a socio-political bloc based on a series of compromises between large industrial employers and unions on a renewed Continental European model, which would allow for a higher degree of employment flexibility in exchange for extended social protection on a more universal model, i.e. moving away from the traditional Conservative systems which have characterized the model so far. This compromise would put stake-holders at the forefront and would imply a limit to the principles of shareholder value, which might paradoxically be easier to implement now that market finance has spread over Europe, in the wake of the Enron and WorldCom scandals and the subsequent depreciation of the principles of market-based corporate governance, and the obvious limits of 'transparency'. This implies an active role for the State in the promotion of social protection and education as well as infrastructures. This calls for a high rate of taxation which would be difficult to apply should tax competition intensify. This strategy is thus bound to lead sooner or later to a step in the direction of tax harmonization, i.e. a political confrontation within the EU. It would orient the Continental European productive structure towards the 'high road'—i.e. high skills, high productivity, high wages—supported by coordinated wage bargaining at the EU level, which would prevent social dumping. Such coordination would also prevent a possible upsurge of inflationary pressures in the event of a tightening of labour markets, and would be compatible with the objectives of the ECB. This project of 'regulated capitalism', though not in line with the dominant political thinking of the last decade, could serve as a basis upon which not only the political strategies of the left but also those of the centre-right of the Continental European countries could be built.[38]

---

[38] Hooghe (2002) shows that support for European-regulated capitalism is far greater than support for market liberalism among the European Commission's top officials, and European big business seems on the whole still favourable to it too, as shown by Cowles-Green (1995) who studied the European Round Table of Industrialists, the major lobby for big business.

APPENDIX

The Methodology behind the Statistical Analysis in Chapter 4

The database is formatted so that individuals are represented by lines of a matrix, and the variables are in columns.

Principal-Components Analysis[1]

All the cluster analyses performed here are based on principal-components analysis. Principal components are linear combinations of initial variables. The objective is to obtain a representation of variables and individuals (countries) on a specific basis, which is generated by the principal components. Principal components are thus synthetic variables which sum up the information contained in the original variables. All variables used are standardized in order to eliminate distortion.

Not all variables need be taken into account in the definition of principal components. In fact, one needs to make a selection of variables in order to come to interpretable results. The selection process is mostly based on the step-by-step elimination of variables which appear to bring little information to the analysis and/or duplicate other variables. The eliminated variables do not entirely vanish however. They can be 'projected' on the factorial plane and actually help *ex post* to interpret the results, i.e. to give a meaning to the factorial axes whose definitions they have not actually contributed to.

The variables left out of the analysis for the definition of the factorial axes are called 'illustrative' variables; the variables contributing to the definition of the factors upon which the analysis is based are the 'active' variables. Both types of variable as well as the first principal components are studied through the analysis of the eigenvalues of the data matrix.

By diagonalization of the matrix of correlation (R) between variables in the standardized case, the principal-components analysis (PCA) provides the eigenelements[2] of R. In general, in a standardized PCA one focuses on axes for which the explained inertia is superior to $1/p$, where p is the number of the variables. In our case, interpretation is limited to the three first factorial axes and to the planes they generate. One can then obtain a projection of continuous variables as well as a simultaneous representation of countries and variables on the axes which have been generated by these factors. The interpretation of countries' positions on the axes is made possible through the study of existing relations between countries' coordinates and variables' coordinates. The quality of the representation of countries in the factorial planes can also be assessed through their contribution to the

---

[1] See Jobson (1992) or Lebart, Morineau, and Piron (1995) for detailed explanations of principal-components-analysis method. One may also mention Escoffier and Pagès (1998).

[2] An eigenvalue is the variance of a principal component.

axes of the relevant factorial plane. The interpretation of the factorial axes also provides a basis for comparing countries with one another.

The interpretation of the axes will be made easier by a representation of the active and illustrative variables on a correlation circle, which gives a representation of the contribution to (active variables) and projection on (active and illustrative variables) the axes defined by the principal components. Each variable will be represented by an arrow vector having the coordinates of the concerned variable in the factorial plane. A variable is the more significant to the analysis the longer the arrow vector is.

Countries' typologies

Typologies of countries are established using the hierarchically ascending classification technique (cluster analysis). The Ward algorithm is used, consolidated by the 'mobile-centred' method. The basic idea behind a cluster analysis is to group 'similar' countries together. In order to do so, one needs to assess similarities and dissimilarities that countries have with one another. In the present case, similarity is defined using the Euclidean distance. Ward's idea consists of a step-by-step aggregation of countries by 'clusters' so that the intracluster inertia varies as little as possible. Yet total inertia is the sum of intra- and intercluster inertia. One tries to get the minimal intracluster inertia or the maximal intercluster inertia. The principle of cluster-characterization is to consider the distance between the average of one variable in a cluster and its general average. The more significant this distance, the more characteristic the variable of this group is for the clustering.

The quality of the typology is considered acceptable if:

- the variability inside each cluster is low; in other words, if the variance between the individuals of the cluster is (relatively) low for each variable
- the variability is strong between clusters; in other words, if for each variable the average of all individuals of a cluster significantly differs between clusters.

The direct hierarchical classification is established on the basis both of the 'reciprocal-neighbours' algorithm and of the utilization of some aggregation criteria. This classification gives a representation of clustering according to the 'hierarchical tree'. Making a typology means cutting this tree at a certain level. This may be done either 'manually'[3] or automatically according to a predetermined statistical criterion. In what follows we used a preset statistical criterion; this allows for the choice of a certain clustering pattern. Suppose, for instance, that two clusterings are deemed statistically significant, one which identifies three groups of countries and one with five groups. Then, which typology of country will be used is a matter of choice. The choice made was based on the interpretability of the clusters.

---

[3] We can manually cut the tree through the index-levels study. These index levels provide the loss of intercluster inertia generated by the gathering of clusters.

Appendix

Variables

Product markets

Indicator	Description	Source
Product-market regulation	Score 0–6, by	Nicoletti et al. (2000)
Inward-oriented policies	increasing	
Outward-oriented policies	extent of	
State control	regulation	
Public ownership		
Involvement in business operation		
Barriers to entrepreneurship		
Administrative burdens on start-ups		
Regulatory and administrative opacity		
Barriers to competition		
Barriers to trade and investment		
Explicit barriers		
Other barriers		
Administrative regulation		
Economic regulation		
Regulation of economic structure		
Regulation of economic behaviour		
Regulation of competition		
Scope of public-enterprise sector		
Size of public-enterprise sector		
Special voting rights		
Control of public entreprises by legislative bodies		
Use of command and control regulation		
Price controls		
Licence and permit system		
Communication and simplification of rules and procedures		
Administrative burdens for corporations		
Administrative burdens for sole-proprietor firms		
Sector-specific administrative burdens		
Legal barriers		
Antitrust exemptions		
Ownership barriers		
Discriminatory procedures		
Regulatory barriers		
Tariffs		

Labour market

Indicator	Description	Source
Employment-protection procedures	Score 1–3, by increasing degree of firing difficulty	OECD Employment Outlook
Delay to start of notice	Number of days	
Notice period (after 9 months)	Number of months	
Notice period (after 4 years)		
Notice period (after 20 years)		
Severance pay (after 9 months)		
Severance pay (after 4 years)		
Severance pay (after 20 years)		
Unfair-dismissal definition	Score 1–3, by increasing degree of firing difficulty	
Trial period	Number of months	
Unfair-dismissal compensation (after 20 years' seniority)		
Extent of reinstatement (in case of unfair dismissal)	score 0–3 (0 = never; 3 = always)	
Employment-regulation rigour (synthetic indicator)	Score 0–6, by increasing degree of rigour of regulations	
Dismissal notice and pay-offs (synthetic indicator)		
Firing difficulties (synthetic indicator)		
Employment protection (synthetic indicator)		
Fixed-term contracts (valid cases)	Score 0–4, by increasing ease of use	
Fixed-term contracts (maximum number of successive contracts)	Maximum number of successive contracts	
Fixed-term contracts (maximum cumulated duration)	Score 0–6, maximum cumulated duration	
Temporary-work agencies (breadth)	Score 0–6	
Temporary-work renewal restrictions		
Temporary work (maximum cumulated duration)		
Labour share of value added— manufacturing		OECD Compendium 1998–2, main industrial indicators

Indicator	Description	Source
Research and development personnel (%)	Percentage of total labour force	OECD Compendium 1998
Ratio of activity—total	Employment/labour force ratio	
Ratio of activity—men		
Ratio of activity—women		
Non-wage labour costs as percentage of total labour costs		
Rate of union membership		
Collective-agreement coverage		
Precariousness feeling		
Seniority—less than 1 year		
Seniority—more than 20 years		
Average seniority		
Compensation per employee		
Centralization degree		
Coordination degree		
Public expenditures on employment administration as percentage of GDP		
Public expenditures on professional formation as percentage of GDP		
Public expenditures on youth programmes as percentage of GDP		
Public expenditures on hiring aid as percentage of GDP		
Public expenditures on handicapped persons' programmes as percentage of GDP		
Public expenditures on unemployment indemnity as percentage of GDP		
Public expenditures on early retirement as percentage of GDP		
Public expenditures on labour-market programmes, total, as percentage of GDP		
Employment-protection legislation (EPL) on regular contracts		Nicoletti, Scarpetta, Boylaud (2000)

Indicator	Description	Source
EPL on temporary contracts		Nicoletti, Scarpetta, Boylaud (2000)
EPL global index		
Wage-bargaining-coordination index		Elmeskov, Martin, and Scarpetta (1998)
Wage-bargaining-centralization index		
Wage-bargaining corporatism index		
Union density (percentage)		
Average effective tax wedge	*Ex post* wedge percentage computed from national accounts	OECD national accounts
Ratio of minimum to median wage		OECD
Gross replacement rate		
Tax wedge—single		
Tax wedge—married		
Payments—single		
Payments—married		
Industrial disputes	Working days lost per 1,000 inhabitants per year	*World Competitiveness Forum Yearbook* (1987, 1992, 1997)
Manager–employee relations	Industrial relations between managers and employees are generally fragile/productive	
Seniority—less than 1 year	Percentage	OECD Employment Outlook
Seniority—more than 20 years	Percentage	
Average seniority	Years	

Finance

Indicator	Description	Source
Accounting standards	Number of accounting standards on a scale from 0–90 normalized to lie in the range 0–1	Center for International Financial Analysis and Research; reported by Rajan and Zingales (1998)
Equity owned by banks	Proportion of total equity-market capitalization in different countries held by banks	OECD financial accounts, various years
Ownership concentration 1	Percentage of the twenty largest publicly traded firms that were widely held in 1995	La Porta et al. (1998)
Ownership concentration 2	Average percentage of common shares owned by the three largest shareholders in the ten largest non-financial, privately owned domestic firms in a given country	
Market capitalization	Market capitalization to GDP ratios averaged over the period 1982–91	Reported in the IFC *Emerging Stock Market Factbook* (1992)
Credit to GDP	Bank credit to GDP ratios averaged over the period 1980–90	Reported in IMF international financial statistics
External capitalization to GNP	Ratio of stock-market capitalization held by minorities to GNP for 1994. The stock-market capitalization held by minorities is computed as the product of the aggregate stock-market capitalization and the average percentage of common shares not owned by the top three shareholders in the ten largest non-financial, privately owned domestic firms in a given country	La Porta et al. (1998)
IPOs to population	Ratio of the number of initial public offerings of equity in a given country to its population (in millions) for the period 1995–7	La Porta et al. (1998)
Debt to GNP	Ratio of the sum of bank debt of the private sector and outstanding non-financial bonds to GNP in 1994	

Indicator	Description	Source
Venture-capital investment (value)	Venture-capital investment in million USD.	Baygan and Freudenberg (2000)
Venture-capital investment as percentage of GDP	Venture-capital investment as percentage of GDP	
Venture-capital—country of management, total	Total venture-capital investment (country of management) as percentage of GDP	
Venture-capital—country of management, early stage	Venture-capital investment in early stage projects (country of management) as percentage of GDP	
Venture-capital—country of management, high-tech	Venture-capital investment in high-tech projects (country of management) as percentage of GDP	
Venture-capital—country of management, early stage high-tech	Venture-capital investment in early stage high-tech projects (country of management) as percentage of GDP	
Venture-capital—country of destination, total	Total venture-capital investment (country of destination) as percentage of GDP	
Venture-capital—country of destination, early stage	Venture-capital investment in early stage projects (country of destination) as percentage of GDP	
Venture-capital—country of destination, high-tech	Venture-capital investment in high-tech projects (country of destination) as percentage of GDP	
Venture-capital—country of destination, early stage high-tech	Venture-capital investment in early stage high-tech projects (country of destination) as percentage of GDP	
Stock-market capitalization to GDP	Value of listed shares divided by GDP	Beck, Demirgüç-Kunt, Levine (1999)
Stock-market total value traded to GDP	Total shares traded on the stock-market exchange divided by GDP	

Indicator	Description	Source
Stock-market turnover ratio	Ratio of the value of total shares traded and market capitalization	
Private-bond-market capital-ization to GDP	Total amount of outstanding domestic-debt securities issued by private domestic entities divided by GDP	
Public-bond-market capital-ization to GDP	Total amount of outstanding domestic-debt securities issued by public domestic entities divided by GDP	
Equity issues to GDP	Equity issues divided by GDP	
Long-term private-debt issues to GDP	Long-term private-debt issues divided by GDP	
Concentration	Ratio of the three largest banks' assets to total banking-sector assets	
Foreign-bank share (assets)	Share of foreign bank assets in total banking-sector assets	
Foreign-bank share (number)	Number of foreign banks in total banks	
Overhead costs	Accounting value of a bank's overhead costs as share of its total assets	
Net interest margin	Accounting value of a bank's net interest revenue as a share of its total assets	
Public share	Share of publicly owned commercial bank assets in total commercial bank assets. A bank is defined as public if at least 50 per cent of the equity is held by the government or a public institution	
Mergers and acquisitions	Ratio of the number of deals and population averaged over 1990–7	Pagano and Volpin (2001)
Corporate taxes on undistributed profits (1)	Average effective tax rate on undistributed profits	La Porta et al. (1999)
Corporate taxes on distributed profits (2)	Average effective tax rate on distributed profits	

Indicator	Description	Source
Personal tax on capital gains (3)	Average effective tax rate on capital gains to local-resident minority stakeholders	
Personal tax on dividends (4)	Average effective tax rate on dividends to local-resident minority stakeholders	
Imputation rate (5)	Shareholder's tax credits for distributed earnings	
Capital gains	$(1 - (1)) \times (1 - (3)/4)$	
Dividend tax preference	$(1 - (2) + (5)) \times (1 - (4))/(\text{capital gains})$	
Efficiency of judicial system	Assessment of the 'efficiency and integrity of the legal environment as it affects business, particularly foreign firms'. Average 1980–3. Scale 0–10	La Porta et al. (1998)
Rule of law	Assessment of the law and order tradition in the country. Average of the months of April and October of the monthly index between 1982 and 1995. Scale 0–10	
Corruption	Assessment of the corruption in government. Average of the months of April and October of the monthly index between 1982 and 1995. Scale 0–10	
Risk of expropriation	Assessment of the risk of 'outright confiscation' or 'forced nationalization'. Average of the months of April and October of the monthly index between 1982 and 1995	
Risk of contract repudiation	Assessment of the 'risk of modification in a contract taking the form of a repudiation, postponement, or scaling down' as a result of 'budget cutbacks, indigenization pressure, a change in government, or a change in government economic and social priorities'. Average of the months of April and October of the monthly index between 1982 and 1995	
Control (10 or 20 per cent) of large publicly traded firms, widely held	Equals 1 if there is no controlling shareholder. A firm has a controlling shareholder if the sum of her direct and indirect voting rights exceeds alternatively 20 or 10 per cent	

Indicator	Description	Source
Control (10 or 20 per cent) of large publicly traded firms, family	Equals 1 if a person or a family is the controlling shareholder, and 0 otherwise	
Control (10 or 20 per cent) of large publicly traded firms, State	Equals 1 if the (domestic or foreign) State is the controlling shareholder, and 0 otherwise	
Control (10 or 20 per cent) of large publicly traded firms, widely held financial	Equals 1 if a widely held financial company is the controlling shareholder, and 0 otherwise	
Control (10 or 20 per cent) of large publicly traded firms, widely held corporation	Equals 1 if a widely held non-financial company is the controlling shareholder, and 0 otherwise	
Control (10 or 20 per cent) of large publicly traded firms, miscellaneous	Equals 1 if widely held, family, State, widely held financial, and widely held corporation are all equal to 0, and 0 otherwise	
Control (10 or 20 per cent) of medium- sized publicly traded firms, widely held	Equals 1 if there is no controlling shareholder. A firm has a controlling shareholder if the sum of her direct and indirect voting rights exceeds alternatively 20 per cent or 10 per cent	
Control (10 or 20 per cent) of medium- sized publicly traded firms, family	Equals 1 if a person or a family is the controlling shareholder, and 0 otherwise	
Control (10 or 20 per cent) of medium- sized publicly traded firms, State	Equals 1 if the (domestic or foreign) State is the controlling shareholder, and 0 otherwise	

Indicator	Description	Source
Control (10 or 20 per cent) of medium-sized publicly traded firms, widely held financial	Equals 1 if a widely held financial company is the controlling shareholder, and 0 otherwise	
Control (10 or 20 percent) of medium-sized publicly traded firms, widely held corporation	Equals 1 if a widely held non-financial company is the controlling shareholder, and 0 otherwise	
Control (10 or 20 per cent) of medium-sized publicly traded firms, miscellaneous	Equals 1 if widely held, family, State, widely held financial, and widely held corporation are all equal to 0, and 0 otherwise	
Control, one share one vote	Equals 1 if the company law or commercial code of the country requires that ordinary shares carry one vote per share, and 0 otherwise	
Family or financial institutions controlled, pyramids	Equals 1 if the controlling shareholder exercises control through at least one publicly traded company, and 0 otherwise	
Control, cross-shareholdings	Equals 1 if the firm owns shares in its controlling shareholder or in a firm that belongs to her chain of control, and 0 otherwise	
Family, State or financial institutions controlled, share market capital	Ratio of the sum of the market value of common equity of all firms controlled by the relevant type of owner to the total market value of common equity of the largest twenty firms in a given country	
Family or financial institutions con-trolled or widely held, N firms	Average number of firms controlled by the relevant type of owner	
Family controlled, management	Equals 1 if the controlling family is also the CEO, Honorary Chairman, Chairman, or Vice-Chairman of the Board, and 0 otherwise	

Indicator	Description	Source
Financial institutions controlled, independent	Equals 1 when a (widely held) financial institution controls at least 10 per cent of the votes and its control chain is separate from that of the controlling owner, and 0 otherwise	
Financial institutions controlled, associated	Equals 1 when a (widely held) financial institution controls at least 10 per cent of the votes and its control chain overlaps with that of the controlling owner, and 0 otherwise	
Family or State controlled, widely held financial or corporation and all firms, probability that the controlling shareholder is alone	Equals 1 if the firm has a 20 per cent controlling owner and no other shareholder has control of at least 10 per cent of the votes through a control chain that does not overlap with that of the controlling shareholder	
Regulatory framework	Composite indicator capturing the capacity of the State to implement sound policies	Kaufmann, Kraay, and Zoido-Lobaton (1999)
Rule of Law (World Bank)	Composite indicator capturing the respect of citizens and the State for the rules which govern their interactions	
Control rights	Fraction of the firm's voting rights, if any, owned by its controlling shareholder	La Porta et al. (2002)
Cash-flow rights	Fraction of the firm's ultimate cash-flow rights, if any, owned by its controlling shareholder	
Wedge	The difference between control rights and cash-flow rights	
Anti-director index	An index aggregating shareholder rights. 0–6	La Porta et al. (1998)
Total assets of banks as percentage of GDP	National currency, three years' average	OECD financial statistics
Banks' net interest income/average balance-sheet total		
Banks' net non-interest income/average		

Indicator	Description	Source
balance-sheet total		
Banks' net income/average balance-sheet total		
Banks' profit before tax/average balance-sheet total		
Banks' loans as percentage of year-end balance-sheet total		
Banks' securities as percentage of year-end balance-sheet total		
Banks' capital and reserves as percentage of year-end balance-sheet total		
Non-banks' deposits as percentage of year-end balance-sheet total		
Banks' bonds as percentage of year-end balance-sheet total		
Banks' short-term securities as percentage of year-end balance-sheet total		
Banks' bonds as percentage of year-end balance-sheet total		
Banks' shares and participations as percentage of year-end balance-sheet total		

Indicator	Description	Source
Banks' profit rate	Profit after tax/capital and reserves (equity)	
Banks' net non-interest income/net interest income		
Financial assets of insurance companies as percentage of GDP		
Financial assets of pension funds as percentage of GDP		
Financial assets of investment companies as percentage of GDP		
Financial assets of institutional investors, total, as percentage of GDP		
Percentage of bonds in portfolio of institutional investors		
Percentage of loans in portfolio of institutional investors		
Percentage of shares in portfolio of institutional investors		
Percentage of other financial assets in portfolio of institutional investors		
Financial assets of insurance companies/financial assets of institutional investors		
Financial assets of		

Indicator	Description	Source
pension funds/financial assets of institutional investors		
Financial assets of investment companies/financial assets of institutional investors		
Total tax revenue as percentage of GDP		OECD financial statistics
Total tax revenue (excluding social security) as percentage of GDP		
Taxes on income and profits as percentage of GDP		
Taxes on income and profits as percentage of total taxation		
Taxes on personal income as percentage of GDP		
Taxes on personal income as percentage of total taxation		
Taxes on corporate income as percentage of GDP		
Taxes on corporate income as percentage of total taxation		
Social-security contributions as percentage of GDP		
Social-security		

Indicator	Description	Source
contributions as percentage of total taxation		
Employees' social-security contributions as percentage of total taxation		
Employees social-security contributions as percentage of GDP		
Employers social-security contributions as percentage of GDP		
Employers social-security contributions as percentage of total taxation		
Taxes on payroll and workforce as percentage of GDP		
Taxes on payroll and workforce as percentage of total taxation		
Taxes on property as percentage of total taxation		
Taxes on property as percentage of GDP		
Taxes on goods and services as percentage of GDP		
Taxes on goods and services as percentage of total taxation		
Consumption taxes		

Indicator	Description	Source
as percentage of GDP		
Consumption taxes as percentage of total taxation		
Taxes on general consumption as percentage of GDP		
Taxes on general consumption as percentage of total taxation		
Taxes on specific goods and services as percentage of GDP		
Taxes on specific goods and services as percentage of total taxation		

Social Protection

Indicator	Source
Public expenditure alone as percentage of GDP	OECD social expenditure statistics*
Public expenditure alone as percentage of public expenditure	
Mandatory public and private expenditure as percentage of GDP	
Mandatory public and private expenditures as percentage of public expenditure	

*For old-age cash benefits, disability cash benefits, occupational-injury and -disease benefits, sickness benefits, services for the elderly and disabled people, survivors' benefits, family cash benefits, family services, unemployment benefits, health benefits, housing benefits, other-contingencies benefits.

Appendix

Education

Indicator	Description	Source
Students abroad	Number of students enrolled in other countries in tertiary education as percentage of students enrolled in tertiary education *in the country of origin* (head counts) (1995)	OECD
Public expenditure— tertiary (as percentage of GDP)	Direct public expenditure, ISCED 567, as percentage of GDP	
Private expenditure— tertiary (as percentage of GDP)	Private expenditure, ISCED 567, as percentage of GDP	
Public and private expenditure—tertiary (as percentage of GDP)	Total expenditure, ISCED 567, as percentage of GDP	
Public share expenditure— tertiary		
Total expenditure— tertiary (as percentage of GDP)	Total expenditure and subsidies, ISCED 567, as percentage of GDP	
Aid to students	Aid to students, ISCED 567, as percentage of GDP	
Total expenditure— primary	Expenditure on education institutions, ISCED 1, as percentage of GDP	
Total expenditure— secondary	Expenditure on education institutions, ISCED 23, as percentage of GDP	
Total expenditure— university	Expenditure on education institutions, ISCED 67, as percentage of GDP	
Total education expenditure	Expenditure on education institutions as percentage of GDP, all levels	
Expenditure per pupil—early	Expenditure per student, ISCED 0	
Expenditure per pupil—primary	Expenditure per student, ISCED 1	
Expenditure per pupil—secondary	Expenditure per student, ISCED 23	
Expenditure per student—tertiary	Expenditure per student, ISCED 567	
Expenditure per student—all levels	Expenditure per student, all levels	

Indicator	Description	Source
Expenditure ratio— early/primary	Relative expenditure per student, ISCED 0	
Expenditure ratio— primary/secondary	Relative expenditure per student, ISCED 23	
Expenditure ratio— secondary/tertiary	Relative expenditure per student, ISCED 567	
Expected years of schooling	Expected years of schooling for a five-year-old child	
Enrolment rate	Enrolment rates, ISCED 123567	
Enrolment rate— secondary	Enrolment rates, ISCED 3	
Enrolment rate— tertiary	Enrolment rates, ISCED 567	
Enrolment rate— general programmes	Enrolment rates, general programmes	
Enrolment rate— vocational/technical	Enrolment rates, vocational and technical programmes	
Relative teachers' salaries—primary	Teachers' starting salaries, ISCED 1, ratio of starting salary to per capita GDP	
Relative teachers' salaries—lower secondary	Teachers' starting salaries, ISCED 2, ratio of starting salary to per capita GDP	
Relative teachers' salaries—general secondary	Teachers' starting salaries, ISCED 3, general programmes, ratio of starting salary to per capita GDP	
Relative teachers' salaries—vocational	Teachers' starting salaries, ISCED 3, vocational programmes, ratio of starting salary to per capita GDP	
Experienced teachers' salaries—primary	Experienced teachers' salaries, ISCED 1, ratio of salaries at fifteen years' experience to per capita GDP	
Experienced teachers' salaries—lower secondary	Experienced teachers' salaries, ISCED 2, ratio of salaries at fifteen years' experience to per capita GDP	
Experienced teachers salaries—general secondary	Experienced teachers' salaries, ISCED 3, general programmes, ratio of salaries at fifteen years' experience to per capita GDP	
Experienced teachers salaries—vocational	Experienced teachers' salaries, ISCED 3, vocational programmes, ratio of salaries at fifteen years' experience to per capita GDP	
Relative employment— all levels	Relative employment/population ratio, ISCED 12	

Indicator	Description	Source
Relative employment —upper secondary	Relative employment/population ratio, ISCED 3	
Relative employment— non-university tertiary	Relative employment/population ratio, ISCED 5	
Relative employment— university	Relative employment/population ratio, ISCED 67	
Percentage of graduates—secondary	Graduates, ISCED 3	
Relative unemployment rate— below secondary	Relative unemployment rate, ISCED 12	
Relative unemployment rate— upper secondary	Relative unemployment rate, ISCED 3	
Relative unemployment rate— non-university tertiary	Relative unemployment rate, ISCED 5	
Relative unemployment rate— university	Relative unemployment rate, ISCED 67	
Percentage of graduates— non-university tertiary	Graduates, ISCED 5	
Percentage of graduates—university	Graduates, ISCED 67	
Education as percentage of public expenditures		
Employment ratio— below secondary	Employment ratio, ISCED < 3	
Employment ratio— secondary	Employment ratio, ISCED 3	
Employment ratio— non-university tertiary	Employment ratio, ISCED 5	
Employment ratio— university	Employment ratio, ISCED 6–7	
Employment ratios— all levels	Employment ratio, all levels of education	
Unemployment rate—below secondary	Unemployment ratio, ISCED < 3	

Indicator	Description	Source
Unemployment rate—secondary	Unemployment ratio, ISCED 3	
Unemp. rate—non-university tertiary	Unemployment ratio, ISCED 5	
Unemp. rate—university	Unemployment ratio, ISCED 6–7	
Unemp. rate—all levels	Unemployment ratio, all levels of education	
Percentage of labour force—primary	Percentage of the labour force 25–64 by the highest completed level of education—early childhood/primary/lower secondary	
Percentage of labour force—secondary	Percentage of the labour force 25–64 by the highest completed level of education—upper secondary	
Percentage of labour force—tertiary	Percentage of the labour force 25–64 by the highest completed level of education—tertiary	
Percentage of labour force—non-university tertiary	Percentage of the labour force 25–64 by the highest completed level of education—non-university tertiary	
Percentage of labour force—university	Percentage of the labour force 25–64 by the highest completed level of education—university	
Expected years in employment—men	Expected years in employment—men	
Expected years in employment—women	Expected years in employment—women	
Expected years in unemployment—men	Expected years in unemployment—men	
Expected years in unemployment—women	Expected years in unemployment—women	
Relative expected years out of employment—men/primary	Relative expected years out of employment—men, ISCED 12	
Relative expected years out of employment—women/primary	Relative expected years out of employment—women, ISCED 12	
Relative expected years out of employment—men/secondary	Relative expected years out of employment, men, ISCED 3	

Indicator	Description	Source
Relative expected years out of employment women/secondary	Relative expected years out of employment—women, ISCED 3	
Relative expected years out of employment men/tertiary	Relative expected years out of employment—men, ISCED 567	
Relative expected years out of employment women/tertiary	Ratio of expected years in unemployment and out of the labour force for women, ISCED 567—all levels of education	
Higher-education enrolment	Percentage of 20–4-year-old population enrolled in higher education	World Bank (*World Development Report: the Challenge of Development*), UNESCO (*World Education Report*)
Public expenditure on education per capita		WCR
Availability of skilled labour	Skilled labour is hard/easy to get in your economy	
Availability of qualified engineers	There is a lack of/are enough qualified engineers on the market	
Total direct public expenditure per student		Eurostat science, technology, and key figures innovation 2000 and 2001
Total public expenditure tertiary per student		
Total direct public expenditure per student—tertiary		
Higher education RSE growth		
Share of science and technology students		

Indicator	Description	Source
Pupils' and students' enrolment rate		
Tertiary students' enrolment rate		
Technical-orientation (tertiary) enrolment rate		
Academic and advanced (tertiary) enrolment rate		
Students per teacher—tertiary		
Total graduates as percentage of the 20–4 population		
Total graduates—growth		
Total science and technology graduates as percentage of the 20–4 population		
Total science and technology graduates' growth		
Total doctorates as percentage of the 25–9 population		
Total doctorates' growth		
Science and technology doctorates as percentage of the 25–9 population		
Science and technology doctorates' growth		

REFERENCES

ABRAMOVITZ, M. (1986), 'Catching up, Forging Ahead, and Falling Behind', *Journal of Economic History*, 46/2: 385–406.

ACEMOGLU, D., and S. PISCHKE (1998), 'Why Do Firms Train? Theory and Evidence', *Quarterly Journal of Economics*, 113: 79–119.

——(1999a), 'The Structure of Wages and Investment in General Training', *Journal of Political Economy*, 107: 539–72.

——(1999b), 'Beyond Becker: Training in Imperfect Labor Markets', *Economic Journal*, 109: F112–42.

——(2000) 'Certification of Training and Training Outcomes', *European Economic Review*, 44: 917–27.

AGHION, P., and P. HOWITT (1998), *Endogenous Growth Theory*, Cambridge, Mass.: MIT Press.

——, N. BLOOM, R. BLUNDELL, R. GRIFFITH, and P. HOWITT (2001), 'Empirical Estimates of Product Market Competition and Innovation', Paper presented at the Saint-Gobain Conference on Institutions and Innovation, Paris, June.

AGLIETTA, M. (1979), *A Theory of Capitalist Regulation: The American Experience*, London: New Left Books, first French edn. pub. 1976.

——(1998), 'Le capitalisme de demain', *Notes de la fondation Saint-Simon*, 101, Paris.

ALBERT, M. (1991), *Capitalisme Contre Capitalisme*, Paris: Seuil.

ALLEN, F., and D. GALE (2000), *Comparing Financial Systems*, Cambridge, Mass.: MIT Press.

ALLMENDINGER, J. (1989), 'Educational Systems and Labor Market Outcomes', *European Sociological Review*, 5: 231–50.

AMABLE, B. (2000), 'Institutional Complementarity and Diversity of Social Systems of Innovation and Production', *Review of International Political Economy*, 7/4: 645–87.

——, P. ASKENAZY, A. GOLDSTEIN, and D. O'CONNOR (coordinated by D. COHEN) (2002), 'Internet: The Elusive Quest of a Frictionless Economy', Paper presented at the Rodolfo Debendetti conference on 'The Information Economy: Productivity Gains and the Digital Divide', Catania, 15 June.

——, R. BARRÉ, and R. BOYER (1997), *Les Systèmes d'innovation à l'ère de la Globalisation*, Paris: Economica.

——, Y. CADIOU, and P. PETIT (2000), 'On the Development Paths of Innovation Systems', Work package D, TSER-CDIS project, Mimeo CEPREMAP.

——, J. B. CHATELAIN, and O. DE BANDT (2002), 'Optimal Capacity in the Banking Sector and Economic Growth', *Journal of Banking and Finance*, 26: 491–517.

——, and E. ERNST (2002), 'Specific Investments and Interactions between Financial and Labour Markets', Draft paper, CEPREMAP.

——, ——, and PALOMBARINI S. (2001), 'How do Financial Markets Affect Industrial Relations: An Institutional Complementarity Approach', Paper presented at the SASE Conference, Amsterdam.

—— (2002), 'Institutional Complementarities: An Overview of the Main Issues', Paper presented at the Seminar on Institutional Complementarity and the Dynamics of Economic Systems, Paris, April 5–6.

——, and D. GATTI (2002*a*), 'Macroeconomic Effects of Product Market Competition in a Dynamic Efficiency Wage Model', *Economics Letters*, 75/2: 39–46.

—— (2002*b*), 'Product Market Competition, Job Security and Aggregate Employment', Draft paper, CEPREMAP.

——, and B. HANCKÉ (2001), 'Innovation and Industrial Renewal in France in Comparative Perspective', *Industry and Innovation*, 8/2: 113–33.

——, and M. JUILLARD (1999), 'The Historical Process of Convergence', Draft paper, CEPREMAP.

——, and P. PETIT (2002), 'La diversité des systèmes sociaux d'innovation et de production dans les années 1990', in Centre Saint-Gobain pour la Recherche Economique (eds.), *Institutions et Innovation*, Paris: Albin Michel.

AOKI, M. (1994), 'The Contingent Governance of Teams: Analysis of Institutional Complementarity', *International Economic Review*, 35: 657–76.

—— (1995), 'Towards a Comparative Institutional Analysis', *Japanese Economic Review*, 47/1: 1–19.

—— (2000), *Information, Corporate Governance, and Institutional Diversity*, Oxford: Oxford University Press.

—— (2001), *Towards a Comparative Institutional Analysis*, Cambridge, Mass.: MIT Press.

——, and H. PATRICK (eds.) (1994), *The Japanese Main Bank System: Its Relevance for Developing and Transforming Economies*, Oxford: Oxford University Press.

ARESTIS, P., and M. SAWYER (2001), 'The Economic Analysis Underlying the Third Way', *New Political Economy*, 6/2: 255–78.

ARNOLD, D. (2000), 'Labour's Economic Policy and the Competition State: A Social Democratic Critique of the Political Economy of the Third Way, Paper presented at the conference on 'The Third Way and Beyond', Sussex University, November.

ARTHUR, B. (1994), 'Increasing Returns and Path Dependence in the Economy', Ann Arbor: University of Michigan Press.

AUST, D. (2001), 'The Party of European Socialists (PES) and European Employment Policies: From "Eurokeynesianism" to "Third Way policies?"', Paper presented at the workshop 'Third Ways in Europe', European Consortium for Political Research, joint sessions, Grenoble.

AVENTUR, F., C. CAMPO, and M. MÖBUS (1999), 'Factors in the Spread of Continuing Training in the European Community', *Training and Employment*, 35: 1–4.

BARRO, R., and D. GORDON (1983), 'Rules, Discretion and Reputation in a Model of Monetary Policy', *Journal of Monetary Economics*, 12: 101–21.

BARRO, R., and SALA-I-MARTIN, X. (1995), *Economic Growth*, London: McGraw-Hill.

BATIFOULIER, P. (ed.) (2001), *Economie des Conventions*, Paris: Economica.

BAYGAN, G., and M. FREUDENBERG (2000), 'The Internationalisation of Venture Capital Activities in OECD Countries: Implications for Measurement and Policies', *STI Working Paper* 2000/7, Paris: OECD.

BECK, T., G. CLARKE, A. GROFF, P. KEEFER, and P. WALSH. (1999), 'New Tools and New Tests in Comparative Political Economy: The Database of Political Institutions', Washington: World Bank.

——, A. DEMIRGÜÇ-KUNT, and R. LEVINE (1999), 'A New Database on Financial Development and Structure', Washington: World Bank.

BECKER, G. S. (1962), 'Investment in Human Capital: a Theoretical Analysis', *Journal of Political Economy*, 70/5: 9–49.

——(2002), 'The Continent Gets It', *Business Week*, 22 April.

BERGLÖF, E. (1997), 'Reforming Corporate Governance: Redirecting the European Agenda', *Economic Policy*, 27: 93–123.

BERLE, A., and G. MEANS (1932), *The Modern Corporation and Private Property*, New York: Macmillan.

BLACK, M. (1962), *Models and Metaphors*, Ithaca: Cornell University Press.

BLAIR, T. (1998), *The Third Way*, London: Fabian Society.

——, and G. SCHRÖDER (1999), *Europe, the Third Way*, French trans. in *Notes de la fondation Jean Jaurès*, xiii. Paris (1999).

BOHM, P. (1987), 'Second Best', in J. Eatwell, M. Milgate, and P. Newman (eds.), *The New Palgrave: A Dictionary of Economics*, London: Macmillan.

BOISMENU, G. (1994), Système de représentation des intérêts et configurations politiques: les sociétés occidentales en perspective comparée, *Canadian Journal of Political Science*, 27/2: 309–43.

BONOLI, G. (2001), 'The Third Way and Political Economy Traditions in Western Europe', Paper presented at the workshop 'Third Ways in Europe', European Consortium for Political Research, joint sessions, Grenoble.

——, and A. MACH (1999), 'Switzerland: Adjustment Politics within Institutional Constraints', in F. Scharpf and V. Schmidt (eds.), *Welfare and Work in the Open Economy, ii. Diverse Responses to Common Challenges*, Oxford: Oxford University Press.

BOYER, R. (1986), *La Théorie de la régulation: une analyse critique*, Paris: La Découverte.

——(ed.) (1988), *The Search for Labour Market Flexibility*, Oxford: Clarendon Press.

——(1997), 'French Statism at the Crossroads', in C. Crouch and W. Streeck (eds.), *Political Economy of Modern Capitalism*, London: Sage.

——(2001), 'Un retard de l'Europe ? Mythes et réalités', in Centre Saint-Gobain pour la Recherche Economique (eds.), *Institutions et Croissance*, Paris: Albin Michel.

——(2002), *La Croissance, début de siècle*, Paris: Albin Michel.

——, and M. DIDIER (1998), *Innovation et Croissance*, Report for the Conseil d'Analyse Economique, Paris: La Documentation Française.

——, and J. P. DURAND (1998), *L'Après-Fordisme*, Paris: Syros.

——, and J. MISTRAL (eds.) (1986), *Capitalismes fin de siècle*, Paris: Presses Universitaires de France.

——, and T. YAMADA (eds.) (2000), *Japanese Capitalism in Crisis*, London: Routledge.

BRADSHAW, J., J. DITCH, H. HOLMES, P. WHIETFORD, and J. RAY (1994), 'Une comparaison internationale des aides à la famille', *Recherches et Prévisions*, 37: 11–26.

CAIRNCROSS, F. (2001), *The Death of Distance*, Cambridge, Mass.: Harvard Business School Press.

CALMFORS, L., and J. DRIFFIL (1988), 'Bargaining Structure, Corporatism and Macroeconomic Performance', *Economic Policy*, 6: 14–61.

CARLIN, W., and C. MAYER (2002), 'Finance, Investment and Growth', Draft paper, University College, London, and Saïd Business School, University of Oxford.

CEPREMAP-CORDES (1977) (J. P. Benassy, R. Boyer, R. M. Gelpi, A. Lipietz, J. Mistral, J. Munoz, C. Ominami), 'Approches de l'inflation: l'exemple français', Convention de Recherche, xxii.

CIOFFI, J. (2002), 'Control, Transparency, and the Politics of Company and Takeover Law Reform in Germany and the European Union', Paper presented at the 13th International Conference of Europeanists, 'Europe in the New Millennium: Enlarging, Experimenting, Evolving', Chicago.

COASE, R. (1937), 'The Nature of the Firm', *Econometrica*, 4: 386–405.

COMMISSION EUROPÉENNE (1993) Livre blanc de la Commission sur la croissance, la compétitivité et l'emploi—COM (93) 700, *Bulletin de l'Union Européenne 12—1993*, Brussels.

COWLES-GREEN, M. (1995), 'Setting the Agenda for a New Europe: The ERT and EC 1992', *Journal of Common Market Studies*, 33: 501–26.

CRAWFORD, S., and E. OSTROM (1995), 'A Grammar of Institutions', *American Political Science Review*, 89/3: 582–600.

CROUCH, C. (1993), *Industrial Relations and European State Traditions*, Oxford: Oxford University Press.

CUKIERMAN, A., and F. LIPPI (1999), 'Central Bank Independence, Centralisation of Wage Bargaining, Inflation and Unemployment', *European Economic Review*, 43: 1395–434.

CUMINGS, B. (1987), 'The Origins and Development of the Northeast Asian Political Economy: Industrial Sectors, Product Cycles, and Political Consequences', in F. Deyo (ed.), *The Political Economy of the New Asian Industrialism*, Ithaca: Cornell University Press.

DAVID, P. (1985), 'Clio and the Economics of QWERTY', *American Economic Review*, 75: 332–7.

DEEG, R. (2001), 'Institutional Change and the Uses and Limits of Path Dependency: The Case of German Finance', MPIfG Discussion Paper 01/6, Max Planck Institut für Gesellschaftforschung, Cologne.

DERTOUZOS, M., R. LESTER, and R. SOLOW (eds.) (1989), *Made in America: Regaining the Productive Edge*, Cambridge, Mass.: MIT Press.

DEWATRIPONT, M., and E. MASKIN (1995), 'Credit and Efficiency in Centralised and Decentralised Economies', *Review of Economic Studies*, 62: 541–55.

DRAZEN, A. (2000), *Political Economy in Macroeconomics*, Princeton: Princeton University.

DUFRESNE, A., and E. MERMET (2002), 'Trends in the Coordination of Collective Bargaining in Europe', *DWP 2002.01.02(E)*, Brussels: ETUI.

DURLAUF, S. (1996), 'On the Convergence and Divergence of Growth Rates', *Economic Journal*, 106 (July): 1016–18.

EBBINGHAUS, B. (1998), 'European Labor Relations and Welfare-State Regimes: A Comparative Analysis of their "Elective Affinities" ', Paper presented at the Conference on 'Varieties of Welfare Capitalism in Europe, North America, and Japan', Cologne.

—— (1999), 'Does a European Social Model Exist and Can It Survive?', in Gerhard Huemer, Michael Mesch, and F. Traxler (eds.), *The Role of Employer Associations and Labour Unions in the EMU: Institutional Requirements for European Economic Policies*, Aldershot: Ashgate, 1–26.

—— (2002), 'Trade Unions' Changing Role: Membership Erosion, Organizational Reform, and Social Partnership in Europe', *Industrial Relations Journal*, 33/5: 465–83.

——, and A. HASSEL (1999), 'The Role of Tripartite Concertation in the Reform of the Welfare State', in *State Intervention and Industrial Relations at the End of the 1990s*. Transfer special issue, Brussels: ETUI.

——, and P. MANOW (eds.) (2001), *Comparing Welfare Capitalism: Social Policy and Political Economy in Europe, Japan and the USA*, London: Routledge.

EDWARDS, J., and J. SCHANZ (2001a), 'Faster, Higher, Stronger: An International Comparison of Structural Policies', *Structural Economics Research Papers*, iii, London: Lehman Brothers.

—— (2001b), 'Lehman's Structural Database: Sources and Methods', *Structural Economics Research Papers*, iv, London: Lehman Brothers.

EGGERTSSON, T. (1990), *Economic Behavior and Institutions*, Cambridge: Cambridge University Press.

—— (1996), 'A Note on the Economics of Institutions', in L. J. Alston, T. Eggertsson, and D. C. North (eds.), *Empirical Studies in Institutional Change*, Cambridge: Cambridge University Press.

EGUCHI, K. (2000), 'Unions, Job Security, and Incentives of Workers', Discussion Paper CIRJE-F-91, University of Tokyo.

ELMESKOV, J., J. MARTIN, and S. SCARPETTA (1998), 'Key Lessons for Labour Market Reforms: Evidence from OECD Countries' Experiences', *Swedish Economic Policy Review*, 5/2: 205–52.

ELSTER, J. (1986), *Rational Choice*, Cambridge: Cambridge University Press.

ESCOFFIER, B., and J. PAGÈS (1998), *Analyses factorielles simples et multiples*, 3rd edn., Paris: Dunod.

ESPING-ANDERSEN, G. (1990), *The Three Worlds of Welfare Capitalism*, Princeton: Princeton University Press.

ESTEVEZ-ABE, M., T. IVERSEN, and D. SOSKICE (2001), 'Social Protection and the Formation of Skills: A Reinterpretation of the Welfare State', in P. Hall and D. Soskice (eds.), *Varieties of Capitalism: The Institutional Foundations of Comparative Advantage*, Oxford: Oxford University Press.

ETZIONI, A. (1995), *The Spirit of Community: Rights, Responsibilities and the Communitarian Agenda*, London: Fontana.

EUROSTAT (2001), *Towards a European Research Area: Key Figures 2001*, Luxembourg: Office for Official Publications of the European Communities.

FAJERTAG, G., and POCHET, P. (eds.) (1997), *Social Pacts in Europe*, Brussels: European Trade Union Institute and Observatoire social européen.

FAVEREAU, O. (1999), 'Salaire, emploi et économie des conventions', *Cahiers d'economie politique*, 34: 163–94.

FLORA, P. (1986), 'Introduction', in P. Flora (ed.), *Growth to Limits: The Western European Welfare States since World War II*, Berlin: De Gruyter.

FRANKS, J., and C. MAYER (1997), 'Ownership and control', *Journal of Applied Corporate Finance* (1997), 9: 30–45.

FREEMAN, R. (2000), 'Single-peaked vs. Diversified Capitalism: The Relation between Economic Institutions and Outcomes', *NBER* Working Paper No. 7556.

GANGHOF, S. (2001), 'Global Markets, National Tax Systems, and Domestic Politics: Rebalancing Efficiency and Equity in Open States' Income Taxation', MPIfG Discussion Paper No. 01/9.

GARVEY, G., and P. SWAN (1992), The Interaction between Financial and Employment Contracts: A Formal Model of Japanese Corporate Governance, *Journal of the Japanese and International Economies*, 6/3: 247–74.

GATTI, D. (1999), 'Equilibrium Unemployment, the Nature of Competence, the Organization of the Firm', *Economia Politica*, 1611.

—— (2000), 'Unemployment and Innovation Patterns: The Critical Role of Coordination', *Industrial and Corporate Change*, 9/3: 521–44.

——, and C. VAN WIJNBERGEN (2001), 'Co-ordinating Fiscal Authorities in the Euro-zone: A Key Role for the ECB', *Oxford Economic Papers*, 54: 56–71.

GIDDENS, A. (1994), *Beyond Left and Right*, Cambridge: Polity Press.

—— (1998), *The Third Way*, Cambridge: Polity Press.

—— (2000), *The Third Way and its Critics*, Cambridge: Polity Press.

GLYN, A., and S. WOOD (2000), 'New Labour's Economic Policy: How Social-Democratic is the Blair Government?', in Glyn (ed.) (2000), *Economic Policy and Social Democracy*, Oxford: Oxford University Press.

GOES, E. (2000), 'The Third Way and the Politics of Community', Paper presented at the conference 'The Third Way and Beyond', Sussex University, November.

GONENC, R., M. MAHER, and G. NICOLETTI (2000), 'The Implementation and the Effects of Regulatory Reform: Past Experience and Current Issues', Economic Department Working Paper No. 251, OECD, Paris.

GOUREVITCH, P., and M. HAWES (2002), 'The Politics of Choice among National Production Systems', Draft paper, University of California at San Diego.

GOYER, M. (2002), 'The Transformation of Corporate Governance in France and Germany: The Role of Workplace Institutions', MPIfG Working Paper No. 02/10, Max Planck Institut für Gesellschaftforschung, Cologne.

Grundwertekommission beim Parteivorstand der SPD (1999), *Dritte Wege—Neue Mitte*, Berlin: SPD.

GUILLEN, M. (2000), 'Corporate Governance and Globalisation: Is There Convergence Across Countries?', Draft paper, Wharton School and Department of Sociology, University of Pennsylvania.

HALL, P. (1993), 'Policy Paradigms, Social Learning and the State: The Case of Economic Policymaking in Britain', *Comparative Politics*, 26: 275–96.

——, and D. GINGERISH (2001), 'Varieties of Capitalism and Institutional Complementarities in the Macroeconomy: An Empirical Analysis', Draft paper, Harvard University.

——, and D. SOSKICE (eds.) (2001), *Varieties of Capitalism: The Institutional Foundations of Comparative Advantage*, Oxford: Oxford University Press.

——, and R. TAYLOR (1996), 'Political Science and the Three New Institutionalisms', *Political Studies*, 44: 936–57.

HANNAN, D., D. RAFFE, and E. SMYTH (1996), 'Cross-National Research on School to Work Transitions: An Analytical Framework', Draft paper.

HART, O. (1995), *Firms' Contracts and Financial Structure*, Oxford: Clarendon Press.

HASSEL, A. (2001), 'The Politics of Social Pacts: A Framework for Analysis', Draft paper, MPIfG, Cologne.

HAYEK, F. (1967), 'Notes on the Evolution of Systems of Rules of Conduct', in *Studies in Philosophy, Politics, and Economics*, Chicago: Chicago University Press.

HELLWIG, M. (1998), 'Banks, Markets, and the Allocation of Risks in an Economy', *Journal of Institutional and Theoretical Economics*, 54: 328–45.

HEMERIJCK, A., and P. MANOW (2001), 'The Experience of Negotiated Reforms in the Dutch and German Welfare States', in B. Ebbinghaus and P. Manow (eds.), *Comparing Welfare Capitalism: Social Policy and Political Economy in Europe, Japan and the USA*, London: Routledge.

HOLLINGSWORTH, J. R. (2000), 'Doing Institutional Analysis: Implications for the Study of Innovations', *Review of International Political Economy*, 7/4: 595–644.

HOOGHE, L. (2002), *The European Commission and the Integration of Europe*, Cambridge: Cambridge University Press.

——, and G. MARKS (1999), 'The Making of a Polity: The Struggle over European integration', in H. Kitschelt, P. Lange, G. Marks, and J. D. Stephens (eds.), *Continuity and Change in Contemporary Capitalism*, Cambridge: Cambridge University Press.

HÖPNER, M. (2001), 'Ten Empirical Findings on Shareholder Value and Industrial Relations in Germany', Draft paper, MPIfG, Cologne.

——, and G. JACKSON (2001), 'An Emerging Market for Corporate Control? The Mannesmann Takeover and German Corporate Governance', MPIfG Discussion Paper No. 01(4), Cologne.

IMF (1998), 'The Asian Crisis: Causes and Cures', *Finance and Development*, 35/2 (June).

IVERSEN, T., and T. CUSACK (2000), 'The Causes of Welfare State Expansion: Deindustrialisation or Globalisation?', *World Politics*, 52: 313–49.

——, and D. SOSKICE (2001), 'An Asset Theory of Social Preferences', *American Political Science Review*, 95/4: 875–93.

JACKSON, G. (2002), 'Varieties of Capitalism: A Review', Draft paper, RIETI.

JOBSON, J. D. (1992), *Applied Multivariate Data Analysis, ii: Categorical and Multivariate Methods*. Springer Texts in Statistics, New York: Springer-Verlag.

JOSPIN, L. (2000), *Le Socialisme Moderne*, note de la Fondation Jean Jaurès, N° 15, Paris.

KAUFMANN, D., A. KRAAY, and P. ZOIDO-LOBATON (1999), 'Aggregating Governance Indicators', World Bank Policy Research Department Working Paper No. 2195.

KITSCHELT, H. (1999), 'European Social Democracy between Political Economy and Electoral Competition', in H. Kitschelt, P. Lange, G. Marks, and J. D. Stephens (eds.), *Continuity and Change in Contemporary Capitalism*, Cambridge: Cambridge University Press.

KNIGHT, J. (1992), *Institutions and Social Conflict*, Cambridge: Cambridge University Press.

KRIPKE, S. A. (1982), *Wittgenstein on Rules and Private Language*, Cambridge, Mass.: Harvard University Press.

KYDLAND, F., and E. PRESCOTT (1977), 'Rules Rather Than Discretion: The Inconsistency of Optimal Plans', *Journal of Political Economy*, 85: 437–91.

LAFONTAINE, O. (1999), *Das Herz schlägt links*, München: Econ Verlag.

LA PORTA, R., F. LÓPEZ-DE-SILANES, and A. SHLEIFER (2002c), 'Investor Protection and Corporate Valuation', *Journal of Finance*, 57/3: 1147–70.

——, ——, ——, and R. VISHNY (1997), 'Legal Determinants of External Finance', *Journal of Finance*, 52: 1131–50.

—— (1998), 'Law and Finance', *Journal of Political Economy*, 106: 1113–55.

—— (2000a), 'Agency Problems and Dividend Policies Around the World', *Journal of Finance*, 55: 1–33.

—— (2000b), 'Investor Protection and Corporate Governance', *Journal of Financial Economics*, 58: 3–27.

——, ——, and —— (2002), 'Investor Protection and Corporate Valuation', *Journal of Finance*, 57/3: 1147–70.

LAYARD, R., S. NICKELL, and R. JACKMAN (1991), *Unemployment: Macroeconomic Performance and the Labour Market*, Oxford: Oxford University Press.

LEBART, L., A. MORINEAU, and M. PIRON (1995), *Statistique exploratoire multidimensionnelle*, Paris: Dunod.

LEVINE, R. (1997), 'Financial Development and Economic Growth: Views and Agenda', *Journal of Economic Literature*, 35: 688–726.

LEWIS, D. (1969), *Convention: A Philosophical Study*, Cambridge, Mass.: Harvard University Press.

LIJPHART, A. (1999), *Patterns of Democracy: Government Forms and Performance in Thirty-Six Countries*, New Haven: Yale University Press.

LÜTZ, S. (2000), 'From Managed to Market Capitalism? German Finance in Transition', MPIfG Discussion Paper No. 00/2, Cologne.

MCCULLEN, P., and C. HARRIS (2000), 'Generative Equality, Work and the Third Way: A Managerial Perspective', Paper presented at the conference 'The Third Way and Beyond', Sussex University, November.

MADDISON, A. (1995), *Monitoring the World Economy 1820–1992*, Paris: OECD.

MADSEN, P. K. (2002), 'The Danish Model of "Flexicurity"—A Paradise with some Snakes', Paper presented at the Conference of the European Foundation for the Improvement of Living and Working Conditions on 'Interactions between Labour Market and Social Protection', Brussels, 16 May.

MAYER, C. (2001), 'Structures de financement et organisation des enterprises', in Centre Saint-Gobain pour la Recherche Economique (eds.), *Institutions et Croissance*, Paris: Albin Michel.

MILGROM, P., and J. ROBERTS (1992), *Economics, Organization and Management*, Englewood Cliffs: Prentice Hall.

MOENE, K. O., and M. WALLERSTEIN (1999), 'Social Democratic Labor Market Institutions: A Retrospective Analysis', in H. Kitschelt, P. Lange, G. Marks, and J. D. Stephens (eds.), *Continuity and Change in Contemporary Capitalism*, Cambridge: Cambridge University Press.

MORIN, F. (1998), 'La Rupture du modèle français de détention et de gestion des capitaux', *Revue d'économie financière*, 50: 111–32.

NICKELL, S. (1997), 'Unemployment and Labour Market Rigidities: Europe versus North America', *Journal of Economic Perspectives* , 11/3: 55–74.

—— (1999), 'Product Markets and Labour Markets', *Labour Economics*, 6: 1–20.

NICOLETTI, G., S. SCARPETTA, and O. BOYLAUD (2000), 'Summary Indicators of Product Market Regulation with an Extension to Employment Protection Legislation', OECD Working Paper No. 226.

NORTH, D. (1990), *Institutions, Institutional Change and Economic Performance*, Cambridge: Cambridge University Press.

OECD (2000), *A New Economy? The Changing Role of Innovation and Information Technology in Growth*, Paris: OECD.

—— (2001), *Connaissances et compétences: des atouts pour la vie: Premiers résultats du programme international de l'OCDE pour le suivi international des acquis des élèves (PISA) 2000*, Paris: OECD.

OKAWA, K., and H. ROSOVSKY (1973), *Japanese Economic Growth*, Stanford: Stanford University Press.

OLSON, M. (1982), *The Rise and Decline of Nations, Economic Growth, Stagflation, and Social Rigidities*, New Haven: Yale University Press.

ORRU, M., N. W. BIGGART, and G. G. HAMILTON (1997), *The Economic Organization of East Asian Capitalism*, Thousand Oaks: Sage.

OSANO, H. (1997), 'An Evolutionary Model of Corporate Governance and Employment Contracts', *Journal of the Japanese and International Economies*, 11: 403–36.

OSTROM, E. (2001), *Understanding Institutional Diversity*, Draft.

PAGANO, M., and P. VOLPIN (2001), 'The Political Economy of Corporate Governance', Discussion paper No. 2682, London: CEPR.

PALIER, B. (2002), 'The Necessity for French governments to Negotiate Welfare State Reforms with the Social Partners', Paper presented at the 13th Conference of Europeanists, Chicago, 14–16 March.

PALOMBARINI, S. (1999), 'Vers une théorie régulationniste de la politique économique', *L'Année de la régulation*, 3: 97–125.

——(2001), *'La Rupture du compromise social italien: Un essai de macroéconomie politique'*, Paris: Editions du CNRS.

——, and B. THÉRET (2001), 'Le Politique, l'économique et la difficile émergence des nouvelles régulations', Paper presented at the Forum de la Régulation, Paris, November.

PIERSON, P. (2001), 'Coping with Permanent Austerity: Welfare State Restructuring in Affluent Democracies', in P. Pierson (ed.) *The New Politics of the Welfare State*, Oxford: Oxford University Press.

PISTOR K., Y. KEINAN, J. KLEINHEISTERKAMP, and M. WEST (2001), 'The Evolution of Corporate Law', Background paper prepared for the World Development Report 2001, *Institutions for a Market Economy*.

PLANT, R. (1991), *Modern Political Thought*, Oxford: Blackwell.

——(1998), 'The Third Way', Working Paper FES 5/1998, London.

POLLACK, M. A. (1998), 'Beyond Left and Right? Neoliberalism and Regulated Capitalism in the Treaty of Amsterdam', in Working Paper Series in European Studies ii/2, Department of Political Science, University of Wisconsin.

——(1999), 'Blairism in Brussels: The "Third Way" in Europe since Amsterdam', Draft paper, University of Wisconsin.

POWELL, M. (2001), 'Third Ways in Europe: Concepts, Policies, Causes and Roots', Paper presented at the workshop 'Third Ways in Europe', European Consortium for Political Research, joint sessions, Grenoble.

RAJAN, R., and L. ZINGALES (2000), 'The Great Reversals: The Politics of Financial Development in the Twentieth Century', Draft paper, University of Chicago.

REGINI, M. (2000), 'Between Deregulation and Social Pacts: The Response of European Economies to Globalisation', *Politics and Society*, 28/1: 5–33.

RHODES, M. (1999), 'Restructuring the British Welfare State: Between Domestic Constraints and Global Imperatives', in F. Scharpf and V. Schmidt (eds.), *Welfare and Work in the Open Economy, ii. Diverse Responses to Common Challenges*, Oxford: Oxford University Press.

——(2001), 'The Political Economy of Social Pacts: "Competitive Corporatism" and European Welfare State Reform', in P. Pierson (ed.), *The New Politics of the Welfare State*, Oxford: Oxford University Press.

——, and B. VAN APELDOORN (1997), 'Capitalism versus Capitalism in Western Europe', in M. Rhodes, P. Heywood, and V. Wright (eds.), *Developments in West European Politics*, London: St. Martins Press.

ROE, M. (1993), 'Some Differences in Corporate Structure in Germany, Japan, and the United States', *Yale Law Journal*, 102: 1927–2003.

ROE, M. (2000), 'Political Preconditions to Separating Ownership from Corporate Control', Columbia Law School, Center for Law and Economic Studies Working Paper No. 155.

—— (2001), 'The Shareholder Wealth Maximisation Norm and Industrial Organisation', Harvard Law School Public Law Working Paper No. 019.

ROGOWSKI, R. (1987), 'Political Cleavages and Changing Exposure to Trade', *American Political Science Review*, 81/4 (Dec.): 1121–37.

ROMER, P. (1986), 'Increasing Returns and Long Run Growth', *Journal of Political Economy*, 94: 1002–37.

—— (1993), 'Ideas Gaps and Object Gaps in Economic Development', *Journal of Monetary Economics*, 32.

RUTHERFORD, M. (1994), *Institutions in Economics*, Cambridge: Cambridge University Press.

SAINT-PAUL, G. (2001), *The Political Economy of Labour Market Institutions*, Oxford: Oxford University Press

SARGENT, T., and N. WALLACE (1975), ' "Rational" Expectations, the Optimal Monetary Instrument and the Optimal Money Supply Rule', *Journal of Political Economy*, 83/2: 241–54.

SCHARPF, F. (2000), 'Institutions in Comparative Policy Research', MPIfG Working Paper No. 00/3, Cologne.

SCHELLING, T. (1960), 'The Strategy of Conflict', Cambridge, Mass.: Harvard University Press.

SCHLUDI, M. (2001), 'The Politics of Pensions in European Social Insurance Countries', Paper presented at the 13th SASE Annual Meeting, Amsterdam.

SCHMIDT, R., A. HACKETHAL, and M. TYRELL (1998), 'Disintermediation and the role of Banks in Europe: An International Comparison', Working Paper Series: Finance and Accounting No. 10, Johan-Wolfgang Goethe Universität, Frankfurt am Main.

SCHMIDT, V. (2002), *The Futures of European Capitalism*, Oxford: Oxford University Press.

SCHOTTER, A. (1981), *The Economic Theory of Social Institutions*, New York: Cambridge University Press.

SCHULTEN, T. (2001), 'A European Solidaristic Wage Policy? Conceptual Reflections on a Europeanisation of Trade Union Wage Policy', Paper prepared at the 6th IIRA European Congress, Oslo, 25–9 June.

—— (2002), 'Europeanisation of Collective Bargaining. An Overview on Trade Union Initiatives for a Transnational Coordination of Collective Bargaining Policy', WSI Discussion Paper No. 101, Wirtschafts- und Sozialwissentschaftliches Institut der Hans-Böckler Stiftung, Düsseldorf.

SHINN, J. (2001), 'Private Profit or Public Purpose? Shallow Convergence on the Shareholder Model', Paper presented at 'Varieties of Capitalism' discussion at University of North Carolina at Chapel Hill.

SHONFIELD, A. (1965), *Modern Capitalism: The Changing Balance of Public and Private Power*, Oxford: Oxford University Press.

SIEBERT, H. (1997), 'Labor Market Rigidities: At the Root of Unemployment in Europe', *Journal of Economic Perspectives*, 11/3: 37–54.

SINGH, A. (1998), ' "Asian Capitalism" and the Financial Crisis', CEPA Working Paper, Series iii, No. 10.

SOSKICE, D. (1999), 'Divergent Production Regimes: Coordinated and Uncoordinated Market Economies in the 1980s and 1990s', in H. Kitschelt, P. Lange, G. Marks, and J. D. Stephens (eds.), *Continuity and Change in Contemporary Capitalism*, Cambridge: Cambridge University Press.

STEINER, P. (2001), 'De Simiand à l'école de la regulation', *L'Année de la Régulation*, 5: 147–70.

STEVENS, M. (1996), 'Transferable Training and Poaching Externality', in A. L. Booth and D. J. Snower (eds.), *Acquiring Skills: Market Failures, their Symptoms and Policy Responses*, Cambridge: Cambridge University Press.

STREECK, W. (1997*a*), 'Beneficial Constraints: On the Economic Limits of Rational Voluntarism', in R. Hollingsworth and R. Boyer (eds.), *Contemporary Capitalism: The Embeddedness of Institutions*, Cambridge: Cambridge University Press.

—— (1997*b*), 'Industrial Citizenship under Regime Competition: The Case of the European Works Councils', *Journal of European Public Policy*, 4/4: 643–64.

—— (2001), 'Explorations into the Origins of Nonliberal Capitalism in Germany and Japan', in W. Streeck and K. Yamamura (eds.), *The Origins of Nonliberal Capitalism*, Ithaca: Cornell University Press.

—— (2002), 'Notes On Complementarity: How It Comes About, And How We Should Analyze It', Paper presented at the seminar on 'Institutional Complementarity and the Dynamics of Economic Systems', Paris, 5–6 April.

SUGDEN, R. (1986), *The Economics of Rights, Cooperation and Welfare*, Oxford: Blackwell.

SUPIOT, A. (1999), *Au delà de l'emploi*, Paris: Flammarion.

SVALERYD, H., and J. VLACHOS (2000), 'Financial Markets, the Pattern of Specialisation and Comparative Advantage', evidence from OECD countries, Draft paper, University of Stockholm.

SWANK, D. (2002), '21-Nation Pooled Time-Series Data Set: Political Strength of Political Parties by Ideological Group in Capitalist Democracies', http://www.marquette.edu/polisci/swank.htm.

TEULINGS, C., and J. HARTOG (1998), *Corporatism or Competition?: Labour Contracts, Institutions and Wage Structures in International Comparison*, Cambridge: Cambridge University Press.

THÉRET, B. (1997), Méthodologie des comparaisons internationales, approche de l'effet sociétal et de la régulation: fondements pour une lecture structuraliste des systèmes nationaux de protection sociale', *L'Année de la régulation*, 1: 163–228.

TITMUSS, R. (1974), *Social Policy: An Introduction*, London: Allen and Unwin.

TOPKIS, D. M. (1998), *Supermodularity and Complementarity*, Princeton: Princeton University Press.

TRAXLER, F. (1995), 'Farewell to Labour Market Associations? Organized versus Disorganized Decentralization as a Map for Industrial Relations', in C. Crouch and F. Traxler (eds.), *Organized Industrial Relations in Europe: What Future?* Aldershot: Dartmouth.

TSEBELIS, G. (1995), 'Decision-Making in Political Systems: Veto Players in Presidentialism, Pariliamentarism, Multicameralism, and Multipartyism', *British Journal of Political Science*, 25: 289–326.

——(2002), *Veto Players: How Political Institutions Work*, Princeton: Princeton University Press/Russell Sage Foundation.

——, and E. CHANG (2001), 'Veto Players and the Structure of Budgets in Advanced Industrialised Countries', Draft paper, UCLA.

VANDENBROUCKE, F. (2001), 'European Social Democracy and the Third Way: Convergence, Divisions and Shared Questions', in Stuart White (ed.), *New Labour and the Future of Progressive Politics*, London: Macmillan.

WHITLEY, R. (1999), *Divergent Capitalisms: The Social Structuring and Change of Business Systems*, Oxford: Oxford University Press.

WILLIAMSON, O. (1985), *The Economic Institutions of Capitalism: Firms, Markets, Relational Contracting*, New York: Free Press.

WREN, A. (2001), 'The Challenge of De-industrialisation: Divergent Ideological Responses to Welfare State Reform', in B. Ebbinghaus and P. Manow (eds.), *Comparing Welfare Capitalism: Social Policy and Political Economy in Europe, Japan and the USA*, London: Routledge.

YOUNG, H. P. (1998), *Individual Strategy and Social Structure*, Princeton: Princeton University Press.

INDEX

.